"Anyone concerned for the futur̲ ̲ ̲ ̲ ̲ ̲ ̲ ̲ and especially anyone in business m̲ ̲ ̲ ̲ ̲ ̲ power training, or policy-making—should read this inspiring book! Bereiter and Scardamalia convey a wonderfully clear understanding of expertise, combining psychological, epistemological, educational, and social perspectives. The major thrust is that we can achieve a society where expertise flourishes and is naturally used for the common good. The chapter on schools is a remarkable critique of current efforts at educational reform."

—HANS A. SCHIESER
   Professor Emeritus,
   De Paul University

"A better society won't just happen. Individuals with powerful problem-solving capabilities are key. Surpassing Ourselves calls out to those experts and calls for our support of them in quest of the best society."

—ROBERT W. GALVIN
   Motorola Corporation
   Author of *The Idea of Ideas*

"Bereiter and Scardamalia masterfully explicate the poorly understood concepts of problem solving and expertise. Drawing upon some of the latest research in cognitive science and psychology, they argue that the capacity to acquire expertise is uniquely human. They ask how society can and should take better advantage of expertise to address social problems and enhance personal growth, and present intriguing, provocative suggestions in areas as diverse as medical care, environmental protection, and industrial productivity. Their description of current schools as non-expert societies and their critque

of reform efforts as offering (at best) change with no improvement are compelling."

—JOHN T. BRUER
President, James S. McDonnell Foundation
Author of *Schools for Thought*

"*An uncommonly thoughtful and imaginative book, this probing examination of the nature and sources of expertise leads us to valuable insights into learning, instruction, and the ways we conceive of education reform. Bereiter and Scardamalia point the way toward schools from which expertise could be the normal result rather than a rare and almost accidental byproduct.*"

—CHESTER E. FINN JR.
Former Assistant Secretary of Education
Professor of Education, Vanderbilt University
Founding Partner and Senior Scholar, The Edison Project

"*Anyone with a serious interest in improving America's schools must read* Surpassing Ourselves. *Bereiter and Scardamalia have given us more than insight into expertise. They have given us insight into a knowledge-based school capable of serving a post-industrial society.*"

—TED SANDERS
Superintendent, Ohio Department of Education

Surpassing Ourselves

Surpassing Ourselves

AN INQUIRY INTO
THE NATURE AND IMPLICATIONS
OF EXPERTISE

Carl Bereiter
Marlene Scardamalia

OPEN COURT

Chicago and La Salle, Illinois

OPEN COURT and the above logo are registered in the U.S. Patent and Trademark Office.

© 1993 by Open Court Publishing Company

First printing 1993

Printed and bound in the United States of America.

Library of Congress Cataloging-in-Publication Data

Bereiter, Carl.
　　Surpassing ourselves / Carl Bereiter and Marlene Scardamalia.
　　　　p. cm.
　　Includes bibliographical references and index.
　　ISBN 0-8126-9204-7. — ISBN 0-8126-9205-5 (pbk.)
　　1. Expertise. 2. Expertise—Social aspects.
I. Scardamalia, Marlene, 1944– . II. Title.
　　BF378.E94B47 1993
　　001—dc20   93-28840
                                                            CIP

Contents

Preface

It happens often in the physical and biological sciences, seldom in the behavioral sciences, that a line of research pursued for its theoretical interest intersects with a growing societal concern. Research on expertise is such a case. It started with efforts to understand what enables chess grandmasters to excel. Now it is being applied to finding out what it takes to be good at computer programming, medical diagnosis, instrument repair, sports of all kinds—virtually every skill that feeds society's rampant needs for high performance.

The main thing this research shows is that expertise requires enormous amounts of knowledge—far more than anyone, even the experts, had supposed. We should not minimize the importance of this finding. It radically changes the whole scale of problems related to expert knowledge and skill. But its practical upshot is the need for years of training and experience. This, it is fair to say, we already knew.

There is an important respect in which research on expertise has failed to make contact with society's interest. Virtually all the research compares experts with many years' experience to novices with very little. But as a society, we are not concerned with novices. Eventually they will quit being novices, without our having to do anything about it. The important question is what they will become. Will they become experts in their lines of work or will they swell the ranks of incompetent or mediocre functionaries? As scientists, engineers, or managers, how will they compare with their counterparts in other countries that seem to be gaining the upper hand in world commerce? As the builders of tomorrow, will they have creativity and breadth of vision? Will they be able to grasp, and make headway against, the large problems that face us? These are social concerns related to expertise, and expert-novice comparisons do not address them. We need to know what separates expertise from mediocrity and what is needed— besides training and experience—to foster continuing growth in competence. Those are the kinds of issues we hope at least to illuminate in this book.

There is a whole other set of social concerns about expertise that get summed up in statements like, 'Today's problems are too serious to be left to the expert', or—one that we especially like—'If you define a problem in such a way that only experts can solve it, you have just made the problem unsolvable.' Some readers will feel that we do not pay enough attention to these concerns. Others may feel that we pay too much. Priority, we believe, should be given to the more fundamental task of *understanding* expertise. Statements like those just quoted seem really to be referring to specialists, not experts; and treating expertise as if it were synonymous with specialization reveals a misunderstanding that can only lead to bad thinking. The capacity to acquire expertise is, we shall argue, one of the great and peculiar strengths of the human species. The challenge for social thought is how best to use this capacity to the benefit of all. But to meet that challenge, we need to understand better what it means to acquire expertise, what fosters and what stunts its development, and how it functions in people's lives and work.

We came to the study of expertise from an unusual direction, through the study of writing. Writing, as it happens, violates the conventional wisdom about expertise on a number of counts. Conventional wisdom has it that practice makes perfect and that expertise is the natural outcome of years of practice. But few people become good writers, no matter how much they write. For many, the effect of years of practice is simply to produce increasingly fluent bad writing. Conventional wisdom, backed by scores of experiments comparing novices and experts in various fields, sees experts doing quickly and easily what novices do laboriously, if they can do it at all. Novices have to reason things out, whereas experts know what to do without thinking. Yet in our research we found consistently that, given the same assignment, experts would work harder and do a great deal more thinking. The paragons of effortless performance were fifth-graders who, given a simple topic, would start writing in seconds and would produce copy as fast as their little fingers could move the pencil.

What can be observed in expert writers is something rarely observable in typical expert-novice comparisons. One observes the *growing edge* of expertise. We assume that every expert, in whatever field, has a growing edge. Doctors often remark that the great majority of cases they see are unchallenging. Routine diagnostic and treatment procedures suffice. But then there are the five or ten percent of cases that are challenging. Those cases test the growing edge of the doctor's expertise. The doctor who treats them in a routine way stops growing and is likely to drift into the category of the 15 percent of doctors whom the Ontario College of Physicians and Surgeons tags with "major deficiencies".

There is a growing edge to everyone's knowledge. But the poorer writers we studied approach the task in ways that minimize opportunities for growth, whereas the better writers maximize them. The result is a multiplier effect, where the more expert keep gaining in expertise while the less expert make little progress. Aided by research of our students, we went on to look at learners in other academic areas, and in music and medicine. The same results appeared. When working at the edge of their competence, the more expert people go about things in ways that result in their learning still more. Doesn't this suggest something about how they got to be experts in the first place, and why so many people with the time and the opportunities fail to gain expertise? We thought so, and this book is the result of seeing how far this insight could carry us in gaining an understanding of expertise.

We wish the research base for this inquiry were stronger. Despite intense research on expertise during the past decade, hardly any of it contrasts experts with experienced nonexperts or examines the growth of expertise over time—and these are the kinds of research most relevant to issues about the growing edge. However, we suspect that the problem will not be that readers go away from the book unconvinced. The more likely problem, and one we have run into when we introduced early versions of this material in a university course, is resistance to a different way of thinking about expertise. That is thinking about it in terms of process—as something people do rather than as something they have.

Thinking about expertise as a process does not come easily. One has to struggle with a language that keeps wanting to change it into a thing or a state. And thinking about *creative* expertise can get one into a real tangle, because the romantic way we are brought up to think about creativity makes expertise seem like an impediment. Really to understand expertise, we shall argue, you have to pry it loose from ideas like specialization and from the individualistic bias most of us westerners are heir to. But among the rewards for doing so is ability to take a sane view of something that, according to contemporary criticism, we need much more of but already have too much of, that is the source of our gravest problems and is our only hope for solving them.

We sketched out the main ideas of this book while bumping around Southeast Asia on a study leave in 1987 and completed a major rewriting during a current study leave at the Center for Advanced Study in the Behavioral Sciences in California. The bulk of the writing was done during odd moments taken away from research whose immediate objectives were of different sorts—research on intentional learning, knowledge-building, and a computer-based learning environment that we will say a bit about in Chapter 7. But the book would not have been what it is without that research or our earlier research on the psychology of writing. So we are indebted to all the foundations, government agencies, and private corporations that have supported our research at one time or other during the 17 years that we have been working together, specifically: Apple Computer, the Charles R. Bronfman Foundation, IBM, the James S. McDonnell Foundation, the Ontario Ministry of Colleges and Universities' University Research Incentive Fund, the Ontario Ministry of Education, the Alfred P. Sloan Foundation, and the Social Sciences and Humanities Research Council of Canada. Our current stay at the Center for Advanced Study in the Behavioral Sciences enjoys support from the Spencer Foundation and the James S. McDonnell Foundation. The support most directly relevant to the present effort, however, has come from our home institution, the Ontario Institute for Studies in Education, which, through its block research grant from the Ontario Ministry of Education, has provided the continuity over a long span of years that has made it possible for a diversity of research projects to yield something that we hope starts to resemble wisdom. Many people contributed to the research. Here we single out only those whose contributions related most directly to the present work: Jud Burtis, Carol Chan, Pam'la Ghent, Margaret Ogilvie, Evelyn Ng, and Naomi Tal.

We have also profited from two works that have tried to draw general conclusions from the diversity of research on expertise: *The Nature of Expertise*, edited by Micheline Chi, Robert Glaser, and Marshall Farr (1988), and *Toward a General Theory of Expertise*, edited by K. Anders Ericsson and Jacqueline Smith (1991). Building on, rather than duplicating, those solidly research-based contributions, we have felt free to concentrate our own efforts on a layer of psychological, educational, and social questions that research so far has left unanswered.

Chapter One
The Need to Understand Expertise

Alfred North Whitehead said, "The greatest invention of the nineteenth century was the invention of the method of invention."[1] Invention had been going on throughout previous ages, but in the nineteenth century invention itself became sufficiently understood that it would be pursued as a goal, and directed toward particular problems or needs. Without this discovery of invention, the prairie fire of innovations that swept across Europe and America could never have happened.

A discovery of similar importance may be starting to materialize here at the end of the twentieth century, and if it does, then the progress of nations in the coming century will depend in no small degree on how well they are able to capitalize on and advance this discovery. It is the discovery of the method of expertise.

Like invention, expertise has been around since the dawn of civilization, but until recent times the development of experts was able to go on without anyone's having to understand its nature or processes. Social forms such as apprenticeship evolved, whereby expertise could be passed on from one generation to the next. Even when formal education began to play a greater role, it for a long time rested on little more than the notion of a body of knowledge to be passed on to the student—knowledge which was not itself expertise but which, it could be assumed, would combine somehow with experience, natural talent, and guidance to produce an expert in good time.

Increasingly, however, societies are experiencing a need to pursue expertise itself as a goal and to find more systematic ways of doing so. Developing nations want to be able to produce experts straightaway, without having to wait for the gradual evolution of disciplines, professions, and trades. Other nations want to produce more and better experts. They want to open expert domains to previously excluded groups. They worry that the kind of expertise they are fostering may not be what the future requires. New specialties like artificial intelligence and genetic engineering arise rapidly and create sudden demands for new kinds of experts. More and more there is a need for people to acquire new kinds of expertise in mid-career.

All of this adds up to a need to understand expertise itself—what it is and how it develops. More than that, it means that people must become expert at becoming experts. There may or may not turn out to be a general 'method of expertise', but we will not know unless we look for it, and we will not know where to look unless we are guided by a theoretical understanding that goes deeper than mere descriptions of all the things that experts are able to do better than nonexperts.

The Capacity for Expertise

There are some things that human beings almost all do really well—really well, that is, in comparison to nonhumans and in comparison to how well human beings themselves do many other things. Prominent on this list are talking, counting, and reasoning. Of course, there are also other things that some animals do markedly better than we do, such as swimming, leaping about in trees, navigating by the stars, and catching flies with the tip of the tongue. This balance of natural abilities is upset, however, by the fact that human beings are also able, with effort, to acquire an almost unlimited range of other abilities, for which evolution could not possibly have specifically prepared them. To be sure, chimpanzees have learned to ride bicycles, use flush toilets, and execute many other feats alien to their biological heritage, but with nowhere near the versatility or levels of attainment shown by human beings. Among nonaquatic animals, none can swim as well as a human Olympic contender. Among nonarboreal animals, none can perform feats comparable to those of the human trapeze artist. Among nonmigratory animals, none can find its way over long distances as well as a human navigator—even a navigator who, like the Trobriand Islanders, works without instruments.[2] It is these effortfully acquired abilities, abilities that carry us beyond what nature has specifically prepared us to do, that we properly refer to as *expertise*.

What does this capacity to acquire expertise consist of? It isn't enough to say 'learning'. Other animals can learn, often very well. Rats and even cockroaches compete favorably with human beings when it comes to learning mazes. And animal learning is not always simple. The skills acquired by seeing-eye dogs are complex enough to rival some of what gets labeled expertise in humans. The uniquely human part seems to involve intentionality. Human beings, unlike dogs, can set skill as a goal and pursue it, sometimes to extraordinary levels. Or they will set other kinds of goals that lie beyond their present competence—to bake a quiche, to remove a tumor, to explain the movements of the planets—and in the process of pursuing those goals will gain new competence. Once acquired and practiced, these new competencies may become so effortless that we begin to think the person may have been born with them. Some romantics extoll the ease and naturalness of expert performance, treating that as its distinguishing characteristic.[3]

But if ease and naturalness are the criteria, then we have to conclude that fish are expert swimmers and Olympic breast-strokers are not. To our mind, any useful conception of 'expertise' has to take into account the process of acquisition. Olympic breast-strokers are experts and fish are not, precisely because of the intentional effort, through which the human athletes have acquired a competence that would never have come about naturally.

Expertise, we are arguing, is a venture beyond natural abilities. Human beings, unlike other species, may have a natural capacity for such venture, but the venture itself is effortful and chancy, highly dependent on supports that do not come from the everyday milieu.

Dismantling the Stereotypes of Expertise

Our main goal in this book is to provide a way of thinking about expertise that opens up new possibilities for developing, promoting, and dealing with it in society. There is a growing body of research on expertise, and some theory, that we will draw on, but the core difficulties, as we see them, are conceptual. 'Expertise' is a term that comes to us from ordinary language. Like most ordinary language terms, it defies precise definition, and to impose a definition on it at the outset would be a sophomoric exercise almost guaranteed to stifle productive thought.

Instead of coming to us accompanied by a definition, 'expertise' comes to us bundled with a host of social and evaluative connotations. These connotations have been picked up as a result of common experiences with people who are labeled expert, and they reflect common emotions, beliefs, and prejudices that these people excite. In short, we all have stereotypes of experts, much the way we have stereotypes of politicians, drug addicts, animal rights activists, senior citizens, and various ethnic groups. These stereotypes may have some empirical validity, but they are exceedingly mischievous when it comes to constructive thinking. In particular, they block creativity, making it difficult for us to look at things in fresh and promising ways.

In popular thought, expertise is bound up with notions such as the following:

talent	elitism
skill	paternalism
specialization	industrialism
credentialling	technology
(degrees, licensing, etc.)	rationalism (especially
professionalism	'technical rationality')
age	hubris
experience	band-aid solutions
maleness	Western culture
authority	objective truth

Little wonder that expertise has acquired a bad name in some quarters and is generally regarded as a mixed blessing! There may well be an empirical basis for all these connotations. They may represent characteristics that are statistically associated with the experts encountered in real life. One may even go so far as to argue that various of these characteristics are inevitable accompaniments of expertise. But none of this implies that these connotations are an essential part of the *concept* of expertise. Long-haired dogs may inevitably acquire burrs, but it would be a poor zoologist who treated burrs as part of the dog.

We want to disentangle expertise from its stereotypic accompaniments. There are experts who have little formal education, hold no licenses, wield little social power. There are youthful experts, experts who have no truck with modern technology, and experts whose main strength is in going beyond band-aid solutions and tackling issues in all their complexity. We shall even argue that there are experts who are not highly talented and people who, although too inexperienced to earn recognition as experts, nevertheless go about things in a distinctly *expert-like* way. If we are to think about expertise in a nonstereotyped way, we need a concept that embraces these less stereotypic examples.

Must Experts Be Specialists?

Of all the notions that have gotten attached to expertise, none sticks more tightly than the notion that expertise entails specialization. In the past, no great harm has come from thinking of the two as almost the same. But overspecialization has become a social problem. There is a growing feeling that specialization is getting out of hand and that it must somehow be curtailed. It would be unfortunate, possibly catastrophic, if movements to cut back on specialization came to war with efforts to promote expertise. Yet that is just what threatens to happen. To prevent it, we have to be able to think of expertise as something that can exist apart from specialization.

In one sense the concepts are not hard to separate. There are incompetent specialists. One of us (C.B.) had his hearing permanently damaged by an eye, ear, nose, and throat specialist whose only real expertise was in raising beef cattle. So you can have specialization without expertise. But it is more difficult to conceive of expertise without specialization.

One reason that we think of specialists whenever we think of experts is ease of identification. Expertise is easiest to identify when it differs most dramatically from what ordinary people can do. We are inclined to call anyone who can remove brain tumors an expert, because ordinary people cannot do this at all. The same goes for anyone who can play a Chopin etude at full speed without hitting wrong notes. It is much harder to identify expert teachers, because everyone can and does teach in some fashion. Or expert farmers. Here it is not so much a matter of everyone's being able to do it as there not being any particular skill or performance that can be singled out. Nothing that can be observed in the span of an hour may distinguish the expert from the inexpert farmer, and yet novices who try their hands at farming are overwhelmed by the amount of knowledge and skill required.

In order to contemplate expertise divorced from specialization, we have to look beneath the surface of expert performance, beneath the sometimes sensational display of competence, and examine what makes the performance possible. That is what cognitive researchers have been trying to do, and in Chapter 2 we will review some of their more pervasive findings. In the chapters following that, we will try to construct an 'inside view' of expertise, which makes it possible to begin recognizing expertise in areas like teaching, farming, parenting, managing, and even just living one's life—areas in which outer manifestations of expertise are not easy to recognize.

As a foretaste, we will examine an actual case of non-specialist expertise in the next section. This is a general repairman, whose genius is in being able to cope with the full range of repair problems that beset a rural community. You could say he is a specialist in fixing things, but to do so stretches the term beyond meaning. 'Things' is too broad a category to constitute the domain of a specialist. But to say he is an *expert* at fixing things—that makes sense and it can be defended with evidence.

If society is to deal successfully with problems of over-specialization, it is going to require expertise to do so. Environmental protection provides the most widely recognized case in point. Specialization has been and can be blamed for much of the unwitting pollution of the environment and destruction of wildlife habitats—specialization in the form of people pursuing their limited roles as chemists, engineers, and what not, without regard to the wider implications of what they were doing. But much of the money that people are now contributing to environmentalist groups goes to paying experts to enlighten or to combat those other experts. Originally environmentalists were amateurs or scientists venturing beyond their specialties to embrace larger issues. In time environmental studies itself became a specialty. You can major in it in college. Now, perhaps, we need new kinds of experts to overcome the limits of these specialists—for instance, people who can deal coherently with the intersecting problems of wealth creation and environmental preservation.

A similar story can be told about health care, social welfare, international relations, crime prevention, education—and on through the litany of social concerns. Everywhere it can be shown that there is a need to take a broader view of problems than is taken by the specialists involved. Only fanatics believe that solutions to the broader problems are already available and need simply to be enacted. Thinking people all recognize that the roads ahead are arduous, that the best-conceived actions will give rise to further problems that require yet more skill, wisdom, and breadth of conception. But thinking people can get into a terrible muddle and end up chasing their own tails if they persist in confusing expertise with specialization.

Here is an example. It comes from an article by Robert Welker, titled 'Expertise and the Teacher as Expert: Rethinking a Questionable Metaphor'.[4] Welker is criticizing current movements to study and foster expertise in teaching. In referring to expertise as a "metaphor" when applied to teaching, Welker is signaling his main point, which is that teaching is not the sort of occupation in which you want people to be experts. Why not? Welker emphasizes that teachers must be caring, sensitive people and that teaching is a complex human enterprise that cannot be reduced to technique. Teachers ought not to seal themselves off as an elite community of experts, but ought to be involved with and responsive to the communities in which they serve. They should be fostering growth toward independence rather than making people dependent upon them.

All this is undeniable, and makes a good argument against trying to turn out teachers who are narrowly technical specialists—but no one has been proposing that. Welker proposes that teachers need a broad liberal education and training that will prepare them for their complex social roles. But then he notes with concern that this could give rise to "a whole new breed of experts". "Expertise for these specialists," he says, "might possibly include knowledge in personnel, organizational structure, and social institutions as well as techniques in group management skills."[5] The logical conclusion to this line of thought should be, 'So it isn't that teachers should not be experts, it's that they ought to be broadly competent experts.' But having welded expertise to specialization in the opening phrase, Welker cannot proceed to this forthright conclusion, but instead offers the weak homily, "Thus in the final analysis, any efforts to avoid the negative effects of exclusive speciality need to face the questions of attitude and value."

It is generally believed that there are expert teachers, and when identified they are revered. But there is no reliable way of identifying them,[6] much less a reliable way of producing them. In many ways public education typifies the contemporary situation: the need for more expertise, the recognized inadequacy of traditional methods of developing it, and the need for a new conception of expertise that is not confused with specialization, professionalism, technocracy, and the various other notions that make up the common stereotypes.[7]

Who Is an Expert?

Although it may be futile to attempt a precise definition of expertise, we cannot proceed without refining our use of the term somewhat. Everyday uses of the term are so inconsistent as to ensure a hopeless muddle if one sets out to 'explain' or 'foster' expertise. People sometimes speak of fish as expert swimmers, and young children as expert language learners (referring to their apparent superiority to adults in picking up a new language). In other contexts, the term is closely tied to occupational status. Doctors and scientists can be experts, whereas people farther down the socio-economic ladder can only expect to be called 'skilled'. And those at the bottom are denied even that label, although researchers have documented extremely complex skills involved in what is called 'unskilled labor'.[8] Sometimes specialists are called experts, without any implication about the quality of their work. More democratically minded people will sometimes claim, instead, that everyone is an expert at something, it is just that certain kinds of expertise are more highly rewarded than they should be.

Is there anything of substance under this rubble of usages? One might be tempted to look for a dimension of complexity or difficulty along which expertise could be distinguished from more mundane competencies. However, as Paul Attewell has observed, "*all* human activity, even the most mundane, is quite complex. Things that everyone does—such as walking, crossing the road, and carrying on a conversation—are amazing accomplishments requiring a complex coordination of perception, movement, and decision, a myriad of choices, and a multitude of skills."[9] Why would we not want to call people who can successfully cross busy streets experts? We can't say the skill is trivial. Lack of it could be deadly. And it isn't quite right to say anyone can do it. Any normal person with sufficient experience can do it, perhaps. But then, might it not also be true that any normal person with sufficient experience could perform heart transplants?

Rather than trying to define expertise, as if it were some abstract thing existing in a Platonic world of pure ideas, with only distorted shadows of it being cast on our poor world, suppose we start with examples. Rather than asking 'What is expertise?' let us ask 'Who is an expert?' The examples that come immediately to mind, having been primed by contemporary clichés, are rocket scientists and brain surgeons. But these examples, although valid, are too encumbered with the stereotypes we want to overcome. We shall look for examples that may not be typical but that are cleaner.

When we bought our first microcomputer, computer repair was not the industry that it is today. Individuals with a knack for getting the things working again would establish a reputation by word of mouth. Shortly after the guarantee ran out on our machine, it developed the habit of every so often emitting a sparking sound and going dead. We took it to a local repairman whom we'll call Chang, whose shop had grown with his reputation, to the point where it included a staff of technicians. On hearing the symptoms, Chang said, "It must be the power supply. There isn't enough voltage anywhere else to make a sparking sound." He then turned the machine over to his technicians, who ran tests on it for a week and could find nothing wrong. Then began a series of trips to the manufacturer's repair facility. The people there couldn't find anything wrong either, but as the problem recurred, they began replacing parts. When we returned the computer for about the fifth time, still with the same problem, the foreman said, "There isn't anything else we can do. We've replaced everything. There's nothing left of your old computer but the box." "Did you replace the power supply?" "Well, no. . . ." And that, of course, was the problem, just as Chang had said without even looking at it. Once the power supply was replaced, the computer worked fine ever after.

A series of technically-trained people in white lab coats worked on our computer, but we are not tempted to call them experts. They probably did well enough what they had been trained to do, but they demonstrated no ability to rise to the level of the problem that confronted them. In fact, they did not seem to address problems at all, but instead performed their customary tasks, trusting that by performing them the problems would be solved. We believe this distinction is absolutely critical to a useful conception of expertise. The difference between experts and experienced nonexperts is not that one does things well and the other does things badly. Rather, the expert addresses problems whereas the experienced nonexpert carries out practiced routines. Often these routines are carried out very well and are effective in a majority of cases. It is only when the routines fail, as they did with our computer, that the difference between experts and nonexperts becomes manifest. Chang alone actually addressed the problem. Unfortunately, his expertise in electronic diagnosis was not matched by expertise in managing a shop, and so his diagnosis had no effect until we ourselves recalled it months later.

Is expertise, then, just another word for problem-solving ability? One could say yes and then add numerous qualifications, but it is better to reject the question. For the question implies that there is some general quality of intellect that can be called problem-solving ability, and this is both doubtful and beside the point. We want to say that experts and experienced nonexperts, even when they are nominally practicing the same profession, are actually pursuing different careers. *The career of the expert is one of progressively advancing on the problems constituting a field of work, whereas the career of the nonexpert is one of gradually constricting the field of work so that it more closely conforms to the routines the nonexpert is prepared to execute.*

We were reminded of Chang in reading about Willie, in Douglas Harper's remarkable book, *Working Knowledge: Skill and Community in a Small Shop* (1987). Willie is a cleaner example of an expert than Chang, because his expertise is rooted in a pre-electronic age. In fact, Harper likens him to the *bricoleurs* that Lévi-Strauss identified in primitive societies. These are people who can make or fix just about anything and whose tools and materials are the leftovers of previous jobs. Willie lives in a backward rural area, where neighbors for miles around depend on him to fix anything that exceeds their own resources—cars, farm machinery, furnaces, wells. His role in maintaining the mechanical infrastructure of the local society is not unlike the role that country doctors in generations past performed in maintaining the physical health of such societies. But Willie has no formal training, no degrees, no license.

Harper followed Willie closely through many jobs, photographing him at work, in an effort, as Harper put it, to "disassemble" Willie's genius as a fixer. It becomes immediately clear that Willie's skill is primarily mental. But it is not merely a matter of raw mental power, although something like that may also be involved. Willie knows a tremendous amount. He has a deep knowledge of materials, what can be done with them, how they will respond to various treatments. He understands his tools in the same way. His ability to fix things depends on understanding how they were made and why they were designed the way they were, and this often includes understanding shortcomings in manufacture or design that were responsible for the eventual breakdown. With this understanding, Willie is often able to modify the object in the process of repairing it, so that it is better than it was originally. His repair of a broken car door handle, for instance, does not involve simply fixing or reproducing the broken lever. It involves inventing a new lever that fits into the same handle but is less vulnerable to stress. Even Willie's manual skills have a basis in understanding. He understands why filing the teeth on a chain saw often results in rounding the edges, and this enables him to handle the file in such a way that it cuts straight.[10] This is not to say that Willie's knowledge is all conceptual, explainable. He knows how things sound or look or feel under different circumstances, and often there is no way to convey this knowledge except by demonstration. But it is knowledge nonetheless. A brilliant general problem solver, if there is such a thing (it is what Sherlock Holmes purported to be), would be helpless trying to solve Willie's problems without Willie's knowledge.

Douglas Harper's analysis of Willie's expertise conforms with the findings of researchers who study experts in many different fields.[11] What looks on the surface like sheer intellectual brilliance turns out to rest on extraordinary knowledge. To some researchers that finding explains expertise: Study and practice build up the knowledge that makes one an expert. Here the case of an untutored expert like Willie becomes important for moving beyond such a shallow explanation. With Willie, we have to ask how he acquired all his knowledge. He had no specialist training. He learned blacksmithing in apprentice fashion from his father, but his knowledge goes far beyond what his father could have taught him. Clearly, he learned it from experience—and that turns out to be how experts in all fields acquire most of their knowledge, even if they have a great deal of formal training as well.

In Willie's case, it is impossible to separate knowledge acquisition from the problem solving in which the knowledge plays its part. Willie's knowledge is deep because he tackles problems at a deep level. He understands the engineering behind the machinery he works on because he has continually addressed problems at the level of engineering rather than at a superficial, symptomatic level. He has a deep understanding of materials, "knowing how metal, wood, plastic, or even paper and cardboard respond to attempts to alter their shape, density, or pliability",[12] because he has continually tried to solve problems by taking advantage of available "junk". In restoring the badly rusted blower pipe of a field chopper, Willy has to figure out how to weld it "so it wears right, so it will last with a lot of weld and stuff . . . ." His solution is to use high-tensile steel, but then he uses a coat hanger to tack the repaired bar on:

> The high tensile doesn't have much flexibility. The coat hanger is more mild, more flexible. It's less apt to break afterward. Vibrations break the higher tensile a lot easier. But I used it because I'm welding the bar that comes up the side—that's an important place that needs more strength.[13]

Although Willie's expertise as an all-round fixer is becoming obsolete as the machinery of daily life becomes increasingly complex and electronic, there is a deeper sense in which Willie represents the wave of the future. Larry Hirschhorn, using the nuclear reactor breakdown at Three Mile Island as his prime example, argues that the job of human beings in industry is increasingly becoming that of dealing with failures of automatic systems.[14] For automatic systems will break down, like anything else. One can design another automatic system to deal with failures of the first, but there has to be an end somewhere, at which point you need a Willie who can fix things.

Modern aircraft are full of instruments to detect problems automatically, but those instruments occasionally break down. And so back in the hangar is a whole other system of instruments to diagnose what is wrong with the airborne instruments. But that system, too, has failures. There the automation stops. Human technicians have to diagnose failures in the instrument testing equipment. Alan Lesgold headed a group charged by the U.S. Air Force with finding out why some of these technicians were so much better than others at diagnosis. This is one of the few studies we know of where experts were compared, not to novices, but to experienced nonexperts. Lesgold's findings mirror what we have been saying about Willie. The experts were not superior in general problem-solving skills or in knowledge of electronics, and they went about trouble-shooting in the same way as the less expert technicians. But the experts differed from the nonexperts in having a very deep understanding of the particular systems they were working with.[15]

Hirschhorn's analysis of the Three Mile Island near-disaster indicates that the technicians there lacked this overall understanding of the system they were dealing with, were too narrowly specialized to particular tasks, and when an emergency arose they had to go by the book rather than being able to grasp the problem and solve it. Having been conditioned to think of expertise as being based on highly specialized training, we are likely to respond to such findings by recommending more formal instruction. That may be helpful, but will it produce a Willie?

To put it simply, the challenge we are trying to meet in this book is to understand the kind of expertise exhibited by Willie in such a way that we can more reliably produce people like him. They are needed everywhere. If you are wheeled into surgery, you of course want the person wielding the scalpel to be thoroughly trained in modern surgical techniques and to have a thorough knowledge of medical science relevant to your condition. But you also want that surgeon to be a Willie. You want someone who knows tissues and organs in the intimate, resourceful way that Willie knows metals and engines; who knows how things should look, sound, smell, and feel; who can reason out the cause when something is amiss; who can grasp situations as a whole rather than contending with only part of a problem.

But it is not just as 'fixers' that we need Willies. Douglas Harper makes the point that, in the approach to work taken by people like Willie, there is no sharp separation between engineering and manufacture on one hand and diagnosis and repair on the other. The mental activity is essentially the same. We need Willie's kind of expertise in the people who design and build things in the first place. We need it in the people who form laws and policies, where Willie's kind of deep knowledge goes by the name of wisdom—an understanding of people, their aims and constraints, how they will respond to "attempts to alter their shape, density, or pliability".

We want to make it clear that, in using Willie as the exemplar of expertise, we have no intent to disparage formal education and specialization. In many modern occupations these are essential. In these occupations one cannot achieve Willie's kind of deep knowledge without formal knowledge of some discipline, and there is so much to be known that one cannot learn it without specializing. The point of using Willie as the exemplar is to emphasize that formal training and specialization are not defining characteristics of expertise. One can have the necessary formal knowledge yet not acquire the kind of informal knowledge that is so intimately connected with trying to address challenging problems in one's domain.

The world of the twenty-first century will need specialists and it will also need generalists. We need a conception of expertise that applies equally well to both. There are people who resemble Willie in the world of ideas. Society's need for their kind of expertise is coming increasingly to be appreciated, although it is usually not called expertise. Our favorite exemplar here is Jane Jacobs, whose books on city life and economy have had a profound effect on architecture and urban and economic planning.[16] Architects, urban planners, and economists have all criticized her for lack of expertise in their domains. But that is like criticizing Willie because he is not a metallurgist and a mechanical engineer. You can have deep knowledge that is not specialized to any particular discipline. It will look shallow when viewed from the standpoint of neighboring disciplines, but its depth will be appreciated when it is viewed from the standpoint of the problems to which it is connected. In Willie's case the problems are those of sustaining the infrastructure of a particular rural locale, using the tools and materials already available in it. In Jane Jacob's case the problems are those of sustaining the economies and the quality of life of cities in general, again making use of endemic resources. The visible products of Willie's problem-solving efforts are silage blowers and tractors that work again. The visible products of Jane Jacob's efforts are books presenting ideas about why some inner city neighborhoods are safe to live in and how cities become economically strong. But the invisible product in both cases is an ever-deepening knowledge that grows out of problem solving and keeps feeding back into it.

Can There Be a 'Method of Expertise'?

Probably no one is naive enough to believe that there could be some general method, encapsulated in a book with a money-back guarantee, which would enable one to by-pass novicehood in any chosen field and go directly to being an expert. Although differences in talent seemingly make it much easier for some people than others, we know that in general it takes a great deal of time and experience to become an expert. Ten thousand hours is the figure that John R. Hayes comes up with, having studied biographies of experts in many fields.[17]

That being the case, what kind of method could speed up the process? We believe that that is not the right question. Such a question arises from the standard way of thinking about expertise, as a state that is arrived at gradually by progression through one or more pre-expert stages. Dreyfus and Dreyfus, who provide the most thoughtful elaboration of the conventional view, identify five stages of progress toward expertise. There is a novice stage where one rather blindly follows limited rules; then there is a stage of more flexible and situationally sensitive rule use. At the third stage, which Dreyfus and Dreyfus call "competence", one applies goal-directed plans and strategies. At the next stage, one has accumulated enough experience that one can often recognize what needs to be done and so have less need of planning and problem solving. At the final stage, for which they reserve the term "expertise", decision making becomes unnecessary and one just naturally does the right thing without having to think about it.

The trouble with such an analysis is that, when it comes to explaining or fostering expertise, it doesn't lead anywhere except back to the familiar standbys of time and experience. Like most other analyses, it speaks to the difference between experts and novices rather than to the difference between experts and experienced nonexperts. One of the examples the Dreyfuses use to illustrate their five-stage scheme is automobile driving. It nicely illustrates the progression from having to think everything out and being almost blind to situations onward to the state where driving through traffic is second nature and requires hardly any thought. But some drivers go through this same progression and end up being bad drivers. They too reach the state where everything happens automatically, by second nature, but the result is that they are mindless menaces on the highway. In fact, very few people, despite extensive experience, ever become expert drivers in any significant sense—as in, 'It's going to be tough getting back to town in this weather. We'd better let Jeannie drive; she's an expert.' But almost everyone who drives long enough reaches the state of effortlessly doing the right thing, *under normal conditions, most of the time.* It is just that such performance doesn't distinguish the expert from the experienced nonexpert.

The problem is not how to turn novices into experts faster or with less work. The problem is how to ensure that novices develop into experts rather than into experienced nonexperts. In trying to make headway on that problem, we have found it more useful to think of expertise as a characteristic of careers rather than as a characteristic of people. The problem then is how to get people to pursue expert careers and to sustain them in those careers.

As earlier discussion should have made clear, an expert career is not necessarily highly specialized or professionalized or one that requires extensive formal training. It could be law. It could be hairdressing. It could be carpentry. What makes it an expert career is that it is pursued in the manner of a Willie, addressing and readdressing, with cumulative skill and wisdom, the constitutive problems of the job, rather than reducing the dimensions of the job to what one is already accustomed to doing.

Attributing expertise to the career rather than to the person has several virtues: first, it makes better sense of ups and downs. Some people maintain expert careers for years and then they become discouraged or complacent or infirm and their work declines. Actors and artists start imitating themselves. Doctors start processing patients instead of attending to their problems. Clerks and building inspectors start saying 'no' to anything that is out of the ordinary. Should we say that such people have lost their expertise? It seems more reasonable to say that they have ceased to maintain expert careers. Sometimes people's careers will go into a decline and then they will pick up again. It would be bizarre to say that people lost their expertise and then regained it. But there is meaning in saying that someone switched from an expert career to a nonexpert way of carrying on their work and then switched back again.

Secondly, attributing expertise to the career rather than to the person offers a perspective from which there is more to expertise than skill. Is someone who can type accurately at 120 words per minute an expert? The question is too limited to be answerable. One wants to ask about the career of this person who types so rapidly. Has there been a continual investment of effort in achieving greater speed or has the person plateaued years ago and now types as indifferently at 120 words per minute as other typists do at half that speed? Is this a solitary skill or is it part of a more general development of secretarial prowess? Where is it leading? What's the point? These are all legitimate questions to ask about expert careers. Not to ask them is to reduce expertise to skill and to lose much of what makes expertise a lively human concern.

Thirdly, attributing expertise to the career invites us to look for differences between experts and nonexperts across the whole career span, rather than only at the pinnacle. What was Willie like in the early days of his career? It is a reasonable guess that he was much as we have seen him, only less knowledgeable, more liable to make mistakes. We suppose, however, that even then he was tackling problems at a deeper level than his peers, making fuller use of the knowledge he had, and in the process increasing that knowledge. In Chapter 6 we will present evidence that there are in fact people who can be characterized as *expertlike novices*. If these are, indeed, the experts of the future, then they can provide us clues as to how expertise may be fostered in early stages of people's careers.

The notions of career and expertise are closely linked even in ordinary usage. We would not call people who are good at crossing busy streets experts, unless they have managed to make a career of it. (One could imagine someone in Rome making a career of guiding frightened tourists through the torrent of traffic around the Colosseum.) When a hobbyist starts to become expert at model railroading, stamp collecting, or whatever the case may be, the hobby starts taking on the characteristics of a career. Conversely, when people perform their work indifferently, we hesitate to call them experts, even if they are skillful, and by the same token we are inclined not to speak of them as having a career.

Not every job provides scope for an expert career. There are repetitious jobs, which may involve quite complex skills, but the skills, once acquired, need merely be practiced. Traditional assembly-line jobs, data-entry typing, garment-making—these are often-cited examples (although with job restructuring even such jobs are coming to take on more of the challenging character of careers). In most other jobs people have a choice as to the level at which they will approach their work. In all lines of work that involve design, planning, leadership, teaching, or helping people with their problems, the *potential* complexity of problems to be addressed exceeds anyone's capacity. Thus, as Herbert Simon argued in putting forth his idea of 'bounded rationality',[18] people must simplify. But people have a choice of how much they will simplify. They can simplify to the maximum that conditions permit, reducing the work as much as possible to undemanding routines. Or they can simplify to the minimum that their knowledge and talent will permit. (And, of course, there are gradations in between.)

Our conjecture is that in order to be experts, people must choose to address the problems of their field at the upper limit of the complexity they can handle. And they must make this choice early in their careers, or perhaps even earlier, as school children. For it is through such working at the upper edge that people develop the deep knowledge that makes expert performance possible. Most of the rest of this book will be devoted to elaborating the research and thinking that lie behind this conjecture and investigating its implications. If the conjecture is correct, then a 'method of expertise' will need to have both an individual and a societal aspect. For the individual, a method of expertise would consist of personally effective and rewarding ways of living at the edge of one's competence—not necessarily the same ways for all people and all fields. For society, it would mean having a culture that encourages and sustains expert-like endeavors. Modern North American society rewards expert performance, with some exceptions, but it provides hardly any support for the processes that build expert knowledge and thus make expert performance possible. A first step in changing things is to get a clearer idea of what those processes are.

Beyond Individualistic Expertise

We have been at pains to discredit the idea that expertise necessarily involves specialization. Assuming that it does can make it virtually impossible to think clearly about problems of overspecialization. An even more pervasive assumption is that expertise is necessarily a property of individuals. This assumption is harmful in two ways. First, it encourages us to think of expertise as a *thing,* and so to get caught up in questions of how to measure it, how to find out who has it or is likely to acquire it, what its parts are, and so on. These are not pointless questions, but they do tend to lead us away from what we consider to be a much larger question: *How can society take fuller advantage of the human capacity for expertise?* Second, the individualistic assumption limits our ability to think about expertise insofar as it involves two or more agents. Even the most hardened individualist recognizes that there is such a thing as teamwork and that without it a group of individually expert players may produce decidedly inexpert results. But according to this view, expertise is one thing, dependent on certain abilities and dispositions, and teamwork is another, dependent on other traits and on social factors such as compatibility and leadership. We would like to develop a richer conception, which would recognize that teamwork *is* expertise, but it is expertise that can be observed only at the level of the group, not at the level of the individual.

In order to do justice to teamwork as a variety of expertise, we would need to be able to identify expert knowledge that is the property of a group rather than the property of the individuals composing it, and we would need to think of a group's having a career that might follow an expert path, continually advancing the edge of its competence. It is not easy to think this way, especially for those of us brought up in Western traditions with their individualistic bias. Cognitive science does, however, provide us with a way to think along these lines that does not require a complete cultural overhaul. What cognitive scientists have managed to do, in a straightforward rationalistic way, is to separate processes from agents. Thus, it is possible to describe a process of problem solving or object recognition or sentence production, which simply states what functions are performed and with what organization. This process might then be, as it is usually put, 'implemented' by a machine, by a person, by a group of people performing different parts of the process, or by even more esoteric combinations, such as a person and a machine or a person and an animal. (On this latter point, consider the expert performance of teams composed of a human being and a dog—in hunting, in police work, in pedestrian travel—where the dog's superior sensory abilities are essential but where the teamwork involves much more than this.)

In the same way, we hope to develop an idea of expertise as a process that can be implemented or realized in various ways. The most common way is in the career of an individual, but it is also possible for a team or a corporation or, conceivably, a whole society to function in an expert way. In the case of child actors or musicians, it may require a parent-child pair to function collectively in an expert way, but gradually the child takes over more of the process and is eventually functioning as a mature expert. The process, as we shall present it, cannot foreseeably be realized by a machine, despite the growing sophistication of expert systems. But a machine cannot compare to a dog, let alone to a human being, when it comes to such functions as parenting or taking part in a social gathering, and so it should not be surprising that it cannot pursue an expert career, despite being able to do some of the things an expert does. (More of this in the next chapter.) Of more practical importance is the question of whether the process can be realized by people who under present circumstances will not do so. In short, is it teachable or can it be fostered somehow?

Understanding expertise in a way that will enable us to produce more experts is one goal of our undertaking, but it is not the highest goal. The mere proliferation of individual experts does not constitute taking full advantage of the human capacity for expertise. It could even worsen the problems that social critics link to expertise—overspecialization, overdependence on technology and professional care, a widening social and economic gap between an expert class and the lower classes. Rather than seeing these as problems that must be dealt with by restraints and countermeasures, we would hope that a better understanding of expertise might enable us to turn expert careers to better advantage.

An expert career can follow a variety of paths, and some of these are paths that go beyond simply getting better and better at one's occupation—beyond what is sometimes ridiculed as "knowing more and more about less and less." Two paths that are of special social importance are these:

1. Applying expert skills to broader social needs. Knowledge is power. As expert knowledge increases, so does power to do good and to do harm. Instead of increasing specialization, some experts start broadening the use of their talents, into other areas of value to the community. Managers, marketers, and lawyers, among others, will often contribute their expertise to volunteer organizations or social causes. But more important would be for experts to incorporate higher social goals into the main line of their work, and for organizations to develop in ways that made this a normal rather than a subversive way to go.

2. Giving expertise away. This expression is adopted from George Miller, who in his presidential address to the American Psychological Association in 1969 urged members to "give psychology away". What Miller advocated is the polar opposite of what professions are often accused of. Instead of hoarding specialized knowledge and making the public more dependent on it, Miller was urging psychologists to share their knowledge so as to make the public less dependent on them. The ideal would be for professions to do away with themselves by disseminating their knowledge or the fruits of their knowledge until there was no longer a need for their specialized expertise. It is important to appreciate that this sort of effort is not an aberration, a reaction *against* expertise.

Rather, it is one particularly admirable way in which expert careers can develop. It represents progressive advancement on the problems of a field, where progress means going beyond the individual delivery of professional services and trying to do something about the conditions that give rise to a need for those services in the first place. There is no evidence that psychology has moved significantly in that direction, but, as we shall discuss in Chapter 8, there are other professions where advances have been made in giving expertise away.

None of this is to deny the importance of expertise of the kind manifested by individuals. They can be found, though sometimes rarely, in every field. Jean Lave has said that most people don't have problems, they have predicaments. If you have a predicament and have to look for help from someone—be it a hardware store proprietor, a priest, a courthouse clerk, or an airline ticket agent—you dearly hope that you will encounter an expert. For an expert will turn your predicament into a problem and then help you solve it. The nonexperts will provide you with a standard course to follow, more likely than not adding further complications to your predicament. A tenfold increase in society's supply of experts would not mean that experts are in the employment lines looking for work. It would mean that all the world's work was being done better, that people's predicaments were being eased, that life was becoming more livable for practically everyone. And so we shall start there, trying to understand expertise at the individual level, but trying to understand it in a way that does not keep us bound to that level.

Chapter Two
Experts are Different from Us:
They Have More Knowledge

To F. Scott Fitzgerald's suggestion that the very rich are "different" from the rest of us, Ernest Hemingway gave the famous rejoinder, "Yes, they have more money." Hemingway's implication, of course, was that the rich are not different in any fundamental or interesting way. Their seemingly great differences from the common herd are merely a consequence of their wealth, not a larger constellation of differences of which wealth is only a part. Just so, there is a view of expertise according to which all the ways in which experts appear to differ from novices are merely a consequence of greater knowledge of their specialties. Yet psychologists who have pursued this way of thinking about expertise have found the differences between expert and nonexpert knowledge and the consequences thereof to be intensely interesting. In this chapter we shall try to see why such differences have proved interesting and what questions remain unanswered by the claim that it's all in what you know.

Thinking Better or Knowing More?

The modern study of expertise dates from de Groot's research on chess masters, which appeared in 1965.[1] To appreciate the impact of this research, one must take account of the mystique that has surrounded the game of kings. A game of strategy, it has been played by militarists with the notion that it would perfect the mental skills needed to plan battles. Even today chess finds its way into school curricula aimed at teaching children to think.[2] If ever there were a domain in which expertise rested on thinking abilities rather than knowledge, chess would seem to be it. The rules, though a bit complicated, can be mastered in an hour or so. Becoming expert at the game takes years.

What de Groot found was that chess masters did not think ahead farther than lesser players, nor did they consider more possibilities. If anything, they considered fewer, but they tended to consider only good moves. De Groot's most pregnant finding, however, had to do with ability to remember chessboard configurations. Given only a few seconds to examine an arrangement of pieces on a board, chess masters could accurately reproduce the arrangement from memory, whereas less accomplished players were much less able to do so. Superior memories? Not in the sense of superior brain hardware, certainly, for de Groot found that the superiority of the chess masters held only when chessboard configurations were meaningful ones—configurations that might occur in a real game. Experts were no better than lesser players at remembering random arrangements. In a later replication, Chase and Simon neatly demonstrated the difference by in one case using chessboard configurations taken from reports of tournament games and in the other case using the same configurations of occupied squares but randomly changing which pieces occupied which squares.

In a series of experiments Chase and Simon tried to pin down the nature of the chess masters' mysterious memory for chess configurations.[3] Did they have whole chessboard scenes stored in their heads, so that they could recognize one as—*aha!*—number 1267? Not quite. Judging from the order in which experts placed pieces on the board when trying to recreate a configuration and the kinds of errors they made, Chase and Simon concluded that chess masters had stored in memory a large number of 'chunks' consisting of arrangements of eight pieces or so that were related in a strategically significant way. These then represented a kind of huge alphabet—numbering beyond ten thousand items, according to Chase and Simon's estimate. With it, any chessboard arrangement could be represented as a 'word' composed of no more than six or seven of these chunks. This didn't work with random arrangements, of course, because they aren't composed of these recognizable chunks. This huge alphabet clearly constitutes knowledge. Although it cannot be said that the Chase and Simon studies proved that knowledge accounts for chess expertise, they did shift the burden of proof onto those who would claim otherwise—and two further decades of research have not turned up a strong competing explanation.

The research on chess experts did more than contribute insight into the contents of the chess master's mind. It also provided an experimental strategy that could be applied to expertise in many other areas, limited only by the ingenuity of experimenters in devising relevant arrangements of something or other that can be presented for a few seconds of inspection, then whisked away, leaving the subject with the task of recalling the arrangement. Results similar to those in chess have been obtained in electronics, when experts and nonexperts are shown wiring diagrams that do or do not represent reasonable circuits. Experts surpass less advanced specialists in recalling sensible diagrams but not in recalling meaningless ones.[4] There has been a rash of studies having to do with team sports, where instead of chess pieces on a board you can present diagrams of football players in action on a field, hockey players swarming around the goal, and so on. The same general result is reproduced again and again: Experts in the sport are much better than nonexperts at reconstructing a briefly examined scene provided it portrays a realistic state of affairs in a game, but not if it portrays an arbitrary or random placement of players.[5] The finding shows up again in music, when the task is to remember passages of numerical notation. Experts are better at remembering 'good' melodies than 'bad', whereas nonexperts show no difference.[6]

Studies after Chase and Simon, with more extensive sampling of chess players, have shown that matters are not quite so tidy as the preceding account suggests. There is evidence that better players do, in fact, think ahead somewhat further, and they are somewhat better at remembering both random and meaningful arrays of chess pieces.[7] Nevertheless, the original findings live on as a turning point in thinking about expertise. The image of the chess master as a supreme reasoner remains demolished and in its place we have the more banal image of an expert with a head chock full of knowledge—knowledge not of any very exalted kind, just the kind of knowledge that you would expect to result from increasing familiarity with the objects of one's trade, but far greater in quantity than anyone had imagined.

The Knack for Being Right

Interesting as it may be, pattern knowledge does not explain everything about expertise. By itself it does not explain anything. Through special training, non–chess players have been brought up to the same level of skill in memory for chessboard configurations as chess masters. This does not make them experts at chess. In fact, their skill is irrelevant. They recognize the chessboard configurations by features that have nothing to do with chess—for instance, by the resemblance of one arrangement to a candlestick.[8] Chess experts do not merely recognize thousands of chessboard patterns, they recognize them in ways that are relevant to playing the game.

Studies of pattern recognition in sports show how finely tuned it is to the requirements of the game. Expert field hockey players are better at recognizing offensive arrangements of players while basketball players are best at recognizing defensive arrangements. This difference corresponds to the different character of the games. In hockey, defense tends to be fluid, but players must quickly recognize when an attack is being mounted. In basketball, on the other hand, quick recognition of the defensive formation is important for taking advantage of openings. Expert volleyball players are not distinctly better than novices at memory for arrangements of players, but they are exceptionally quick at detecting presence or absence of the volleyball in scenes that are flashed before them. This, say sports psychologists Allard and Starkes, makes sense in view of how fast the ball travels in championship volleyball and the fact that players' movements are often intended to deceive opponents as to the path of the ball.[9]

Thus there is more to experts' knowledge of patterns than just familiarity based on repeated exposure to common configurations. The patterns experts learn to recognize are ones of high *significance*. This fact seems to relate to de Groot's other fascinating finding, that chess masters do not consider unusually large numbers of possibilities but that the possibilities they consider tend all to be good ones. That too is a finding that has been replicated in other fields. Expert medical diagnosticians do not consider more symptoms than do novices, but they attend to more important ones—that is, to symptoms that point to the underlying disease—and they do not consider more possible diagnoses but rather consider only the more plausible ones.[10]

When we start talking about the ability of experts to recognize what is significant or promising, it begins to sound as if superior mental powers are beginning to worm their way back in to the characterization of expertise. It is as if experts possess a sixth sense. Some commentators go so far as to suggest something like a sixth sense, a knack defying the ordinary rules of reasoning, as a defining characteristic of expertise.[11] Neil Charness, who has carried forward experimental research into chess expertise in the tradition of de

Groot and Chase and Simon, has gone some distance toward demystifying this aspect of chess expertise. Although memory for chessboard patterns is a good predictor of level of chess expertise, Charness has found a better one. It is textbook knowledge about chess. There is a vast literature devoted to analysis of chess openings, middle, and end games, and chess experts devote a great deal of time to studying it. And so one answer to how chess masters know what are significant patterns and what are promising possibilities to consider is that they have read about them in books.[12]

Because there are computer programs now that play chess at expert levels, we can use them to gain some insight into the knack for being right. For whatever computers may have going for them, it is certainly not a sixth sense. They are still a long way from having mastered the first five. The most successful programs, according to Charness, do not work the way a human chess expert does. By exploiting superior computing power and speed, they do in fact think farther ahead and consider more possibilities than human opponents. Thus they are more like what people used to imagine human chess masters to be. The knowledge they use for making decisions tends, on the other hand, to be simplistic compared to that of the human expert. Charness offers the intriguing idea that human beings rely on knowledge to compensate for their limited computing power. Given that we cannot weigh many different possibilities in mind at once and cannot think far ahead along different paths, we have to build up and use kinds of knowledge that enable us to act intelligently despite the limited scope of our reasoning.

This is the deeper meaning of the claim that expertise is knowledge. Expert knowledge is not just a head full of facts or patterns, a reservoir of data for the intellect to operate upon. Rather, it is information so finely adapted to task requirements that it enables experts to do remarkable things with intellectual equipment that is bound by the same limitations as that of other mortals. In a sense, knowledge takes the place of intellect rather than being the stuff it uses. At one level this is not a very radical notion. Everyday experience provides numerous instances in which having the appropriate knowledge relieves us of the need for hard thinking or, conversely, lacking critical knowledge turns an otherwise straightforward task into a difficult problem. Household repairs figure prominently in our experience in this regard. But behind these commonsense observations lie three issues that are problematic for understanding expertise:

First, the idea that knowledge replaces thought implies that experts, contrary to popular beliefs, may actually do *less* thinking than novices. That, in fact, is what expert-novice comparisons tend to show. The second issue is the domain specificity of expert knowledge. If the knowledge that makes expertise possible is so finely adapted to performance, it cannot have much generality outside its domain. And so this raises the question of whether there is anything interesting to be learned from studying expertise across different domains. The third issue is how such marvellous knowledge comes about.

The third issue is by far the most neglected in research on expertise, whereas the first has gotten more attention than it deserves. We have already intimated, and will try to show more fully in this chapter, that it is largely a false issue that can be disposed of by drawing some useful distinctions. The second issue, whether there is anything worth finding out about experts *in general,* is one that cannot be settled without investigating the third issue, how expert knowledge comes about. That will be the task for most of the remaining chapters of the book. For the present, however, let us consider what is to be learned from studies that have compared the way experts and novices tackle problems in their fields.

Do Experts Think Less?

In their classic work on problem solving, Newell and Simon examined how people went about solving puzzles such as missionary-and-cannibal problems. (There are, say, three missionaries and three cannibals who must cross a river using only a two-passenger boat. If at any time cannibals outnumber missionaries on either side of the river, the missionaries turn into dietary supplements.) A powerful strategy employed by the more successful problem solvers was that of reasoning backward from the goal. Start with the goal of all the missionaries and cannibals having arrived on the far side of the river. Then consider what states could come immediately before that end state. Then consider what states could precede each of these, and so on. If you do that with the problem of three missionaries and three cannibals, you will discover that in order to get to the final state of having everyone safely across the river you will have to achieve a situation in which all the missionaries are across the river with none of the cannibals there. This state then becomes a new goal, or subgoal, that you must figure out how to achieve. This setting of subgoals that bring you in reach of the end goal is part of what Newell and Simon called "means-end analysis", and which they saw as the heart of intelligent problem solving.[13]

Means-end analysis is hard work. It requires holding two situations in mind while thinking about how one can be changed into the other. After you had solved a number of missionaries-and-cannibals problems you would probably acquire some standard procedures that would allow you to start right in moving toward a solution, without such taxing analysis. You would then be working forward rather than working backward.

Comparisons of experts and novices in several different areas show that novices typically use a difficult working-backward approach whereas experts tend toward the less effortful forward procedure. It has been found to be true in mathematics, physics, and medical diagnosis.[14] Research on medical diagnosis is particularly interesting, because it demonstrates more clearly than any other research we know of how knowledge influences problem-solving strategies.

In the typical medical expertise study, interns or residents are compared with experienced specialists by presenting them with case descriptions and asking them to think aloud as they arrive at a diagnosis. Inexperienced diagnosticians make extensive use of reasoning backward from hypothesized diagnoses. That is, they will select a candidate diagnosis and then check out the description to see whether it contains facts that support or contradict that diagnosis. This approach manages to be both laborious and unreliable. It involves going back over the facts repeatedly to check out different possibilities. Errors can arise from accepting a diagnosis because there is some evidence to support it and no evidence against it, although some other diagnosis, not yet considered, would more fully accommodate the facts. Experts, by contrast, reason forward by noting significant facts and what they may suggest or imply, thus converging on a diagnosis in a straightforward manner.

Why do novices do things the hard way? Would they not be better off using the forward-reasoning approach of the experts? Almost certainly not. Evidence against such a notion comes from the finding that when experts encounter difficult diagnostic problems, they too resort to reasoning backward. The most telling demonstration comes from a study by Guy-Marie Joseph and Vimla Patel, in which expert endocrinologists and cardiologists tackled a diagnostic problem in cardiology. In this circumstance, whether physicians reasoned forward like experts or reasoned backward like novices depended on whether the problem was in their specific area of expertise.[15]

It seems that what is a good problem-solving strategy depends on how much you know, and that experts and novices alike tend to employ the strategy best suited to their state of knowledge. If you do not have much relevant knowledge, you can compensate to a degree by making maximum use of the knowledge you do have. This may mean struggling to recall partly forgotten knowledge and searching afield for analogies that you can apply in the unfamiliar situation. It may mean testing many leads. It may mean holding several items of information in mind at once (a demanding task for human beings) while you try to connect them. When you have ample knowledge, much of this mental effort can be avoided. Relevant knowledge comes immediately to mind. You have orderly procedures ready to apply. You recognize promising leads. You know what relationships to look for and therefore don't have to discover them. Instead of analyzing, you need merely recognize.

The Limitations of Expert-Novice Comparisons

Without too much exaggeration, we hope, we have presented the picture of expertise that emerges from a large body of research on expert-novice comparisons. It is a picture of increasingly effortless proficiency. The expert becomes a kind of oracle, able to draw forth from inner knowledge an answer to anything within his or her specialty. This on-top-of-it image fits some flesh-and-blood experts one is likely to know, but not others. Many experts we know are active, striving people. They work long hours, usually at something they consider to be quite difficult, and they tend to set standards for themselves and others that are always at least slightly beyond reach. When at liberty to do so, one of the first things they will admit is that they are deplorably ignorant. When such people start to act as if they have effortless access to the answers, it is sometimes a sign that they are over the hill.

The issue is not which is the more typical variety of expert. The issue is that an adequate description of expertise ought to span all varieties, and expert-novice studies seem to fail on this count. The difficulty can be traced to inherent limitations of the research method. First, comparisons of experts and novices give us a static picture. They show what experts know and do at a given moment, but they show nothing about how experts got to where they are or how they maintain their expertise. The presumptive answer is "through practice", but the research doesn't really tell us that or give us any basis for inferring whether more is involved. Second, expert-novice comparisons almost always employ tasks that are easy for the experts, comfortably below the limits of their competence.[16] This is done in order that the novices can also handle the tasks in some fashion. Comparing expert mathematicians with undergraduates on problems that truly challenged the mathematicians would be pointless; the typical undergraduate would have no inkling of what the problem was, let alone be able to work at solving it. Yet what may be most important to understand about experts is what goes on at the edge of their competence.

There are, however, some tasks on which both experts and novices can work at the edge of their competence. These are tasks that permit latitude in how people will define them or at what level they will approach them. Writing is one such task. Give people a topic to write on and they are free to treat it as a simple matter of putting down what they know about the topic or as a challenging task of producing an original essay. Or ask people to discuss an issue of policy. You may get anything from an instant opinion to a careful analysis of the issue's complexity. The two tasks combine when people are assigned to write a brief essay on an issue such as 'Should students be allowed to choose what they study in school?' Thinking-aloud transcripts of people composing essays on this topic have shown that the more expert writers use five or six times as many words in thinking through the task than they use in the actual essay, whereas the least expert writers do little more than think of the actual words they will put down. The more expert writers (those whose essays are rated as having the most fully developed main points) are found to engage in all sorts of effortful searching, evaluating, and reconsidering in the process of arriving at a main point, whereas the least expert writers settle on their main points in less than a minute of thought. In this context, then, it is clear that experts do work harder and that they do more rather than less thinking than the less competent.[17]

Fluid and Crystallized Expertise

There is a concept in the field of intelligence measurement that we can borrow to make sense of the findings on expertise and effort. It is a distinction between fluid and crystallized abilities. Among tests of intelligence, some employ tasks that manifestly demand reasoning, problem solving, or some such component of what people normally think of as intelligence. Examples are analogies tests or tests that require you to identify the missing element in a figure or a number series or a set of objects. But then there are other intelligence tests, equally valid according to psychometric evidence, that simply test knowledge. Vocabulary tests are the prime example, but tests of cultural knowledge or of world events are equally effective when applied to people of similar backgrounds. How could such fundamentally different kinds of tests measure the same thing?

According to the fluid/crystallized distinction they do not measure quite the same thing. Reasoning tests and the like measure fluid intelligence, which consists of mental processes active at the moment. A vocabulary test does not require much in the way of active mental processing, but it reflects the residue of past mental activity. Put more precisely,

> crystallized intelligence represents previously constructed assemblies of performance processes retrieved as a system and applied anew in instructional or other performance situations not unlike those experienced in the past, whereas fluid intelligence represents new assemblies, or the flexible reassembly, of performance processes needed for more extreme adaptations to novel situations.[18]

Applying the same concepts to expertise, we can distinguish a crystallized form of expertise consisting of intact procedures, well learned through previous experience, that can be brought forth and applied to familiar kinds of tasks. Then there is fluid expertise, consisting of abilities that are brought into play on novel or challenging tasks or tasks that the expert has elected to treat in a challenging way. It is in the nature of expert-novice research that the tasks assigned are usually ones that call on crystallized expertise in the experts and on fluid abilities in the novices. It is little wonder then that the novices are found to think more and work harder. It takes a different kind of task to give us a view of what fluid expertise is like. Essay writing is such a task, and it shows experts to think more.

Crystallized and fluid expertise interact. By giving us a picture only of crystallized expertise, the expert-novice research fails to give us a dynamic picture of fluid expertise being converted into crystallized and crystallized expertise providing a basis for the further growth of fluid expertise. That is the sort of picture we will hope to begin developing in later chapters, when we consider expertise as a process.

The fluid/crystallized distinction helps us make sense of some of the varied images that exist of expert careers. In the young expert-on-the-rise we may see much of the effortful, fluid part of expertise, whereas crystallized expertise is more evident in the mature person. As with intelligence in general, crystallized expertise may continue to function when old age has diminished fluid expertise—hence the wise old expert who may, however, have trouble adapting to new developments. In some fields like championship athletics and very fast-moving science, fluid expertise may be pre-eminent. Energetic striving, in full view of one's audience and associates, is the socially approved image. There is no such thing as having acquired enough skill that one can begin to take it easy, because there are always too many talented younger competitors coming up. In some professions, on the other hand, crystallized expertise may be the only kind presented to public view. Physicians, especially, are traditionally expected to do their problem solving and learning behind the scenes and present an all-knowing facade to their clients.

Where Expert-Novice Comparisons Leave Us

It is easy both to overrate and to underrate what expert-novice comparisons tell us about the nature of expertise. To infer from these studies that expertise is nothing but the inevitable residue of practice is surely to endow these studies with more force than they deserve. It also seems unwise to make very much of such findings as the expert's use of forward reasoning versus the novice's reliance on reasoning backward. We have to keep in mind that what expert-novice studies show before anything else is people behaving in perfectly reasonable ways given the knowledge at their disposal.

But it would be equally unfortunate to write this research off as showing only the obvious—that experts know a lot and do well at their trades. We have expert-novice research to thank for revealing the extent to which knowledge penetrates to all aspects of expert functioning. It is not just a mental library that the expert consults. It provides the categories or cognitive chunks with which the expert apprehends situations. In effect knowledge enables experts to see the world differently, to parse it automatically into elements that they know how to deal with.

Can Aritificial Intelligence Explain Expertise?

There is a close tie between the study of expertise and the design of artificial expert systems. 'Knowledge engineers' study live experts in order to translate their knowledge into rules that a computer program can operate on. It might seem, therefore, that a successful expert system—one that in some significant way performs on a par with human experts—ought to represent a good working theory of expertise.

Unfortunately, matters are not that simple. There are important things to be learned about human expertise from looking at expert systems, but there are also two major obstacles to drawing inferences about human expertise from its electronic counterpart. One is a part-whole problem and the other is a level-of-abstraction problem.

The part-whole problem is the more obvious one. No expert system tries to do everything a human expert does or to embody all the human's knowledge and abilities. It tries to handle a limited range of tasks and to get by on knowledge closely related to those tasks. But what parts of human expertise are left out and what is their significance? Obviously the expert system cannot tell us that; we would need a more comprehensive theory that told us how the part of human expertise embodied in an artificial system related to the whole.

One thing we can say is that the part of human expertise that gets represented in present-day expert systems is crystallized expertise, which we defined earlier as "intact procedures, well learned through previous experience, that can be brought forth and applied to familiar kinds of tasks". The success of expert systems, in areas like medical diagnosis, is a testimony to the power of crystallized expertise. *Mycin,* a bundle of software that contains no fundamental knowledge about germs or the immune system, has nevertheless won a place for itself as an intellectual tool in the diagnosis of infectious diseases.[19] Such systems get better and better, just by adding more rules or replacing fallible rules with less fallible ones. By providing concrete proof of how much it is possible to accomplish with superficial knowledge and simple reasoning, expert systems stand as a challenge to psychologists to come up with equally solid evidence of what else is required to constitute human expertise. But by being limited to crystallized expertise, artificial systems prove to have the same limitations as do expert-novice comparisons when it comes to enlightening us about the nature of human expertise. They tell us nothing about how expertise is acquired or about how experts function at the leading edge of their competence.[20]

Even if an expert system were created that functioned all around like a human expert, we would still be a large step away from having an adequate understanding of expertise. We might suppose that whoever designed that expert system understood human expertise, but they might or might not be able to convey their understanding to the rest of us. Their computer program alone would not do it, because it would be only one instance, not enough to convey the generality. If they produced a series of instances, expert systems in different domains, each duplicating the full range of human expertise in that domain, someone would have to do the work of extracting a set of general principles from those instances. That is the level-of-abstraction problem.

A theory of expertise has to be built at one level of abstraction higher than the models which represent actual expert competence. If you wanted to implement a theory of architecture, you would not write a program that simulates a house. You would write a program that simulates an architect—in other words, one that designs houses. But if you want to implement a theory about *expertise* in architecture, then you do not want a program that simulates an architect. You want a program that, as it were, designs architects. The model implemented in such a program is not a model of an expert architect nor even the model of a generic expert. If it simulates anything it should simulate the intuitions of designers of expert systems or of teachers who are successful at making experts out of novices.

One implication of this argument is that we are some way off from having an adequate theory of expertise, even if we already know quite a bit about the knowledge and intelligence that go into expert performance. If there were already people who were consummately skillful at producing experts, artificial or natural, then we could try to figure out what they intuitively know and try to formalize it into a theory. But people actually engaged in the business of producing experts are limited by lack of the very theory we would like to educe from them. In areas where understanding of expertise is severely limited, this situation represents a real and serious impasse. Efforts to train more expert teachers, for instance, often amount to insisting that trainees receive more and more coaching and instruction from people who may or may not be expert teachers themselves but who in any case are likely not to have the slightest idea of what it takes to produce an expert teacher. In many other areas the situation is better in that fairly reliable procedures have evolved for transmitting expertise from one generation to the next, but efforts to improve those procedures remain hampered by ignorance.

Most likely, progress in understanding expertise is going to have to come about through an interplay of practical and basic research activity, with the practical including both educational experiments and efforts to advance the design of artificial systems. There seems little prospect that any one of these activities could continually lead the others.

What Should a Theory of Expertise Look Like?

Probably everyone doing expert-novice studies would agree to the need for a coherent theory. Questions like *What is the relative importance of domain knowledge and general skills in expertise?* and *Under what circumstances do experts reason forward and reason backward?* serve to give empirical researchers something to do, but they are the kinds of questions one asks when wandering in a theoretical wilderness.

It is not that expert-novice research has been atheoretical. Rather, what researchers have done is to import theory from elsewhere—from areas such as problem solving, skill, and knowledge representation—and try it out on expert-novice data. The effort has often proved fruitful. Much of what we will have to discuss in later chapters comes from having looked at expertise from these various perspectives. But the overall result is a genuine blind-men-and-elephant situation. That folk tale is a story about applying imported schemas—trying to make sense of an elephant by applying a tree schema, a snake schema, and so on, no one having a schema applicable to the whole elephant.

What kind of schema, in the case of expertise, would help us to make sense of the whole elephant? In cognitive science these days, the presumption always is that the desirable theory will be computable. We have already indicated, however, why we cannot look to expert systems to present us with theories of expertise. At best they will provide cases that may be easier to get hold of theoretically than the ones that come on two feet.

If this assessment is correct as to the present state of knowledge in relation to what a real theory of expertise would require, then we ought not to be in a hurry to formalize what we already know. Instead, we ought to be trying to build up our understanding in more modest ways. Not just by gathering more facts, of course (expert-novice comparisons seem already to be yielding diminishing returns) but by pursuing interesting questions that just seem as if they might lead to theoretically interesting results. Some of the questions we will be dealing with in the next few chapters are the following:

Why don't experts dig themselves deeper into ruts through practice?

How does formal knowledge get converted into knowledge an expert can think with?

Is there such a thing as expertise in learning, distinct from expertise in performance?

These are not questions whose theoretical significance can be established in advance. But they look like questions we ought to be able to answer if we claim to understand expertise. And they are questions that do not spring from looking at expertise merely as a state that exists in contrast to novicehood. They do, however, arise quite naturally if one considers expertise as a process—if one starts to investigate how it comes about, what people do differently who become experts from those who do not, and how the knowledge that seems to be the basis of expertise is generated from experience.

Summary

Are experts really different from other people, or are they merely the beneficiaries of the knowledge that comes inevitably from experience? Taken at face value, the great bulk of research on expert-novice differences favors the latter conclusion. Repeatedly it is shown that experts are not better thinkers. They are better at solving problems in their domains because of the knowledge they can draw on, knowledge which is so effective that it enables experts to get by with *less* thinking than their lowlier colleagues.

These findings are misleading, however. They say nothing about how the experts' superior knowledge came about or how it could be that people with the same amount of experience might differ greatly in knowledge. Also, they deal with experts working comfortably below their limits, whereas what may be most important to understand about experts is what goes on at the edge of their competence. On tasks where experts have a chance to extend themselves, research gives quite a different picture. Experts work harder, rely less fully on routines, and seem to be engaged in extending their knowledge rather than merely exploiting it.

There is an obvious need for theory in the study of expertise. But the kind of theory most needed is not one that can be represented in computer programs that simulate experts. It needs to be one level of abstraction higher, at a level that could, hypothetically at least, be represented in computer programs that *design* experts. To develop theory at that level, we need to know not only what experts are like generically but also how expertise works, how it comes about, and how it is maintained.

Chapter Three
Expert Knowledge and How It Comes About

Most people we talk to do not want to believe that research shows expert performance is mainly a matter of knowledge. They do not necessarily have an alternative explanation ready, but they feel there has to be more to expertise than that.

Let us be clear that no one is claiming that knowledge is all there is to expertise. Everyone recognizes that characteristics such as persistence, industry, and desire for excellence are relevant. Most people also acknowledge a role for innate talents. And then there are the social conditions that permit expertise to develop and flourish. But knowledge deserves a special status for two reasons:

1. Other factors may contribute but they are not essential. There are lazy experts, and experts who seem to

pursue their careers more for fun than for higher purposes. There are experts who overcome limitations of talent or physical constitution, and experts who sustain themselves in unsupportive or even hostile working environments. But there are no experts who lack expert knowledge of their fields. They may lack formal knowledge. The village fiddler of old may have been unable to read music and may have known little of the history or technical characteristics of the tunes he played, but he surely had a great deal of knowledge essential to his craft: a repertoire of tunes; mental representations of how they should sound, of their appropriateness to different occasions, of the effects on listeners that could be achieved, and how to achieve those effects. Take any substantial part of that knowledge away and you would no longer have an expert.

2. Knowledge is not just one more factor to be added in with personality, aptitude, and social factors to account for expertise. These other factors also enter into explaining how the knowledge was acquired. Thus the knowledge is part of expertise—a large part of what must be explained—and not something that lies in the background as part of a pattern of causes.

The main reason people feel that knowledge cannot be an adequate basis for expertise, we suspect, is that they have too limited a conception of knowledge. We were visited a while back by a scholar who was touring the world collecting academic views on thinking skills. When we started arguing that knowledge, not skill in thinking, is what counts, our visitor's genial smile grew increasingly strained. Finally he burst out with, "But people who know a great deal are often so dreadfully dull!" Our visitor apparently had in mind what we will call 'formal knowledge'—statable facts and principles, often of the kind found in textbooks. A person whose knowledge was only of that kind would very likely be dull, not to mention impractical and socially inept. In common usage, such knowledge is contrasted with know-how or skill. But cognitive psychologists —especially the ones who are equating expertise with knowledge—generally count skill as knowledge, too.[1] Formal knowledge belongs to the category of what these psychologists call *declarative* knowledge,whereas skill belongs to the category of *procedural* knowledge. These are roughly the same things that the philosopher, Gilbert Ryle, distinguished somewhat more felicitously as *knowing-about* and *knowing-how.*[2]

The conventional view of knowledge is not only limited as to what knowledge includes but it is also limited in its conception of how knowledge is acquired and how it works. In the traditional view, the mind is like a filing cabinet. Items get added to it or removed from time to time, through learning and forgetting. Otherwise, the knowledge just sits there until an occasion arises for particular items of it to be taken out and used. So long as that view is retained, it is impossible to understand the centrality of knowledge in expertise. If knowledge is just items in a mental filing cabinet, then it is easy to acknowledge that an expert must have a well-stocked filing cabinet, but that is like saying that a cook must have a well-stocked pantry. The pantry is not the cook, and the filing cabinet is not the expert. What counts with cooks and experts is what they do with the material in their pantries or memory stores. Thus are we led to posit things like thinking ability, practical sense, taste, intuition, flexibility, or perseverance as the essential components of expertise.

According to modern memory research, however, the mind isn't anything like a filing cabinet.[3] Learning, remembering, perceiving, and understanding are situational variants of the same process which, crudely put, is a process of getting on in the world. Someone else could stock your pantry for you, and then it would be up to you as a cook to exhibit expertise in what you are able to do with it. But there is no imaginable means whereby someone could stock your memory for you, leaving it up to you to exhibit expertise in what you did with the contents. There isn't any 'you' existing separate from your knowledge. Past experience has not left a residue in your mind called knowledge. Past experience has made you what you are, and knowledge is an aspect of what you are. It therefore makes no sense to look for the essence of expertise in mental traits supposed to influence what you do with knowledge. Rather, we have to find it in the ongoing process in which knowledge is used, transformed, enhanced, and attuned to situations.

English being a 'thing' language, we have no choice but to speak of knowledge as a thing. The closing sentence of the preceding paragraph demonstrates that weakness. We are struggling toward a dynamic conception of expertise in which what experts *do* accounts simultaneously for what, at a given point in time, will be described as the expert's knowledge and abilities. Unavoidably, however, we must talk of knowledge as something experts *have*. That immediately implies the dualism between what you have and what you do with it and encourages people to go baying down the trail of mental traits. Although it may be impossible to overcome the 'thingness' of our language, we can at least keep its perversity in mind as we proceed to examine this non-thing that we call expert knowledge.

The Hidden Knowledge of Experts

It might seem that, once both formal knowledge and skills are counted as knowledge, we have pretty much included all there is to human competence, and so equating expertise with knowledge becomes tautological. We want to argue, quite to the contrary, that these two kinds of knowledge do not begin to encompass expert knowledge and that they miss the most distinctive parts. Declarative and procedural knowledge are kinds of knowledge that show. Declarative knowledge manifests itself in explanations, lectures, and justifications. Procedural knowledge manifests itself in performance. But there are important kinds of knowledge that do not show in these ways, and these are the kinds of knowledge that most profoundly distinguish experts from nonexperts.

The philosopher Michael Polanyi has done the most to make us aware of the invisible knowledge lying behind intelligent action. He has called it "tacit" knowledge. Anyone who feels uneasy or skeptical about the notion of unconscious knowledge, or who is inclined to mystify it, would do well to read Polanyi.[4] Here we will not follow Polanyi's analysis, but will discuss three kinds of hidden knowledge that play a role in expertise and that we believe must be recognized if one is to understand expertise in a productive way. These are kinds of knowledge that we all have and rely on, but that are developed to a high degree in areas of expertise. Let us begin, however, with common examples that characterize everyday knowledge:

1. **Informal knowledge.** Suppose you were given a test in which many different kinds of cups were dropped from various heights on to various surfaces. The task is to predict on each trial whether the cup will break. Even allowing for the fact that in some instances you would just have to guess, you would probably score well above chance level on the whole. You would employ a great deal of knowledge about materials, their strength, hardness, and brittleness; also knowledge about force of impact as it relates to weight and distance of fall; also, back in your mind, would be vague recollections of actual instances of dropped cups in your experience. This knowledge is not skill. You aren't having to do anything except make predictions. And it is not formal knowledge. You would find little of relevance to this task in textbooks, and what you did find—elastic constants, gravitational formulas, and the like—would be of almost no help because you would have no way of applying it to cases. The various factors that you take into account are combined in ways for which you could provide no formula. And yet this is just one small sample of knowledge you have of the physical world that extends over the whole range of natural and manufactured things that you deal with in daily life.

2. **Impressionistic knowledge.** Suppose you have to select books as gifts for a number of acquaintances whose actual reading habits are unknown to you.

Although you may do a certain amount of reasoning from facts and prior opinions, you will probably have to do a great deal of matching of impressions—your impression of a book matched with an impression of the person. Furthermore, if you do not know a particular book, you will need to form an impression of it from bits of information—the title, the jacket blurb, sampling of a few lines here and there, perhaps even the cover illustration (that's what it is there for). You would find it impossible to explain what your impression of a long-time acquaintance is based on. It seems to be a distillation of your whole experience, perhaps dominated by a few salient events. But your impression is knowledge. You can use it, as in selecting a gift or predicting the person's behavior. Impressionistic knowledge can outlast other kinds of knowledge. If you have read a novel long ago, you may not remember a single definite fact about it, but sight of it in the bookstore will still bring back an impression that you can use in estimating the novel's appropriateness for someone else. 'Sort of crude and raunchy. Fred wouldn't like it, but Harry might.'

3. Self-regulatory knowledge. This term comes from the world of child-development research, where it is found that children often lack knowledge of how to manage themselves so as to attain their goals. They may not know about rehearsing when trying to remember something. Or they may not know how to avoid being continually tempted by a forbidden prize. An adult example of self-regulatory knowledge may be drawn from the previous example. If you are a frequent browser of bookshelves, you have probably learned how to manage your self so as to form more accurate impressions of books. You may have learned how to suppress attention to the seductive art and the one-word reviews decorating the covers of paperbacks. You may have learned how to skim pages rapidly, picking up bits of text here and there. Not everyone can do this. We have done tests in college classrooms, where the students knew that in the short time available they would be best off skimming a text, but many of them were unable to overcome the ingrained habit of reading continuously. In a job, self-regulatory knowledge is not knowing how to do the job but knowing how to manage yourself so that you do the job that way. The farmer who declined to attend a county agent's lecture on new agricultural techniques, saying, 'I don't farm half as well as I know how already, so why should I learn more?', was in effect indicating that what he lacked was self-regulatory rather than technical knowledge.

We have used mundane examples of these three kinds of hidden knowledge to emphasize that there is nothing mysterious about them. The aura of mystery appears when the hidden knowledge is knowledge that someone else has but we don't. We have no trouble with the fact that experts in other fields possess skills and formal knowledge that we lack. The evidence is plain and easily accounted for, or so we imagine. But when the knowledge attributed to experts is knowledge they may not even be aware of themselves and that often defies statement or description, some people start to get uneasy and others start to rhapsodize about intuition or 'feel'.

Hubert and Stuart Dreyfus have said some very cogent things about the tendency of people in Western culture to assume that everything in the mind consists of rules.[5] They trace this tendency back to Plato. Its upshot is that we feel we understand behavior if we can explain it by specifying a set of rules, which we then assume the behaver is following, explicitly or implicitly. Until quite recently, cognitive science and artificial intelligence have been committed to this assumption. Simulations of human intelligence have worked by means of rules representing human knowledge, translated into program code. Conversely, however, intelligent behavior that could not be formulated as rules tended to be ignored or banished to the realm of the inexplicable.

In the 1980s a new direction in artificial intelligence emerged, motivated partly by the fact that in the brain, at the level of neuronal activity, the only 'rules' are laws of physics and chemistry, not rules of logic or statements of principle. Simulations of intelligence, going by the name of connectionist or neural programming, have been carried out at rough approximations to this neural level of functioning.[6] These simulations produce kinds of behavior that we are accustomed to attribute to rules, yet no such rules are in the programs. Moreover, connectionist programs have been able to simulate competencies that have proved difficult or impossible to reduce to rules—pattern recognition, for instance, as in the recognition of distorted alphabet characters and human faces. Pattern recognition, as noted in the preceding chapter, figures very prominently in expert competence. But it tends to be part of hidden knowledge, neither formal knowledge nor skill.

Connectionist programs will sometimes behave in ways that make them seem as if they contain rules. For instance, one program will distinguish bedrooms, bathrooms, kitchens, and so on, when given information about items found in the room. Thus it appears to operate on the basis of definitions or perhaps rules like, 'If it contains a bed then it's probably a bedroom.' But no rules will be found in the program, only connections of different strengths between elements representing various rooms and items of furnishing. The author of the program cannot say for sure how the program will classify various inputs—say a room that contains both a bed and a stove—and the program, in fact, may not classify them the same way every time. The program shows a human tendency to make reasonable guesses on the basis of limited information, but it does not do so by applying rules.[7]

The 'connectionist revolution', so called, is causing a serious rethinking of previous assumptions about the mind.[8] The connectionist approach turns the classical, Platonist view on its head: The part of human knowledge that is hard to explain is the part that makes use of explicit facts and rules; the part that is fairly clear is the part we refer to by the names of informal, impressionistic, and self-regulatory knowledge. The question, 'Why is some knowledge hidden?' gets turned into the question, 'Why is some knowledge overt?'

Connectionist programs are a long way from simulating expertise. Some cognitive scientists doubt that they ever will.[9] Connectionism's importance to our topic at this time is in providing a scientifically plausible picture of the vast sea of mental life that lies beneath the wharf of facts and rules that we have constructed over it.

The following sections deal with how each of the three kinds of hidden knowledge play a part in expertise. We then turn to look at the sometimes disputed role of formal knowledge in expertise and at the intriguing, although little understood, phenomenon of formal knowledge becoming transformed to informal knowledge. We reserve the discussion of procedural knowledge, or skill, until the next chapter. Its relevance to expertise is too obvious to require discussion, but skill development requires serious consideration when it comes to dealing with the 'cognitive economy' of expertise—the allocation of mental resources in learning and doing, which is the focus of Chapter 4.

Informal Knowledge as Educated Common Sense

In their day-to-day work empirical scientists must continually make sense of real-world happenings, make quick predictions, explain unusual phenomena, troubleshoot, and argue points of interpretation and procedure with their colleagues. In fields like physics, where formal knowledge may consist largely of a set of equations, day-to-day activities would seem to require a body of knowledge that can be applied more directly, without the need to compute solutions to equations. As de Kleer and Brown observed,

> Although the modern mathematics in which most physical laws are expressed is relatively formal, the laws are all based on the presupposition of a shared unstated commonsense prephysics knowledge. . . . The knowledge presented in textbooks is but the tip of the iceberg about what actually needs to be known to reason about the physical world.[10]

There is now an active area of work within artificial intelligence concerned with building models of such informal scientific knowledge. They are called qualitative models, because their most distinctive characteristic is that they generate predictions on the basis of qualitatively distinct states of a system rather than on the basis of quantitative variables: If this happens, such and such will be the result; a reduction here will lead to an increase there; and so on. These qualitative models function much like common sense. Indeed, it may be fair to say that they *are* the expert's common sense. Like ordinary common sense, they represent what to the knower is obvious and not in need of consideration. The qualitative models are not deliberately applied, the way explicitly formulated models are; instead, they operate through perception itself, determining the way situations are apprehended. Unlike much of ordinary common sense, however, the qualitative models of experts are profoundly influenced by formal knowledge. They are consistent with it and could not possibly have developed without study of the formal discipline.

Qualitative models are in one respect simpler than formal quantitative models: Whereas the quantitative models typically deal with continuously varying quantities, qualitative models deal with a small number of values such as *increase, decrease, no change* or *greater than, less than, equal.* In other respects, however, qualitative models are more complex, incorporating more knowledge about the physical world.

The knowledge embedded in expert systems is largely informal knowledge. That is why it takes knowledge engineers to dig it out. It can't be found in textbooks. Experts often cannot explicate it. When asked to explain their craft they are likely to restate formal knowledge. But the success of expert system developments indicates that such informal knowledge is in their heads and that it potentially can be explicated. The most striking anecdote illustrating this point comes not from science but from the trade of steam-fitting. An expert steam-fitter worked for a canned soup manufacturer, maintaining the intricate network of pipes involved in the processing of this liquid product. On repeated attempts, however, the expert proved unable to teach his craft to anyone else. As he approached retirement, the manufacturers became alarmed and called in an expert system designer. Knowledge engineers set to work observing and questioning the steam-fitter until they were able to document in explicit form the quantity of informal knowledge that the steam-fitter drew on in his work, finally incorporating this knowledge into an expert system that could guide other people through the maintenance tasks.

Note that the steam-fitter's informal knowledge was not ineffable. It *could* be stated explicitly, and eventually was. In fact, it had to be rendered very explicit in order to work in an expert system. It is just that the steam-fitter had not formulated the knowledge explicitly in his own mind and was unable to do so without help. Why not? The question is something of a puzzler, if we assume that the knowledge already existed as facts and rules in the steam-fitter's mind. What was it about the facts and rules that made them inaccessible? But if we scrap that assumption, as connectionist theorizing suggests we should do, the puzzle disappears. The steam-fitter's informal knowledge did not exist as facts and rules. It existed as patterns of neural connections that had no direct correspondence to propositions and rules. The facts and rules had to be *created* by the knowledge engineers as an *approximation* to the steam-fitter's knowledge, an approximation that was amenable to a rule-based expert system. Over the course of years, the steam-fitter himself might have formulated a set of explicit statements to represent his knowledge, but he hadn't done so—probably because he never had any need to, and perhaps because he had little talent for that sort of analysis.

The steam-fitter's informal knowledge would not appear in a textbook on steam-fitting—not because it could not be formulated but because it was too much tied to the specifics of a particular manufacturing plant. It was what is coming to be called 'situated' knowledge.[11] This means not only that its range of application is limited to certain real-world situations but that the knowledge gains strength from those situations. Sylvia Scribner has detailed, for instance, how dairy workers develop short-cut systems for assembling dairy orders that take advantage of the numbers and arrangements of items in cases—systems that not only make calculation easier than it would be by using standard arithmetic procedures but that also have the effect of minimizing the amount of lifting and moving that has to be done.[12]

There may be informal knowledge that can never be satisfactorily captured by explicit statements. The knowledge that enables us to recognize people we have not seen for decades is a likely example. The important point is that all explicit formulations of informal knowledge are approximations—some good, some bad, some helpful, some useless, but all are representations of the knowledge and not the knowledge itself.

The informal knowledge that everyone has we call common sense. We are saying that experts have a great deal of knowledge that has the same informal character as common sense, but it is much more highly developed and usually more heavily influenced by formal knowledge. Besides that, of course, experts have ordinary common sense in large or small amounts and it may or may not be in harmony with the informal knowledge that is part of their expertise.

Impressionistic Knowledge: Its Role in Expert Judgment

Probably all individual knowledge has feelings connected with it. There are pleasant facts and unpleasant facts, appealing ideas and offensive ideas. Studies using rating scales have shown that, presented with virtually anything—material or immaterial—people will register impressions of it as good or bad, strong or weak, active or inactive.[13] Typically, however, feelings associated with knowledge operate in the background. Your feelings about numbers and mathematical ideas may influence your behavior in large and small ways, affecting your choice of school subjects and career, your mental state when trying to balance a checkbook, and how you respond socially when someone poses a numerical problem. But these feelings do not usually figure as part of your mathematical knowledge. In some circumstances, however, feelings are an essential and inseparable part of knowledge. That is what we are referring to as impressionistic knowledge.

An example is wine-tasting. Professional wine-tasters have an extensive vocabulary of wine characteristics, which is displayed to the wine-drinking public on the little cards merchants affix to shelves beneath their pricier wines. *Lemon, melon, butterscotch; big, light, lingering*—customers naturally wonder whether these terms mean anything or whether they are just cast out at random to snare buyers. As it happens, there has been detailed research on this subject. Expert wine-tasters evidently do use these terms in precise ways. They will independently assign similar terms to a wine, and in blind tests they are able to pick out a wine from its description. But these terms all refer to impressions. The impressions may have a basis in chemistry, but chemical analyses cannot take the place of the wine-taster's highly refined discriminations.

Amateurs of wine have impressions, too, and often they will use the vocabulary of the professional wine-tasters to describe their impressions. But evidently the terms have no consistent meaning for them. Amateurs fail the tests that experts pass. Not only do different amateurs describe the same wine differently, the same amateur will describe it quite differently on different trials. One amateur's description does not enable another to pick out the wine it refers to. An amateur may express a strong preference for one wine over another and yet be unable to identify the preferred wine in a blind test.

Wine amateurs, we might say, have impressions but they do not have much impressionistic knowledge. Their impressions are not stable or clear enough or consistently enough related to actual instances that they can play a useful role in communication or judgment. Experts do have such impressionistic knowledge, and it would appear that it serves them not only in doing their jobs but also in heightening their enjoyment of wine.

More generally, *connoisseurs* are experts who possess highly developed impressionistic knowledge of whatever their specialty entails—food, art, dance, horses, poetry, baseball. It may or may not be accompanied by other kinds of expert knowledge. What must be recognized, however, is that other kinds of expert knowledge do not take the place of impressionistic knowledge. The sort of 'dreadfully dull' person referred to earlier is epitomized by Mr. Casaubon in George Eliot's *Middlemarch*. Casaubon knows a great deal about Italian art, including the approved opinions. He says to his young bride,

> "Should you like to go to the Farnesina, Dorothea? It contains celebrated frescoes designed or painted by Raphael, which most persons think it worth while to visit."
>
> "But do you care about them?" was always Dorothea's question.
>
> "They are, I believe, highly esteemed. . . . "

Of Dorothea's disappointment with her husband's pedantry, Eliot remarks,

> There is hardly any contact more depressing to a young ardent creature than that of a mind in which years full of knowledge seem to have issued in the blank absence of interest or sympathy.[14]

The contribution of impressionistic knowledge to the enrichment of life is an important one; but there are other functions of impressionistic knowledge that bear more directly on the development of expertise. One function is to support the acquisition of formal knowledge. The Casaubons of the world not withstanding, it may be very difficult for most people to accumulate vast stores of formal knowledge unless it is accompanied by strong impressionistic knowledge. This is not just a matter of motivation to learn. It is a matter of providing connections, without which formal knowledge tends to be rapidly forgotten. According to some modern theories of memory, we do not so much recall information as *relive* events. Strong impressions make memorable the experiences out of which we reconstruct knowledge as we need it.[15]

Perhaps the most vital function of impressionistic knowledge in expertise, however, is to provide a basis for practical and theoretical judgments. Administrators often have to make numerous decisions on rather small matters. But the mark of expertise in administration is to make decisions that not only take care of the immediate problem but that at the same time support the higher-level goals of the organization. What do you do when an employee wants time off during a period of heavy work demand? The immediate circumstances are important: How much does the employee need the time off? How much does he or she deserve it? How will this affect the current task? Each of these is a question that cannot be answered definitively, by any amount of rational analysis. Moreover, there probably isn't time or resources for such analysis. Instead, the administrator will have to rely on *impressions* of need, merit, difficulty, and cost. These impressions do not come out of nowhere; they come from the administrator's entire past experience, which constitutes a body of impressionistic knowledge that may be relevant or irrelevant, valid or distorted, scanty or rich. Besides evaluating the immediate circumstances, however, the expert administrator will try to take account of effects of the immediate decision on the morale and future performance of the employee, effects on the morale of other employees, consequences to the organization of delay in completing a task, and so on. These considerations, all involving projection into an uncertain future, are even less amenable to rational problem solving. Even if all the pertinent facts were available, the sheer computational burden of trying to take all of the factors into account would defeat any human intellect. Faced with such complexity, some administrators will simplify the problem. They will go by the book, reiterating whatever the personnel manual says about time off, or they may dodge the problem entirely, putting the responsibility for a decision onto the employee.[16] An expert administrator, we suggest, will try to take the full range of considerations into account, but in order to do so will rely on a rich fund of relevant and trustworthy impressionistic knowledge.

Harry Broudy, an educational philosopher concerned with both cognition and the arts, argues that this kind of amorphous knowledge plays a role in scientific and technical expertise as well. What goes by the name of 'intuition', an attribute often ascribed to brilliant researchers, designers, and trouble-shooters, usually amounts to a strong *impression* that something is interesting, promising, or amiss. The full repertoire of expert knowledge may later be brought into play, but the first move is likely to be on the basis of some impression not tied to any particular item of prior knowledge.[17] For people who do creative work of any kind—artistic, scientific, or practical—an important kind of judgment that must be made continually is judgment of *promisingness*. In Chapter 5 we will argue that this kind of judgment depends crucially on impressionistic knowledge, and that such 'knowledge of promisingness' is the main thing that distinguishes creative from noncreative expertise.

Self-Regulatory Knowledge: How Experts Know Themselves

Frequent fliers have all witnessed this scene: The weather is bad and flights are delayed, some of them canceled. The waiting room is filled with angry and desperate passengers wanting some immediate action to help them get on a flight. But behind the counter the airline agents work calmly and patiently, taking whatever time is necessary to help one passenger at a time, occasionally addressing a soothing word to the others who are seething with impatience. How do we explain this ability to, as Kipling put it, "keep your wits when all about you are losing theirs and blaming it on you"? One common explanation is temperament. Another is habit, simply 'being used to it'. Neither explanation quite does justice to the fact that this ability to sustain methodical problem solving under severe conditions is an important part of the airline agent's competence.

Careful analysis would probably reveal that the airline agents have learned to regulate their attention so that almost all of it is concentrated on the immediate task, with just enough attention to the surrounding turmoil to keep them aware of it. This is no doubt easier for some temperaments to learn than for others, but it does require learning. What precisely is learned may vary from agent to agent, because what works for one person in controlling attention may not work for another. This is the main way that self-regulatory knowledge differs from other kinds of expert knowledge. The ticket agent who discovers a good way to get passengers from Madrid to Toronto when the direct flight has been canceled can pass this knowledge on to other agents, confident that it will work for them as well. But the ticket agent who has discovered a way to remain calm while dealing with a hoard of Toronto passengers alarmed at the prospect of spending a night in New York cannot be sure that this knowledge will be helpful to other ticket agents. Self-regulatory knowledge is self-knowledge relevant to performance in some domain. It is part of an expert's knowledge in a domain, but it is not knowledge *of* that domain. It is knowledge that works *for me*. It will not necessarily work for you.

The difference between self-regulatory knowledge and knowledge of the domain stands out especially clearly in the area of writing. Domain knowledge in writing includes knowledge of literary forms and expressions and skill in achieving intended effects through writing—the whole body of skill and lore that traditionally goes by the name of 'rhetoric'. When interviewed about their work, writers seldom discuss this kind of knowledge.[18] They may, however, talk about how they go about the task of writing—how much revising they do, how they get from a vague notion to an actual draft, how they keep going through long writing stints, what sorts of things they read or avoid reading. Nowadays writers usually have strong beliefs about word processors, but they are very much self-related beliefs. Word processors in general or one word processor in comparison to another is good or bad in how it suits their own way of writing. Some writers like to work early in the morning, others late at night. One writer dictates first drafts and then fixes them up whereas another slaves to get each sentence right before attempting the next. Textbooks occasionally try to prescribe a best way to write for everyone, but this is foolish. The best way is a highly individual matter, and finding it means gaining important knowledge for expertise.

For experts who work under time pressures or other strains, some of the most important self-regulatory knowledge has to do with rhythms of work and relaxation, production and reflection, concentration and incubation, and so on. For athletes or university students who drop out for a time, such self-regulatory knowledge may be the hardest kind to recover, harder than the specific skills of the activity.

Self-regulatory knowledge may be thought of as knowledge that controls the application of other knowledge. Thus it is often referred to as 'metaknowledge' or 'metacognition'. Under the latter rubric, a goodly body of research has developed showing how important it is for academic learning.[19] In Chapter 6 we will discuss 'expert-like learners', who often most resemble experts in their self-regulatory knowledge. But the relevance of this kind of knowledge extends well beyond learning, important as that may be in expert careers. In the lore of major league baseball, tremendous importance is placed on whether the players on teams in contention for a championship have had previous experience in championship competition. Managers of teams lacking in this respect will trade off talented younger players for a veteran, well past his prime, who sports a championship ring or two. The game during championship rounds is no different from the game during the regular season. It requires nothing different in the way of baseball skill and knowledge. What is different is the pressure, where every game is crucial and any lapse may be fatal. Knowing how to manage oneself in this situation is evidently thought by many managers to count enough to balance against quite a bit of excellence in regular performance.

Much self-regulatory knowledge is domain-specific. The baseball World Series veteran is not necessarily calmer under pressure in general. Rather, his advantage over the less experienced player in regulating anxiety and concentration are as specific to baseball as his knowledge of how to play his position. On the other hand, self-regulation is the area of expert knowledge where there is the greatest potential for generalization. There are habits of planning and checking, learnable in any number of fields, that should be applicable to the others. And there are very general strategies, such as drawing back to take stock of a difficult situation, that apply to everything from research to plumbing repair, from reading a legal contract to saving a marriage. Applying general self-regulatory strategies in the right way at the right time is likely, however, to depend in turn on domain-specific knowledge. In science, for instance, being able at the right time to draw back from concerns with a particular experiment and to consider it from a broader theoretical perspective obviously requires not only self-knowledge but also scientific knowledge that includes the broader perspective. How does one acquire that kind of scientific knowledge? Partly, at least, from efforts to consider local problems from a broader perspective. Thus, self-regulatory knowledge is implicated in the development of all other forms of expert knowledge, since the activities it regulates include those responsible for all kinds of expert knowledge development. Implicated in all the other forms of knowledge, it is nonetheless not reducible to any of them, and therefore requires separate attention.

Formal Knowledge as Negotiable Knowledge

Because formal knowledge is what schooling and textbooks are about, because it is overt and almost tangible, we tend to think that we know what it is and that its role in expertise is obvious. That is mostly an illusion. As to what formal knowledge is, this has preoccupied epistemologists since ancient times, and it is perhaps no closer to being a settled issue today. And as for its role in expertise, there is hardly a professional school that does not house continuing struggles between those who think there should be more of it and those who think it should be de-emphasized in favor of more practical or clinical training.

Legitimate questions may be asked about how much and what kind of formal knowledge are needed to be a good electrician, plumber, or doctor. Licensing examinations tend to overemphasize formal knowledge, because it is so easy to test.

But arguments about whether this or that category of formal knowledge is important for practice tend to be fruitless. Those in favor can always show that the knowledge is, in principle, relevant. Those opposed can show that experts seldom make direct use of it. In order for such arguments to be useful— and they do deal with important issues of training and certification—we need to consider how formal knowledge functions in its relation to the broader body of informal knowledge and skill that go to make up expertise.

We have been referring to formal knowledge loosely as 'the kind of thing that is found in textbooks'. This is just a shorthand way of referring to the kind of publicly represented knowledge that has been the main concern of epistemologists since ancient times. As we have noted, when people speak about 'knowledge' they usually mean formal knowledge. For present purposes, the important thing about it is that, being formulated in texts, equations, and the like, it can be dis- cussed, criticized, amended, compared, and rather directly taught. All this is in sharp contrast to the other kinds of knowledge we have been discussing.

Although the right way to think about formal knowledge is unsettled, it is possible with some assurance to identify a common wrong way to think about it. The wrong way is to think of formal knowledge as some kind of abstraction from the knowledge existing in individual minds. Karl Popper and a host of more recent philosophers have taught us to look at it the other way around.[20] Formal knowledge is created through social processes of justification, criticism, and argument. In other words, it starts life as something public, rather than becoming public after having gestated in individual minds. We refer to formal knowledge as 'negotiable' knowledge, using that term in several senses: formal knowledge arises through proc- esses akin to negotiation, it is something people can negotiate about, and it is negotiable in the sense that it can be trans- ferred, exchanged, even purchased for money. It is these negotiable properties that give formal knowledge its unique place among kinds of expert knowledge.

The Uses of Formal Knowledge

Back in the 1920s, Alfred North Whitehead coined a term that has recently taken a new lease on life: "inert knowledge."[21] It is knowledge that people have stored in memory and that they comprehend at some level—they can give sensible answers to questions about it—but it serves no function in their lives. It doesn't play any role in practical activity or in making sense of experience in the world. Once we have identified the other kinds of knowledge that do have important functions in daily life and in expert performance, however, the question arises of what functions are left to be served by formal knowledge. There are three functions that have special importance in expertise:

> **1. Formal knowledge is essential for dealing with issues of truth and justification.** There has been a great deal of research devoted to the question of how much medical experts rely on formal biomedical knowledge and how much they rely on 'clinical', or what we have been calling informal knowledge, with different experiments indicating contrary conclusions. There have been suggestions that as physicians gain experience they actually lose their formal knowledge or it becomes dormant, being replaced by informal knowledge and skill. And yet there were instances in which high-level specialists made outstanding use of basic scientific knowledge. A recent experiment points to a resolution. Physicians were asked to think aloud while in the course of solving a diagnostic problem, and then afterwards to justify their solutions. When working on the problem, experts referred less to formal knowledge than did their less experienced colleagues, but in justifying their diagnoses they made far more use of formal knowledge than the less expert.[22] It might be argued that the problem solving is what really counts, not the justification, but that would be a short-sighted view. In order for medicine or any other knowledge-based field to advance, its practitioners have

to do more than just do the right thing. They have to be able to give justifications and explanations that will withstand critical examination, so that their colleagues may both grasp the general principle in what has been done and be willing to accept it.

2. Formal knowledge is important for communication, teaching, and learning. Although interactive videodisks and intelligent tutoring systems may permit more of expertise to be communicated through demonstration and coaching, it is likely to remain the case that much of the knowledge which experts convey to prospective experts will be in the form of verbal statements that learners must treat as formal knowledge. That is, they must interpret it, question it, relate it to their existing knowledge, consider its implications. An important corollary to this point is that it takes formal knowledge to get formal knowledge. Even the kind of 'inert', superficial, incidental knowledge that Whitehead lamented has some value insofar as it enables you to read books and enter into discourse that may yield more valuable knowledge.[23] In education circles one frequently hears it said that, instead of stuffing students' heads with knowledge, we should teach them how to find the knowledge they need. Electronic information systems have given this tired notion a new life, but it is just as ill-considered as it ever was. In most fields, the vast stores of information available in electronic databases are inaccessible to people who lack knowledge of the vocabulary and structure of the field. In a practical sense, they don't know what to look for.

3. Formal knowledge provides starting points for the construction of informal knowledge and skills. We are all familiar with how skills become refined through practice, and it is reasonable to suppose that informal knowledge becomes elaborated and refined in much the same way. But how do new skills and new areas of informal knowledge get started? Sometimes just through blundering ahead, of course. But relevant formal knowledge can play a crucial role in hastening the process and getting it going in a direction that will prove successful. Although experts have, as we have emphasized, vast amounts of hidden knowledge that could not have been obtained formally, this hidden knowledge is nevertheless consistent with and influenced by formal knowledge. How this occurs is one of the central issues in understanding expertise, and it is the topic of the next section.

Translating Formal Knowledge into Informal Knowledge and Skill

There is a substantial theory, due mainly to John Anderson, about how the conversion of formal knowledge into skill occurs.[24] The key step is the use of subgoals in solving problems. To start with a mundane example, suppose that, because you have never done it before, *driving to the Smiths-'cottage* is a skill you do not possess. Realizing this, the Smiths dictate to you a series of directions such as, 'Take Highway 400 to Barrie. Stay on Highway 11 until just before Gravenhurst. Turn left where you see a big red antique barn. . . . ' These directions represent a kind of formal knowledge, which makes it possible for you to transform the goal of *driving to the Smiths' cottage* into a series of subgoals which you already have the necessary skills to accomplish. When you set out you may discover that the subgoals are not as readily attainable as you might have hoped. You may have to call on more general formal knowledge of geography, map conventions, and highway conventions, in order to figure out, for instance, that you should not turn off Highway 400 at the first intersection with Highway 11, because 11 joins 400 at that point and continues for a while before separating again, which is what 'Stay on' was meant to convey. On subsequent trips these problems do not occur, although you may still rely on the formal directions for a while. Eventually, though, *driving to the Smiths' cottage* becomes 'proceduralized', as Anderson puts it. You no longer need the Smiths' directions or any other formal knowledge. The relevant facts have become implicit in your procedural knowledge. The Smiths' directions did not include subgoals such as 'Get in your car. Start the engine.' Those skills, they could assume, were already proceduralized and thus implicit in 'Take Highway 400 to Barrie.' Anderson shows that more intellectual attainments, such as learning procedures for proving geometry theorems, proceed in the same way. One uses textbook information to set subgoals that appear attainable, carries out problem solving as needed to attain the subgoals, and retains the solutions as procedures that are applied directly on later occasions and eventually compiled into smoothly-functioning skills.

It seems plausible that formal knowledge should enter into the development of informal knowledge in much the same way that it enters into the development of skill. In brief:

> Formal knowledge is converted into skill by being used to solve problems of procedure.

> Formal knowledge is converted into informal knowledge by being used to solve problems of understanding.

The importance of converting formal knowledge into informal knowledge is most obvious when it fails to happen. For modern adults, the roundness of the earth is part of informal knowledge. It is not merely something we accept as true. It is part of the way we picture events such as space vehicles orbiting the earth or people traveling from North America to Australia. But for many school children this is not the case. If asked, they will tell you that the world is round. They have learned that as formal knowledge. But get them talking or drawing pictures of what they think the world is really like, and you discover that the image that shapes their thoughts is an image based on their own experience. It is likely to be the image of a large platform. To reconcile this image with the formal knowledge they have been taught, they may create bizarre theories, such as two worlds, or the earth as a hollow globe with their platform inside it.[25]

This is an instance—and research on people's scientific understanding has turned up many more—of formal knowledge having no functional relation to informal knowledge. The formal knowledge is what Whitehead referred to as 'inert'. It does no work. It does not enter into people's daily efforts to solve problems and interpret events.

James Voss and his colleagues have done several studies in which people of different knowledge backgrounds were asked to address the problem of how to increase agricultural production in what was then the Soviet Union. Novices—that is, people with no special training or experience in the area—tended to give simplistic answers: mechanize, use more fertilizer. Sovietologists, on the other hand, identified and addressed the circumstances that had tended to frustrate Soviet efforts to improve agricultural production: bureaucracy, distribution problems, and the like. Predictable results, to be sure. One group that Voss studied, however, were what he called "post-novices". These were university students who had recently completed a course on Soviet domestic policy. Despite this highly relevant instruction, they tended to approach the problem the way novices did, with simple direct solutions, rather than with ideas that grew out of informed analysis of the situation.[26]

The post-novices had potentially relevant formal knowledge, which they failed to apply. Assuming that these students also had the normal sort of general problem-solving capabilities, then they must have had both the procedural and the formal knowledge necessary to have produced more sophisticated answers. What they undoubtedly lacked, however, was informal knowledge. An expert, if tempted to offer *use more fertilizer* as a solution, would not just evaluate this idea against stored facts and principles. The expert would, as it were, run the idea through a mental model of the workings of the Soviet system. This mental model would, among other things, generate expectations of appropriation requests stalled on the desks of unheedful bureaucrats and of fertilizer shipments melting away on the platforms of remote railroad stations. The expert need not have experienced these things, or have learned about them in particular. They might all be derivable from knowledge that the post-novices also possessed. The difference, however, is that the expert would not have to go back and derive these notions from particular facts and principles. They would already be available in the expert's highly elaborated informal knowledge of what led to what in the Soviet world.

The question is how such informal knowledge comes about; and for this question, Sovietology offers an especially instructive example. The normal dodge, 'from experience', does not work well in this instance. Your typical American Sovietologist has not had much experience trying to help the Soviets solve their agricultural or any other sort of problem and has never tried to get a load of fertilizer to Tashkent. The Sovietologist's knowledge has mostly bookish origins, and yet it manages to develop beyond its origins. What starts out as formal knowledge must somehow develop into informal knowledge.

How does this happen? It happens, we suggest, in the same way that the adult's formal knowledge about the roundness of the earth eventually becomes part of informal knowledge: It happens through using the formal knowledge to solve problems. Although Voss's expert Sovietologists may have had little occasion to solve practical problems of Soviet economy, they had a great deal of experience trying to interpret news, official pronouncements, technical reports, and the like coming from the USSR. They had made predictions and tried to explain ones that failed. Thus they had been continually solving problems of explanation and drawing on formal knowledge which they tried to weave into causal accounts. The result was a massive build-up of informal knowledge that enabled them to make sense of events and to make predictions about their outcomes. This informal knowledge tends to take the form of qualitative models that are also useful in tackling more practical problems. Much of the thinking that goes into solving a practical problem (like the agricultural problem Voss and his colleagues used) is, after all, predicting what will happen as a result of this or that action. Thus it draws on the same causal knowledge that is used in explanation. It is knowledge consistent with formal facts and principles, but it has much more detailed connections to real conditions and events.

A first-hand experience of how formal and informal knowledge influence each other can be gained by examining what happens when you encounter an inconsistency in your understanding. The following example may turn up such an inconsistency for readers who have a lay person's understanding of space science: How is it possible for a satellite to remain fixed in one spot above the earth? This is a question that might occur to you if you acquire a satellite antenna and learn that you aim it at one spot up in the sky rather than tracking a moving object. If you have no immediate explanation, try puzzling one out before proceeding to the next paragraph.

Most people have the formal knowledge needed to undo the main knot of this puzzle, but their informal knowledge is lacking. The essential items of formal knowledge are that a satellite orbits around the earth and that the earth itself rotates. Explaining the stationary satellite requires bringing these two items of knowledge together, but this is difficult if our informal knowledge represents these items in different mental models. Our mental model for dealing with satellite problems is likely to consist of a small object traveling in a circle around a large object. Our mental model for dealing with problems of day and night, for instance, is likely to be that of a spinning ball with a light source off to one side. Each of these models is suitable for understanding various phenomena and narratives, but neither one alone is adequate for understanding the stationary satellite. Somehow the two models must be combined. A model that does this is a person swinging a heavy object around on a rope. The heavy object rotates around the person, but the person is also rotating, and the two rotations are coordinated so that the object remains in front of the person. With such a model in mind, it is easy to see how a satellite can remain fixed with respect to a point on earth. But how does such a mental model come about?

When the stationary satellite problem was posed to a group of scientifically unsophisticated adults, most of them simply acknowledged that this was a puzzler, and thought no more about it. That is the characteristic nonexpert response to problems of explanation, and one that minimizes growth and revision of knowledge. One student, however, was taken with the problem and toward the end of the class period proposed an explanation of the stationary satellite—that it was suspended between two gravitational forces, those of the earth and of the moon. Although unable to state precisely why, she felt dissatisfied with this explanation, and by the next class period had researched the matter in the library and now offered a scientific explanation, which included information about the distance from the earth and the speed required for a satellite's orbit to be synchronized with the rotation of the earth. Thus she acquired considerable formal knowledge. At the same time, her informal knowledge probably improved as a result of trying to make sense of this formal knowledge in applying it to the problem.

This, we suggest, is how expert formal knowledge and informal knowledge develop together, each contributing to the other. The problem solving efforts of the student we have described do not qualify her as an expert in space mechanics, of course, but they do give evidence of a kind of expertise. It is expertise in learning, in the active construction of knowledge—an important variety of expertise that we shall explore further in Chapter 6.

Informal Sources of Informal Knowledge

In concluding this discussion of informal understanding, let us emphasize that formal knowledge is not the only source of informal knowledge. Old-fashioned farmers have tremendous amounts of informal knowledge, very little of which was first acquired as formal knowledge. Instead, it was acquired through observation, through working under the direction of their elders, and through trying to solve a host of practical problems. Still, we would argue, it arose from trying to solve problems of explanation, and those farmers who tried hardest to make sense of what they experienced developed the greatest amount of it.

We have focused on informal knowledge that comes about through the use of formal knowledge, because it has been little examined and because it has such great potential for the upgrading of expertise. There is a long romantic tradition, strong in public education, that sees formal knowledge and informal knowledge as being at odds with one another. This romanticism has started to flare up in cognitive science recently. The mathematical wisdom of the Third-World child who learned it from selling Chiclets on the street is contrasted with the bug-infested rote knowledge of the American school child. The earthy common sense of the village midwife is contrasted with the bookish stupidity of the medical officer who tries to beat medical science into her. These are unfair comparisons, however. They compare people who have highly developed informal knowledge and skills (the street vendors and midwives) against people who have acquired a certain amount of formal knowledge but who have not done the extensive problem-solving needed to transform it into informal knowledge that they would be able to think with.[27]

Formal knowledge is not at odds with common sense. It is a different sort of knowledge. The relevant comparison is between common sense that has been influenced by formal knowledge and informal knowledge that has not. When that comparison is made, the case is overwhelmingly in favor of informed common sense. Let us consider midwifery as an example. A common problem in home health care in the Third World is contamination. Although folk practitioners may have learned formally about germs, they are notorious for not taking proper account of them. Sometimes they may not really believe what they have been told, but in any event they have not processed this germ knowledge into their working mental models of how the world runs. The city-based medical officers, on the other hand, probably have a workable mental model involving germs, but it is adapted to the conditions of hospital and clinic. They have not used this knowledge to solve problems of sterile procedure when delivering a baby in a mud hut.

Notice that this is not to say that the medical officers' formal knowledge is inapplicable to a village environment. It is as relevant there as anywhere else. It is their informal knowledge, their medical common sense, that is inadequate. They have not thought through, for instance, what available materials might be more sanitary than others. At the Chicago Lying-In Hospital, residents who had to go out into the slums to deliver babies at home were taught to use newspapers. With the top pages removed, these were typically much more sterile than bed sheets or towels were likely to be. That is a bit of informal knowledge that grew out of using formal knowledge in solving local problems. Newspapers might not be a practical solution in a Mexican village, but probably a solution could be found that would be an improvement over existing practices. A solution will not be found, however, by relying on a variety of common sense that ignores or denies the existence of germs and recognizes only the esthetic aspects of sanitation. It requires a variety of common sense in which formal medical knowledge has become transformed by using it to understand and come to grips with the physical and social conditions of village life.

There is no assembly line that methodically converts formal knowledge into informal knowledge. People go through life trying to accomplish tasks and to understand things, using their existing skills and informal knowledge. From time to time these prove insufficient and people must resort to problem solving that draws on formal knowledge. The result is new *ad hoc* mental structures that deal with the present situation. These new mental structures may not survive beyond the moment, or if they do they may survive as local ways of dealing with limited problems, having no overall influence on the way we understand things. But just as repeated physical actions sometimes solidify into habits, and these habits begin to displace or rearrange other habits (on moving from a dry to a rainy climate, your newly acquired umbrella-carrying habit may instigate changes in your handbag-carrying habits, for instance), so may some of these newly acquired ways of interpreting information become established and instigate more widespread changes in people's interpretive habits. When this happens the result is not just a new trick for dealing with particular problems, but a different way of looking at things, which marks a progressive shift in the level of common sense.

Working at the Edge of One's Understanding

Acquiring expert knowledge entails working to some extent at the edge of one's competence, accepting the strains and the risks that go with doing so, but gaining in return progressively higher levels of competence and achievement. It takes more than intellectual curiosity and a willingness to change beliefs. Those are essential, but by themselves they imply a passive response to problems of understanding. In the process of expertise, efforts at understanding take place against a constant background of awareness of the complexities that one is not yet dealing with. Of all scientists, Isaac Newton might have had the most reason to imagine that he had the world figured out, but instead he gave us one of the most vivid literary images of expertise developing against a background of ignorance:

> I do not know what I may appear to the world, but to myself I seem to have been only like a boy playing on the seashore and diverting myself now and then finding a smoother pebble or a prettier shell than ordinary whilst the great ocean of truth lay all undiscovered before me.[28]

Newton's image of the child on the seashore of truth suggests that the expert pursuit of understanding is a solitary one. In some respects it always is, but in other respects it is one of the most social of human activities. A large part of human discourse involves direct or indirect efforts to arrive at mutual understandings. In the learned disciplines such efforts become institutionalized. This has a number of results that have been studied by historians and sociologists of knowledge. The pursuit of knowledge becomes a specialty in itself, so that researchers become distinguished from practitioners. Consensuses develop as to what needs explaining and what constitutes an acceptable explanation (the 'paradigms' so widely discussed since the work of Thomas Kuhn). Conferences, colloquia, and the like provide occasions for negotiating shared informal knowledge as well as for exchanging formal knowledge. Perhaps the most distinctive characteristic of learned disciplines, however, is the existence of journals. These are more than just informational media. They are a medium through which informal knowledge gets recast as formal knowledge, undergoes critical review, and is transmitted to others in the discipline, who then use it in the solution of their own knowledge-related problems, these solutions in turn being recast as formal knowledge, submitted for journal publication, and so on—an endless cyclical process that has well-known shortcomings but that seems to be essential if a field as a whole is to progress in understanding. In effect, it is the process of expertise institutionalized.

Summary

Every kind of knowledge has a part in expertise. The obvious kinds, which therefore receive the most attention, are procedural knowledge (skill) and formal knowledge (as in 'book learning'). Expertise also depends on a great body of less obvious knowledge, however. There is informal knowledge, which is the expert's elaborated and specialized form of common sense. There is impressionistic knowledge, often glorified as 'intuition' or 'instinct' because it is experienced as feeling rather than knowing. Nevertheless, it plays a crucial role in expert judgment. Finally there is self-regulatory knowledge—self-knowledge relevant to functioning in a domain.

Nonexperts as well as experts have all these kinds of knowledge. The difference is in how much they have, how well integrated it is, and how effectively it is geared to performance. There is no magic to how expert knowledge is acquired, but it is not enough to say that it comes about through study, experience, and practice. Those terms explain mediocrity as well as expertise.

We have tried to show how problem solving provides the dynamic element in the growth of all kinds of expert knowledge. Experts do not just solve the objective problems that are part of their work—problems of curing illnesses, selling cars, or whatever. They also solve problems of understanding and problems in which they themselves—their strengths and weaknesses, desires and aversions—are a major part of the problem.

These problems are often interrelated: Difficulties that arise in solving an objective problem may bring out problems of understanding or problems of self-regulation. Solving these problems within the context of the objective problems of a domain helps give expert knowledge its coherence and effectiveness.

Chapter Four
Expertise as Process

Everyone learns, more or less continuously throughout the waking hours of their lives. Yet not everyone becomes an expert. It has been shown that even the factory worker whose job consists of pulling down the handle on a drill press becomes increasingly proficient at this task, year after year. And surely the children sometimes labeled 'non-learners' in school are learning something during their hours at the desk, although perhaps not what was intended or not at the expected rate.

There are several commonsense ways of explaining how it is that everyone learns but not everyone becomes an expert. One way is to attribute the differences to native ability or to quality of training, opportunities for experience, and the like. Another is to say that everyone does become expert at something, except that only certain kinds of skill and knowledge are publicly credited as expertise. These are defensible points, but of a kind that tends to stifle thought. They tell us that there is nothing further to be found out about expertise; expertise is just learning accompanied by other factors of aptitude, opportunity, or social approval.

Our whole approach to expertise centers on the idea that there is more to it than these commonsense views suggest. We believe there is something experts do over and above ordinary learning, which accounts for how they become experts and for how they remain experts, rather than settling into a rut of routine performance. The preceding chapter has anticipated what this special something is that experts do: They solve problems. But everyone solves problems, too; and if we take the rather expansive definition of problem solving that is current among cognitive scientists, people are engaged in problem solving much of the time. In this chapter we shall try to show what is distinctive about the problem solving experts do. The distinction is not in how they tackle a given problem, which is what most research on expert problem solving has investigated. Such research shows, as previously noted, that experts tackle problems more efficiently, making use of their superior knowledge. That almost goes without saying. Of considerably more significance is *the kinds of problems experts tackle*. Experts, we propose, tackle problems that increase their expertise, whereas nonexperts tend to tackle problems for which they do not have to extend themselves.

Expert and Nonexpert Skill Development

To illustrate the general idea, we will start with a comparison of two elementary school teachers. School teaching is an especially good area for bringing out distinctions between expert and nonexpert skill development. Any school teacher who survives for long has necessarily developed a high level of skill in certain aspects of the teaching craft, yet it is widely accepted that a large proportion of school teachers are not expert.

Margot and Cynthia are similar in many respects. They both have been elementary teachers for almost two decades. Both are easy-going, relaxed to the point of being slow-moving, firm but patient and warm with their pupils. If you walk into either classroom you are likely to find all the children pleasantly busy. Principals and supervisors regard both of them as excellent teachers. This only goes to show how misleading appearances can be when it comes to judging teaching, however.

In Margot's classes, reading problems are few and most of the children read well beyond their expected levels. The children are equally at home with numbers, and they often do amazing things in writing and in science, showing sophisticated levels of knowledge and thinking. Although Cynthia's pupils come from much the same social environment as Margot's, many of them have learning problems in reading or mathematics. Mathematics achievement is generally low, writing tends to be legible but drab, and science is not taught at all.

In the early days of their careers, we imagine, there would not have been much observable difference between the two teachers. Both would have been mainly concerned with management, getting their classrooms to run in a peaceful and comfortable way. But as management problems diminished, Margot began turning her attention to problems of learning. Two decades later, she is still advancing—not with great speed, but with considerable cumulative effect. She does not simply try out new ideas. In fact, she is skeptical of most innovations. However, she is sensitive to children's shortcomings in learning—to the things they fail to understand, to the challenges they tend to dodge—and to teaching activities that don't seem to have produced the results she expected. So she is continually experimenting and refining. When she takes up a new idea from elsewhere, she plans carefully how to harmonize it with her teaching, so as not to undo what she has already accomplished. It is not just sensed inadequacies that keep her advancing. These have diminished over the years, and the main stimulus for advancement now is that she keeps discovering new potentialities in the children. Recently, for instance, she has become more aware of children's potential to help one another, and she is cultivating this potential with her characteristic patience and thoughtfulness.

Cynthia, by contrast, has developed into what is referred to by some waggish critics as a 'fanny teacher.' The progress of her skill in managing a classroom could be charted by the increasing proportion of time she spends sitting behind her desk instead of on her feet tending to things. Her pupils spend a good portion of the day doing exercises in workbooks. Cooperative learning in Cynthia's classroom means that she benignly ignores children copying from others, so long as they do it quietly. She eliminated science because it was too messy and difficult to control. She is not idle at her desk. Children bring work to her to be checked, and she coaches those who are on the wrong track. There are always problems arising in a classroom full of young children, but Cynthia has developed reliable ways of dealing with them, ways which characteristically begin with, 'Robert, come up here, please.'

Both teachers are very skillful at what they are trying to do, and so it is tempting to say that both are experts, but with different specializations. Besides compunctions one might have about calling someone an expert whose skill is in avoiding the work she is being paid for, there is a more fundamental reason for not lumping Margot and Cynthia together as experts in the same sense. It has to do with the process they have gone through in becoming what they are. Both of them, we assume, started out with difficult problems to solve. Every school teacher does. Imagine these problems as items on a very long list, with problems at the top having priority. Cynthia's and Margot's lists were initially much the same, let us assume, with the top problems perhaps being those of sheer survival as a teacher. As problems are eliminated, they get checked off. In a profession like teaching, eliminating a problem does not mean it is gone forever. It means that you have a fairly reliable way of dealing with it when it recurs. What Cynthia did, as the top problems were checked off, was move farther down the list, with the eventual goal of eliminating all of them. She is almost there. Only very rarely is the placid routine of her classroom disturbed by an event or condition for which she does not already have a routine response.

Margot, too, has over the years been eliminating problems from her list. She, too, has developed effective routines for preventing or dealing with many kinds of difficulties. To this extent, her progress has been the same as Cynthia's. The difference is that, as problems are eliminated from the list, Margot adds new ones at the top. The problems at the top of her list now are problems she could not even have formulated early in her career. They have to do with distinctions she was not then aware of, such as the distinction between children's telling what they know and explaining what they know. Also, perennial problems, such as children weak in self-esteem or overly demanding of help—problems that she once dealt with in simplistic ways—now appear in much more complex formulations on her list. In fact, most of the problems on her original list have not actually been eliminated but have been replaced by new versions that reflect her increasing wisdom.

To generalize, Cynthia's story represents the normal kind of learning that everyone experiences as they adapt to an environment. Things that were initially difficult become easier. Things that called for problem-solving effort come to be handled by well-learned routines. Things that required deliberate attention and thought come to be second nature. This kind of learning is universal. It distinguishes old-timers from beginners, but it does not distinguish experts from experienced nonexperts.

Margot's story also reflects normal learning, of course, but it shows, in addition two things that we believe constitute the process of expertise. These are *reinvestment* and *progressive problem solving*. In the normal course of learning, as problem-solving effort is taken over by well-learned routines, fewer mental resources are needed to accomplish the same results. For Cynthia, the result is a continual decrease in the amount of activity, mental and physical, that her work requires. The problem solving she does do is aimed at eliminating still more problems, thus reducing activity even further. For Margot, however, the result of normal learning is that she has mental resources available to reinvest in the advancement of her teaching, in the pursuit of new goals or of goals that she did not previously have the resources to pursue. Furthermore, Margot recognizes that there are constitutive problems of her profession that are not eliminated by having a routine way of handling them. These are problems such as maximizing children's learning, helping them realize their full potential, enhancing the quality of their school experience. No matter how effective one may be as a teacher, there is always a higher formulation of these problems that represents a challenge not yet met. This continual reformulation of problems at higher levels, as lower levels are achieved, is what we mean by progressive problem solving.

Reinvestment and progressive problem solving are not separate processes. They are two aspects of the same process, which is what we are calling the *process of expertise*. Reinvestment is the motivational aspect. It is not just willingness to exert effort. There are plenty of teachers who pursue their work more energetically than Margot, responding to the countless demands for their attention, many of which Margot ignores or treats casually. Reinvestment involves both conserving resources, so as to have something to reinvest, and putting those resources back into the activity itself rather than dissipating them or directing them elsewhere. Progressive problem solving is the cognitive aspect of the process of expertise. It is generally not enough just to try to do better. What was learned last time must somehow be translated into a better articulation of the goal or problem so that the next effort will be better conceived. We shall say more in later sections about what progressive problem solving consists of.

Some Psychological Background

The ideas of reinvestment of mental resources and progressive problem solving are built upon some more general concepts that are well known in cognitive psychology but that are somewhat different from their counterparts in everyday psychologizing. Some familiarity with these more general concepts will be helpful in following the discussion in this and later chapters.

Problem Solving

Problem solving has a much broader meaning in contemporary cognitive psychology than it does in ordinary usage. Ordinarily we think of a problem as something being wrong that needs correction or else as a puzzle put to us as a challenge. As the term is currently used in cognitive psychology, however, a problem exists whenever there is a goal which we do not already have a known way of achieving. If you are driving to some out-of-the-way place for the first time, you have a problem. You don't already know a route and will have to find one. The problem may prove quite easy. A few minutes studying a road map may suffice. But you don't know this for certain. There may turn out to be complexities. For instance, there may be no direct route and you will then have to calculate various distances, also taking into account what you can discern about the nature of the roads and the number of towns they pass through. Then it may occur to you that some routes are likely to be more scenic than others, or that one route passes near a cheese factory said to have marvellous cheddar, thus opening the possibility of achieving multiple goals on the trip.

Broadly speaking, any nonroutine purposeful activity is a problem in the sense we are using the term. Buying someone a present is a problem, unless you do it in a completely formulaic way. Arranging flowers in a vase is a problem. So is writing a story or deciding how to spend a day off, but probably not taking out the garbage or paying a restaurant bill with a credit card. Problem solving can be pleasant or unpleasant, creative or mundane. All that is required to constitute problem solving is some amount of searching or deliberation in order to find a way to achieve a goal. So when we talk about the process of expertise as involving progressive problem solving, one must not get the idea that this means going at some grave predicament with knotted brow. We might be talking about progressive problem solving applied to flower arrangement.

The difficulty of problem solving depends on the constraints that are to be honored. Constraints, too, is a very general notion and does not necessarily mean something unpleasant. In fact, pleasantness itself may be a constraint involved in such problems as choosing a place to dine or writing a message on a greeting card. All the same, constraints add to the difficulty and complexity of problems. Choosing a restaurant is much easier if you do not include a constraint that the food must be interesting; it may become extremely difficult if you add constraints so that, in addition to providing interesting fare, the restaurant must be inexpensive, close by, and quiet.

Complexity is a matter of the number of constraints that must be taken into account at the same time in problem solving. It does not take much for a problem to become too complex to cope with. If you have ever tried, as we have recently, to design a house renovation that meets the intricate constraints of municipal building codes, you know what it is to be overwhelmed by complexity. It seems that whatever you do to meet one constraint violates another. You believe there must be a solution, but finding it seems to demand keeping all the constraints in mind at once—the constraints imposed by the building codes, by your own vision, by your budget, and by the laws of nature—and this proves impossible.

Mental Resources

One of the central ideas of modern cognitive psychology is the limited processing capacity of the cognitive system. For present purposes, what this may be taken to mean is that a normal adult can only keep on the order of four things actively in mind at the same time. What accounts for this bottleneck in our mental processes is not settled, and so we use the noncommittal term, "mental resources," to refer to whatever it is that limits the size of mental task we can handle. A great deal of mental activity is not resource-demanding,⋅ meaning that it has little or no effect on the resources available for thinking. Subjectively, it is experienced as activity that does not require conscious attention, that we can perform while thinking about something else. For skilled typists, typing is not resource-demanding, and so they can devote all their mental resources to thinking of what to write. For less skilled typists it does demand some resources, and this interferes with their composing, because they must divide resources between the two tasks. Consequently, they will prefer to write their first drafts longhand, because handwriting is normally not resource-demanding.

Mental resource limitations explain why we are so easily overwhelmed by problem complexity. If a problem can be broken down into steps so that we have to deal with only a couple of constraints at each step, we can handle it. Try multiplying a pair of three digit numbers mentally and you are likely to fail, because you need to keep partial products in mind and remember where you are in the problem, and that is likely to stretch mental resources beyond limit. The paper-and-pencil algorithm you learned at school makes the task manageable because at each step you have to remember only two digits and perhaps a carry, write down the result and forget about it while you move on to the next step.

Most real-world problems are not reducible to step-by-step economizing of mental resources. Take the design of a building renovation referred to earlier. It may help to list all the relevant building code rules and the various other criteria and constraints on a sheet of paper, but there they all are—dozens of them, perhaps—and you have to come up with a design that meets them all simultaneously. How is a poor four-constraint mind supposed to cope? There is little chance that the idea you come up with, which meets the four constraints you happen to be holding in mind, will fortuitously meet the remaining twenty.

Herbert Simon observed that most real-world problems are of the building renovation variety. They are too complex for us to deal with all the constraints in any rational fashion. He coined the term 'bounded rationality' to describe what we do instead. We create a simplified mental representation of the problem and solve it rationally.[1] An obvious simplification of the house renovation problem is to delete all the design ideas that appear to conflict with building codes. This reduces the number of constraints, although it results in a design that is not the design of our dreams but something simpler and more conventional. An even more radical simplification of the problem is to change it from 'design a renovation' to 'engage an architect to produce the design of our dreams'. Now, from the

home-owner's point of view, the design process has been
reduced to a step-wise procedure: Express your ideas to the
architect. When the architect produces a provisional design,
discuss changes to bring it closer to your wishes. The architect
produces a second draft, and the procedure repeats until
something is settled. Of course, in this case the complexity of
the design problem remains, but it has been off-loaded onto
the architect. How it is that the architect can handle design
problems of a much greater complexity than we can is the
question to be addressed in the next section. It is obviously a
question of significance for understanding expertise.

Circumventing Mental Resource Limitations

Given that mental resource limitations are more or less the
same for everyone, how is it that some people can handle much
more complex problems than others? Why is the architect able
to take our specifications and produce a design that meets
them and the building codes as well, whereas our minds are
boggled by the number of constraints that must be taken into
account? More remarkable, perhaps, is the performance of the
building plan inspector at City Hall. Although exhibiting no
other signs of superior intelligence, he glances at one complicated drawing and says, 'That driveway's too wide', glances at
another and remarks, 'Lord only knows what's supposed to
hold this staircase up'. Such performance seems to defy normal
resource limitations and thus immediately suggests expertise.
Indeed, one definition of expertise, proposed by Timothy
Salthouse, is "the process or processes of circumventing normal
human limitations on human information processing."[2]

For reasons to be explained later, we do not accept this as
a sufficient definition, but it certainly points to something of
prime importance in the development of expertise, and that
is acquiring the ability to deal with greater complexity within
one's domain. There is no known way of producing a general
increase in a person's information-processing capacity. Whatever apparent gains are achieved must be due to learning ways
of making more effective use of a fixed capacity.[3] There

are a number of ways that this is done, but we will discuss only two of the most general ones, *pattern learning* and *procedural learning.*

Understanding of the human mind has profited greatly from having something relevant to compare it to, namely, the intelligent machine. Computers have their limitations, but they are not the same ones we have. Holding a number of things in mind at once is not the problem for a computer that it is for us.

Consequently computers are much better than we are at carrying out long chains of reasoning or tracing many different inferential paths to find the one that reaches a goal. That is how computers manage to play chess better than most people. This also means that computers are much better than we are at assessing the combined effect of a number of variables, as must often be done in making predictions or diagnoses. On such tasks, relatively simple statistical operations carried out by computer regularly outperform human experts.[4] For instance, if you want to screen job applications, you are better off feeding the available data into a computer program than handing it to a personnel expert. Although personnel experts may be better than other people at integrating the variety of information contained in a personnel file, they are still not very good compared to a computer, which can process a large number of variables in combination.

As John Anderson has pointed out, however, there are two kinds of processes that human beings are able to carry out much better than today's intelligent machines: pattern recognition and procedural learning. Anderson suggests that the development of expertise is not just a matter of getting better at doing things. It involves changing the way we do them, so that instead of relying on processes that we are inherently poor at, we are able to accomplish tasks through use of the processes we are inherently good at.[5] Novices in a domain have to do a lot of figuring things out, which means relying on their very limited ability to hold constraints in mind and consider numbers of variables in combination. Old-timers in a domain have managed to shift most of the burden on to pattern recognition and learned procedures. which are not hampered by the same mental resource limitations.

Pattern learning. While it has been a challenge to get computers to recognize 26 letters of the alphabet in hand-written form, young children find the irregularities of hand-written forms hardly any obstacle. We are very good at recognizing recurrent patterns despite local variations. The fifty thousand chessboard patterns attributed to the chess master may sound awesome, but an educated adult easily recognizes that many different words, and that is pattern recognition too. What matters most, however, is not the number of patterns learned but the proportion of cases they cover. Skilled internists may or may not recognize fifty thousand disease symptom patterns, but expert diagnosticians commonly report that they recognize enough to cover about 95 percent of the cases they see. Beginning internists will recognize far fewer and so will have to do a great deal more problem solving. At least we hope that is what beginning internists will do. Another possibility, which is discussed further in Chapter 6, is that they will rely on the limited number of symptom patterns they have learned and thus will misrecognize a number of diseases.

How the mind recognizes and uses patterns is only beginning to be understood.[6] Learning patterns is not enough; the right ones need to be recalled at the right time, which is also something that people are much better at than computers. An important part of pattern recognition is recognizing when no available pattern fits—recognizing that the person at the door is a stranger or that the pattern of symptoms is inconsistent with the diseases you are familiar with. For our present discussion, however, the essential point is that pattern recognition processes occur without effort. They do not use up mental resources, and so to the extent that the world we are dealing with consists of familiar patterns, our minds are free for other uses.

Procedural learning. The gain to mental economy that comes from having well-learned procedures was extolled by William James, who referred to it as "habit."[7] Perhaps the most familiar example from modern times is automobile driving—a complicated procedure, which at first takes all one's mental resources and yet eventually takes hardly any at all, enabling some people to transact business by telephone while driving through traffic.

John Anderson's theory of skill acquisition, referred to in the preceding chapter, is currently the most complete theory of how procedural learning works. Anderson's theory links up nicely to ideas about expertise. Skill learning, according to Anderson, starts out as problem solving. The beginning driver is solving dozens of problems, and sometimes having to deal with several at once, such as down-shifting and turning a corner. That is why the demand on mental resources is so great. The learner solves these problems, drawing on remembered facts and rules and piecing together already-available skills. As the same problems recur, however, the learner can begin relying on memory for how they were handled before. Two things start to happen. Procedures that at first must be called up separately, such as *hold down the clutch, grasp the gear lever, move the gear lever up and to the right,* become chunked into a single procedure, such as *shift to third gear.* Also, facts or rules that previously had to be remembered and applied, such as *when turning left onto a two-lane thoroughfare, turn into the inner lane and then cross to the outer lane,* become incorporated into the procedure and no longer need to be considered. Thus, once the correct way of turning onto a two-lane thoroughfare has become habitual, the driver may no longer even be aware that it involves entering one lane and then crossing to another.

These processes of proceduralization continue until the originally problem-fraught activity becomes, as is said, 'automatic'. Automaticity is the great freer of mental resources, but it is obtained at a cost. The cost is loss of conscious access. It becomes difficult to modify a well practiced procedure. Many people, for instance, have not learned the approved way of making a left turn onto a two-lane thoroughfare, and the longer they have been driving the harder it is to get them to change. We should not exaggerate this drawback, however. Automaticity suggests machine-like regularity and inflexibility. Automaticity of human skills is seldom like that at all. The driver whose mind is on a telephone conversation is not driving like an automaton but is making all kinds of flexible adaptations of speed and direction. The inflexible driver is the beginner or the infrequent driver whose skills are not so finely attuned to conditions. Where automaticity is a handicap is not in performance but in the *improvement* of performance. That is why it is problematic in the development of expertise.

The proposed answer, then, to how the architect and the building plans inspector are able to accomplish things that overtax our own mental resources is that they are the beneficiaries of pattern learning and proceduralization. Whereas to us every design configuration is new and requires thought, for them many configurations are familiar and immediately recognizable as legal, illegal, or problematic. This is no more effortful for them than recognizing faces on the street as friends, strangers, or people we want to avoid. They have probably also developed fairly automatic routines for going about the tasks of design or plan inspection, so that the procedures themselves do not require much in the way of resources. This does not mean that the architect produces routine or unimaginative plans. It may mean just the opposite, that by being spared the use of mental resources for coping with mundane problems of code compliance and structural integrity, the architect has resources free to devote to imaginative construction. However, it *could* mean that the architect's plans have become as routine as the procedures that produce them, just as the plan inspector's judgments may become so dominated by learned patterns that anything that does not fit a familiar pattern is judged to be illegal or a mistake.

That is why we cannot go along with Salthouse or Anderson in equating pattern learning and proceduralization with the development of expertise. These processes characterize all learning. They belong as much to the experienced nonexpert as to the expert. Keep at an activity long enough and the patterns and procedures will form themselves. They may be good ones, they may be bad ones, but they will be patterns and chunked procedures of some sort. This is the normal course of learning. Consequently, *if we are to discover anything distinctive about expertise as a process, it must consist of something that goes on over and above this normal course of learning.*

Expertise as Reinvestment: Going Beyond Normal Learning

Accident statistics suggest that it takes two years of driving before skills have developed to the point where people cease to be menaces on the highway. It takes that much learning, evidently, before enough patterns and skilled procedures have been acquired that a driver will automatically do the right thing at the right time and will have enough mental resources available to exercise intelligent judgment when it is required. Most people reach this state of skill, yet few would be counted expert drivers. A course in defensive driving will reveal just how limited the average driver's skills are and how inadequate they are for almost any kind of driving emergency.

Driving thus provides a commonplace illustration of the fact that normal learning is not enough to produce expertise. Although driving skills probably continue to improve indefinitely with experience, in the sense of becoming increasingly smooth and automatic, they do not rise above a level of mediocrity. It is not that we reach the limits of our capacity. With training we could become much better. Rather, it seems that our skills develop up to the level that is required for the environment we drive in and no higher. Some driving environments, such as southern Europe, are more demanding than others, such as rural America, and so people's skills will taper off at different levels, and a change of environment may reopen skill learning. But the essential fact remains the same: Normal learning leads to 'satisficing', as Herbert Simon put it—to performance that is 'good enough' but not to expertise.

The difference between normal learning and the learning that leads to expertise can be traced to what we do with the mental resources that are set free by normal learning. Driving, as we have noted, places heavy resource demands on the beginner's mental resources, but these demands diminish greatly with practice. What do drivers do with these freed-up mental resources? Listen to the radio, talk on the telephone, plan ahead, daydream—all manner of things, which are alike only in that they have nothing to do with driving.

But suppose your ambition is to be a racing car driver. The same sort of normal learning occurs. Initially demanding tasks become automatic, freeing up mental resources. But instead of using these resources for unrelated purposes, you apply them to improving your driving performance. Thus mental resources, as they become available, are reinvested in the activity, leading to further growth in skills and knowledge. This, we propose, is the process by which people move beyond the plateaus of normal learning and acquire expertise.

Now, one might ask, isn't this simply normal learning shifted to a different environment—the environment of the racetrack? This is a question of great significance for understanding expertise, because it brings us to identifying the kind of environment that fosters expertise.

Our answer to the question is both yes and no. Yes, the racetrack is a different environment and the racing car driver's learning can be attributed to adaptation to that environment. But, no, learning to be a racing car driver is not simply normal learning in a higher gear, so to speak. If the racetrack were merely an environment in which one must adapt to very fast-moving traffic, then learning to become a racing car driver would not differ in any essential way from learning to become an ordinary highway driver. Learning would still taper off at a level that was sufficient for getting along in the environment. But a racetrack is not just a highway with very fast-moving traffic. It is a track where drivers race, which means that everyone is trying to get to the finish line ahead of everyone else. Consequently, there is no 'good enough' level at which the race driver's skills can level off. Skills that are good enough to win this year will not be good enough next year, because other drivers will have been working to improve (and engineers and mechanics will have been working to improve the cars, which is a different story with the same plot). The racing car driver is adapting to an environment that is continually changing in ways that require still higher levels of learning. Thus there is not the normal leveling off.

We will say more in a later section about environments that foster expertise. Competitive environments are only one kind. At present, however, we want to focus on the individual and to consider the various ways that mental resources may be reinvested so as to develop expertise. The following are common forms of reinvestment:

1. Reinvestment in learning. The endless practicing that athletes and performing artists do represents reinvestment of this kind. So is the time that professionals put into keeping up with the journals in their field and attending training workshops in new procedures. There seem to be few professions any more where the daily practice of the profession itself provides sufficient learning experience. It is necessary also to put effort into learning itself. Before we got involved in technology projects, we had naively assumed that computer programming was one occupation in which, after some initial training, people learned entirely by doing. But it turns out that expert programmers are voracious consumers of computer literature, readers of bulletin boards, and seekers of advanced training. In general, learning has turned out to be so vital a part of expertise that it warrants examination as an aspect of expertise in its own right, which is how it will be treated in Chapter 6.

2. Seeking out more difficult problems. For athletes and hobbyists this is a common recourse whenever normal learning threatens to reduce life to a routine: Move up to a stiffer level of competition, climb a steeper mountain, build a more complicated birdhouse. Such moves do not just require trying harder. They confront one with problems that cannot be handled by applying previously learned procedures. There are opponents with new tricks; there are new obstacles or constraints. To succeed, new knowledge has to be brought into use, new skills developed, or old skills applied in different ways. Thus using spare mental capacity to tackle more difficult problems produces the kind of learning we associate with expertise. In many occupations, however, seeking out more difficult problems requires a change of job or even a change of specialization, and so it is not a continuously available outlet for surplus mental resources.

3. Tackling more complex representations of recurrent problems. This is the most interesting of the ways of reinvesting mental resources, and the one most central to the process of expertise. Earlier we mentioned Herbert Simon's idea of bounded rationality— the idea that, because of mental resource limitations, we are obliged to work with simplified versions of real-world problems, the actual problem situations being too complex for us to handle. This being the case, then as resources are made available through normal learning, it should be possible to work with less simplified representations of problems. That is what Margot, the more expert of the two teachers described earlier, seems to have done. Each year, with a new class of students, many of the same problems present themselves as in years before. But they are not the same problems to Margot. For instance, a recurrent problem for primary grade teachers is the child who is having trouble with reading and who is showing emotional problems as well. A helpful school psychologist can usually be relied upon to provide a dossier indicating the child has a conglomeration of cognitive deficits, unfortunate home conditions, social maladjustments, a history of possibly damaging illnesses, and so on. We have seen dossiers that went into a grandmother's drinking problem, even though the grandmother had only incidental contact with the child. With so much hard-to-assimilate information, rationality must be bounded indeed. Early in her career, Margot's representation of such a case might have been: *a child with multiple problems of a serious kind requiring professional help*. With that simplified representation, a solution is not hard to find—a solution, that is, which would take responsibility off Margot's shoulders and put it on to the shoulders of specialists. Later in her career, however, when Margot was no longer overwhelmed by the problems of managing a classroom, she might have represented the problem in a way that took account of the child's particular anxieties, including his anxieties about her. With this more complex representation, she would have tried to work out a solution in which she played a role as someone who could do something about the child's anxieties, feelings of failure, and so on. As for the child's reading difficulties, however, her representation might still have been very simplified. For instance: *a child who has a history of failure experiences with reading*. This representation would have suggested solutions along the lines of making reading tasks easier for the child. Such a solution would work well in some cases and badly in others.

In later years, Margot might produce a yet more complex representation of the problem, which takes account of the fact that the child's reading difficulty and anxiety have reciprocal effects on one another, so that an adequate solution will have to deal with both factors at once. This would still be a simplification of the actual state of affairs. One does not escape from bounded rationality. But it would be a substantial advance over the earlier representations. The point we are trying to make is not simply that as Margot becomes wiser she represents problems more intelligently. That may be true, but even if Margot knew as much about reading problems ten years ago as she knows now, she might not have been able to put that knowledge to use because her repertoire of learned patterns and procedures was too limited to provide her with means of bringing the more complex version of the problem within the limits of her mental resources.

Earlier, *child with reading problem* and *child anxious about performance* might have been two separate patterns, giving rise to two factors that would need to be held in mind in working toward a solution. Later, *child afraid to guess at words* might have been learned as an immediately recognizable pattern. This one pattern incorporates elements of the other two and adds something more. It becomes a useful token that can be moved about along with several others on the mental checkerboard in order to solve a problem that would earlier have required too many tokens.

Progressive Problem Solving

Margot's progress in dealing with more and more of the complexity of the same basic problem is an example of *progressive problem solving*. The premise is that the complexity was there from the beginning. She is not making a simple problem more complex. In fact, it is through the simplifications provided by pattern and procedure learning that she is able to keep advancing in dealing with the essential complexities of the problem.

Environmental concerns are adding to the complexity of a great range of problems. Every large building project is rendered more complex because of the need to consider environmental impact. Manufacturing, waste disposal, transportation —all these present more complex problems to engineers and designers than they did in the days before environmental awareness. But the complexities have been there right along, it is just that they were not recognized or attended to. Of course, much of what we know today about the environmental effects of things like fluorocarbons and acid emissions was not known in years back, so it is not simply a matter of people's ignoring the facts. Looking at it more positively, the effect of progressive problem solving is not only to advance in dealing with the complexities already known to exist but also to expand knowledge in ways that bring more complexities to light. Some of these may be complexities created by previous attempts at solution (side-effects of drugs, for instance), but others have always been there (such as the extraordinary complexity of nutrition, where one compound influences the body's utilization of another).

Not all problems are endlessly complex. If they were, we would not be able to gain the benefits from pattern recognition and proceduralization that make it possible for us to keep advancing on those problems that are. If arithmetic were endlessly complex, no one would ever make it to algebra. But there is a certain class of problems that are endlessly complex, where progressive problem solving never approaches an endpoint, and these problems have a special relevance to expertise. We shall call these *constitutive problems of a domain.* A constitutive problem of teaching is the elimination of ignorance. There is obviously no end to this problem, but progress is possible, and expertise in teaching entails making such progress. Similarly, a constitutive problem of medicine is the elimination of disease, a constitutive problem of social planning is the elimination of misery, a constitutive problem of negotiation is an agreement in which all parties consider themselves winners, and a constitutive problem of baseball pitching is to get all batters to strike out, ground out, or fly out.

Professions and other expert domains are in an important sense defined by their constitutive problems. Change the constitutive problem and you change the profession in a fundamental way. That may be happening in medicine, with movements to change the constitutive problem from the elimination of disease to the achievement of health for everyone. The idea of constitutive problems helps us to deal with issues such as whether Margot and Cynthia are both experts but with different skills. We can argue that Cynthia does not engage in the process of expertise, that her skills in classroom management, impressive as they may be, are a result of normal learning and do not involve reinvestment of mental resources into the activity. But one could imagine a teacher who does reinvest mental resources into the task of minimizing teaching. One of us knew a college instructor who made an art out of this, who in essence persisted in working toward the ideal of reducing to zero the amount of thought and effort he put into teaching. He scheduled all his classes at 7 a.m., he said, so that his work day would be over before he was fully awake. One might with justice call such a person an expert, but not an expert teacher. He kept reinvesting mental resources into progressive problem solving, but the problem he invested them in is not a constitutive problem of the teaching profession.

By handling some aspects of a problem more or less automatically, the skilled person has mental resources to spare for paying attention to other aspects of the problem that previously had to be ignored. The physician may go on treating the same illnesses, but can pay attention to a greater range of symptoms and complicating conditions. The small contractor may go on doing kitchen renovations, but can work them out within a larger context of possibilities, paying attention to more constraints, taking more account of clients' preferences and needs. Domains in which expertise can flourish are domains in which there is no inherent limit on progress. There is always a larger context within which the present problem-solving effort is partial and oversimplified.

To the extent that people engage in progressive problem solving they work at the edge of their competence. Studying string quartets, sociologists Murnighan and Conlon remarked of the more successful ones: "The fact that they never quite achieve their ultimate goal—to produce transcendent, glorious sound that is just beyond their reach—keeps them continuously striving to achieve it."[8] Working at the edge of competence is risky and taxing, but it yields two great benefits. It results in superior accomplishments: More being ventured, more is sometimes gained. And it leads to further growth as competence advances. New or redesigned skills are acquired, beyond those developed through normal processes of learning. Moreover, the new skills are not simply added like new books to a library. They combine with the old skills to form super-skills, which make it possible to progress toward still more complex problems calling for still more complex skills, and so on. That, in essence, is the process of expertise.

Progressive Problem Solving versus Problem Reduction
The opposite of expertise is normally thought of as incompetence, bungling, doing things the hard way. Those are

appropriate contrasts when we are considering expertise from the standpoint of performance. When we consider it from the standpoint of process, however, the opposite of expertise is the opposite of progressive problem solving. That is something we may call *problem reduction.*

Problem reduction reflects the commonplace view of problems as things to be gotten rid of, to be *reduced* in number and severity. It also represents a common way in which problems are handled, by *reducing* them to tasks that can be handled with routine procedures. Thus, much of normal learning and adaptation can be put under the heading of problem reduction. Starting out on a job or an enterprise, we expect to encounter a host of problems. Little by little, we expect those problems to diminish, to be solved and eliminated. New problems crop up, of course, but we expect a net decline in the problem-solving load. Prospects would be very discouraging otherwise. Problem reduction occurs in two ways. Some problems, once solved, stay solved. Installing a new piece of equipment and getting it to run is an example. Other problems recur, but we develop routine ways of handling them. In effect, they cease to be problems and become merely tasks.

The ideal toward which problem-reduction efforts strive is a condition where there are no more real problems, where everything that comes along can be handled with existing procedures. Although such an ideal is obviously unattainable, it nevertheless provides useful direction. It encourages planfulness and a search for lasting rather than stop-gap solutions.

Problem reduction sounds so good, in fact, that it sounds like just another word for intelligence. Bhaskar, Herstein, and Hayes go so far as to calibrate expertise according to the proportion of cases likely to be encountered that are already covered by existing knowledge.[9] They see the growth of expert knowledge as an unending but nevertheless diminishing process. The reason is that one first learns to handle the most frequently occurring problems. As time goes on, one develops knowledge of increasingly rare cases, so that there is no end to learning, but the amount of problem solving one has to do gets closer and closer to zero.

Thus Bhaskar, Herstein, and Hayes's analysis would suggest that problem reduction and progressive problem solving are one and the same, whereas we are making them out to be opposites. The seeming contradiction is easily resolved, however. It is no doubt generally true that, with increasing experience, experts less and less often encounter unfamiliar cases; but that is also true of the experienced nonexpert. Thus Bhaskar, Herstein, and Hayes are not really distinguishing expertise. Differences between experts and experienced nonexperts would show up primarily in *how* they deal with unfamiliar cases. To what extent do they try to construct new concepts and methods for unfamiliar cases, as compared to force-fitting them to existing routines? To what extent do they redefine familiar problems at higher levels, so as to take more inherent complexity into account? To what extent do they put more effort into the more difficult cases?

Problem reduction is intelligent behavior. Most of us practice it in most areas of our lives and should probably do more of it. Only in that way can we gain enough time and resources to pursue progressive problem solving where it counts. Paying bills, getting to and from work, keeping an orderly home and workplace—these are all activities that one hopes to reduce to the point where they cease to be problems. To pursue expertise in all areas of our lives would be both suicidal and impractical. The process of expertise is the opposite of problem reduction, but it depends on problem reduction.

One has to know where to pursue problem reduction and where to pursue progressive problem solving. Problem reduction with respect to the core problems of one's career means becoming the equivalent of a 'fanny teacher'. Problem reduction in the area of family life means sterile marriages, neglected children. Problem reduction in one's personal development may mean becoming one-dimensional. In its fullest sense, progressive problem solving means living an increasingly rich life—richer in that more and more of what the world has to offer is taken into one's mental life. But that increasing richness, because of its time and cognitive demands, requires the judicious reduction of peripheral problems. Sages like Henry David Thoreau have been telling us that for a long time.

What Motivates the Process?

In discussing progressive problem solving and how it works to keep expertise developing and to prevent settling into ruts, we have been discussing the cognitive side of the process of expertise. But there is also a motivational side, identified with the continuing reinvestment of mental resources. By definition this takes effort. 'Investing mental resources' is another way of saying 'exerting mental effort'. It implies 'paying attention to', 'thinking about', or 'trying to achieve' something. The effort is not necessarily intense. Margot, the teacher we have been using as an exemplar, is not a high-pressure person by any means. Still, she is continually tackling problems at levels that extend her, even though her skills are good enough that she could function adequately as a teacher by staying comfortably within what she already knows how to do. If we are to understand expertise, we must not only understand what experts do that is special but also why they do it.

Cognitive psychologists are often accused of ignoring motivation. A more generous appraisal would be that they honor the principle that if you don't have something worthwhile to contribute on a topic you should refrain from speaking. Most of what psychologists of any sort have to say about motivation is warmed-over common sense. The part that is not common sense involves the brain, but it is at such a basic level that we cannot expect it to be helpful in distinguishing experts from experienced nonexperts. There are, however, three ideas that seem worth highlighting because of their special relevance to the process of expertise. The first is the idea of 'flow', which suggests that one of the reasons people are willing to put effort into the process of expertise is that it actually *feels* good. The second is the idea of 'second-order environment', which are social environments that, unlike most social environments, provide support for the process of expertise. The third is the idea that there is a heroic element in expertise. This last is not an explanation of why people put effort into the process of expertise, but rather an acknowledgement that the other explanations do not quite do the whole job.

Flow

The term *flow* was coined by Mihaly Csikszentmihalyi to refer to an experience of sustained pleasure that he found to be reported by artists of all kinds, athletes, scientists, mountain climbers, and many others, when they were absorbed in an activity that sounds to us very much like the process of expertise. These people in diverse walks of life, said Csikszentmihalyi, "when they describe how it feels when they are doing something that is worth doing for its own sake, use terms that are interchangeable in their minutest detail."[10] Prominent among characteristics of the flow experience are total absorption in the activity, a feeling of being in control, and a loss of self-consciousness, which Csikszentmihalyi attributes to all mental resources being invested in the activity, so that none are available for self-reflection. Also attributable to the total investment of resources in the activity are escape from the concerns of daily life and loss of normal time monitoring, so that minutes may seem like hours or hours may seem like minutes.

So pleasurable is it to be 'in flow' that people who experience it want to keep experiencing it, but this requires what amounts to progressive problem solving. Flow, according to Csikszentmihalyi, requires a nice balance between ability and challenge. If challenge exceeds ability, the result is anxiety and frustration rather than flow. If ability exceeds challenge, the result is boredom. Combined with the inevitable effects of learning, this means that repetition of the same activity will eventually cease to produce the flow experience. It will get too easy. Something must be done to increase the level of challenge so as to bring it into harmony with the increasing level of ability. Thus there is a progressive element inherent in the quest for the flow experience. As Csikszentmihalyi puts it,

To remain in flow, one must increase the complexity of the activity by developing new skills and taking on new challenges. This holds just as true for enjoying business, for playing the piano, or for enjoying one's marriage, as for the game of tennis. Heraclitus's dictum about not being able to step in the same stream twice holds especially true for flow. This inner dynamic of the optimal experience is what drives the self to higher and higher levels of complexity. It is because of this spiraling complexity that people describe flow as a process of 'discovering something new', whether they are shepherds telling how they enjoy caring for their flocks, mothers telling how they enjoy playing with their children, or artists describing the enjoyment of painting. Flow forces people to stretch themselves, to always take on another challenge, to improve on their abilities.[11]

What Csikszentmihalyi appears to be describing is exactly the same process that we have been talking about as the process of expertise, except that he is describing its subjective aspect. We arrive at the same point, from different starting places. We started with cognitive behavior, asking, 'What do experts *do* that distinguishes them from experienced non-experts?' Having identified the process of reinvesting mental resources in progressive problem solving, we then ask why people do it, and are led to intrinsic pleasure as one explanation. Csikszentmihalyi started with the motivational question. Having identified flow as a motivator of exceptional performance, he then asked what is required to produce this experience, and was led to an idea of progressive challenge that is the subjective counterpart of the process of expertise, this same reinvestment of mental resources into tackling things at higher levels of complexity.

If the process of expertise is so addictively enjoyable, however, why doesn't everyone practice it and thus become an expert? One answer is that flow is much harder to achieve in some situations than others. As Richard Mitchell puts it, "Flow emerges in circumstances that are perceived as both problematic and soluble."[12] In many highly routinized jobs it is difficult to perceive problems. The problems may have to be invented.

Typists working in typing pools have been observed to invent little games and challenges to keep life interesting. Larry Hirschhorn has studied work situations in which people perceive problems as insoluble. There, as Csikszentmihalyi has hypothesized, anxiety is the dominant experience. It occurs with nurses working in wards for terminally ill patients, with executives in enterprises that are failing or out of control, and with nuclear power plant technicians overwhelmed by complexity and sense of risk. The common response that Hirschhorn has observed is for people in such situations to "retreat within the boundaries of their roles."[13] They do their jobs in ways that minimize challenges—the very opposite of the process of expertise. If it worked, this strategy might nevertheless result in flow experience, by bringing challenge down to a level commensurate with ability. But instead the strategy leads to worsening of conditions, increased anxiety, and thus to further retreat.

There appear also to be individual differences in how disposed people are to seek or create flow-inducing levels of challenge. Csikszentmihalyi, studying mathematically talented high school students, found some who were typically bored while others typically enjoyed themselves in doing the same homework. It wasn't that the bored ones were more talented and thus found the homework less challenging, Csikszentmihalyi claims, but rather that the unbored students were able to find challenging aspects in the work that the bored students were not. In Chapter 6, dealing with what we call 'expertlike learners', we will look further into this ability to bring the process of expertise into learning situations.

Expert Subcultures as Second-Order Environments

Experts seldom exist in isolation. Often they are linked together by associations or informal networks, but even when that is not the case they are connected through a tradition in which expertise evolves over generations as well as within the careers of individuals. We may therefore speak of a subculture of expertise existing in a field. This subculture embodies ideals and goals that direct the process of expert development. It provides help and cooperation leading to success, as well as forms of recognition of success—recognition that people out-side the subculture would be unable to give. (We think, for instance, of jazz musicians, most of whom play for little money to naive audiences, but who are sustained by a subculture that provides highly sophisticated mutual admiration.) The sub-culture provides models of expert careers so that novices have a better idea of where their efforts are taking them.

In most social environments, adaptation is adequately served by normal learning of the kind we described earlier. The newcomer suffers from lack of requisite knowledge, skills, and customs, yet as these lacks are remedied through experience in the environment, life becomes less problematic and learning tapers off. But in an expert subculture, one of the requirements of adaptation is to participate in the pursuit of ideal goals of the group, and this necessitates continued progressive problem solving. Adapting to a scientific subculture, for instance, requires more than mastering a body of scientific knowledge and skills. One is expected to make some advance on an unsolved problem between this year's convention and the next. Or if it is an artistic subculture, one is expected to have made some contribution to the cumulative tradition of the art. In nonexpert environments, the process of expertise is deviant. Within an expert subculture, however, progressive problem solving and continued building of competence are not deviant but instead are central to one's participation in the life of the expert community. An expert community, we might say, is one in which to conform is to grow (although to grow is not necessarily to conform).

The distinction we are trying to make here needs to be put at a more general level. For it is not simply that experts inhabit one kind of social environment and nonexperts another. Experts are found in all kinds of environments, only some environments are supportive of the process of expertise and others are inhospitable. And there are supportive environments in which not everyone is an expert.

We may call the ordinary situations of work and everyday life *first-order environments*. They present a relatively fixed set of conditions, and learning tapers off as one adapts to those conditions. Problems occur, of course. In fact, some first-order environments may be crisis-ridden. But in first-order environments problems occur as aberrations that need to be removed. Public transportation systems, custodial institutions, and insurance agencies are common examples of this kind of environment.

Second-order environments are ones in which the conditions to which people must adapt change progressively as a result of the successes of other people in the environment. Every social environment changes, and in retrospect historians may discern pattern in the change, but there is no inner logic, no entelechy. But within the world of auto racing, for instance, there is. Each team's advance in technology or strategy sets a new standard which others try to surpass, with the net result that, except for periodic changes in regulations, lap speeds keep going up and up. Adapting in the world of racing means adapting to a progressive set of conditions. Competition is not the only dynamic force, although it is seldom wholly absent in expert domains. In science, conditions keep changing as a result of continual contributions to knowledge.

The crucial point is that in second-order environments one does not merely adapt to continual change. That is true of first-order environments as well, to the extent that they are unstable. One adapts to changes that keep raising the ante, by setting a higher standard of performance, by reformulating problems at more complex levels, or by increasing the amount of knowledge that is presupposed. Through adapting, one raises the ante for others, and so on. Thus there is a compounding of achievements, much like the compounding of capital by investment. It occurs within the individual career, but it also occurs at the level of the community. Consequently, second-order environments override the rigidifying effects of habit and practice, by progressively altering the conditions to which individuals in the environment must adapt.

An important limitation of expert subcultures is that one typically has to possess some level of expertise already, in order to gain admittance to them. Thus they are good for sustaining and elevating expertise, but not for fostering its early development. In Chapter 7 we will discuss the possibility of turning schools into second-order environments, which they decidedly are not at the present time. Then in Chapter 8 we will consider the idea of a whole society that functions as a second-order environment, so that expertise and its process become normal rather than exceptional.

The Heroic Element in Expertise

People in second-order environments may pursue progressive problem solving merely as a way of conforming. But experts can be found in first-order environments as well. They may be rare, but they exist. They can be found here and there behind shop counters, at government office desks, driving taxis, installing telephones, or at home caring for children. They reinvest mental resources in their work, elevating it or expanding its scope to take in a broader set of concerns—such as the concerns of their clients. They exhibit professionalism in its favorable sense, but without benefit of professional identification or a professional subculture to support them. The intrinsic rewards of flow might partly explain what motivates them, but the nature of their work suggests that they must often pursue an expert course with flow experiences being few and far between. In such cases, pursuing high standards and continuing to advance requires an element of heroism. And we mean heroism literally, in the sense of arduous efforts that benefit society but that are disproportionate to what society provides in the way of rewards and supports.

Heroic expertise is especially to be found in occupations where one person's work does not impinge on or serve as a model for another's. Mail delivery is an example. Letter carriers go off on their respective routes, and if one of them does a particularly good or poor job this has little effect on the others and may not even be known to them. The same is true of school teachers, working away in separate classrooms. In such occupations there is often an official ethos of heroic type: the image of the letter carrier braving storm and flood to deliver the mail, and of the teacher selflessly devoted to nurturing the young mind. The images reinforce the fact that the hero must go it alone; there are few social forces lending support.

Even within expert subcultures, however, there is a heroic aspect to exceptional expertise—the individual, striving ahead beyond the supports of kin and community, pursuing some lonely ideal of excellence or knowledge. When Charlie Chaplin said, "I'm not a genius, I'm just a perfectionist", he was being modest about his talents but at the same time he was subtly laying claim to heroic status. He was suggesting that his many-faceted art, which admirers attributed to natural genius, was instead the result of pursuing fine points of excellence which the public could not recognize, let alone support.

Athletes and performing artists often convey the heroic image by virtue of the arduous training and drill that they sustain. While the rest of us shuffle through life they are off somewhere sweating to bring their performance up to that moment which we will ignorantly applaud as a display of natural talent. Similarly, there are the scientists working their 60- or 80- hour weeks pursuing, not personal excellence, but an advance in knowledge that most of the world is in no position to care about.

The heroic aspect does tend to get overblown, however, partly because it is the superstars who have biographies written about them, and heroic effort is often part of .their story. Undoubtedly the numbers are much larger of people in various walks of life who qualify as experts and who invest substantial effort in the processes that have developed their expertise, but whose efforts are comfortably attuned to life's rewards. The process of expertise may involve continual investment in pro-gressive problem solving, as we propose, but it does not follow that the effort must be arduous. There are all kinds of experts. Some have so much talent that progressive problem solving comes easily to them. Others may pursue their careers along lines of least resistance, yet do so in a line that nevertheless leads upward to increasingly complex problems. The issue in distinguishing expert from nonexpert development is not the intensity of effort, although that may count greatly in determining how far people go and at what speed; rather, as we have emphasized, it is a matter of what the effort is invested in.

Even with the most laid-back and convivial of experts—like the teacher, Margot—it seems that there must be some element of heroism. For if expertise involves progressive problem solving and progressive problem solving entails working at the edge of one's competence, then at least a bit of daring is inevitably required. It is always tempting to stay with tasks that fall comfortably within one's competence. Working at the edge risks failure and loss of esteem (especially in professions where the expert image is of always knowing the right answer). But it also provides a certain excitement, which is probably addictive.

How Experts Stay Out of Ruts

The normal learning that makes expertise possible also endangers it. Pattern learning and procedural learning free mental resources so that they are available for reinvestment but at the same time they build up bodies of pattern knowledge and habits which, with continuing practice, become increasingly difficult to modify. This suggests that experts, through the very practice that makes them skillful, may be deepening a rut that will eventually entrap them.

There is a real-life problem here, not just a theoretical conundrum. People do get into ruts. Experts past their prime come to be labeled as 'deadwood' or as members of an 'old guard', resistant to new ways of doing things. But even if rigidification is inevitable, it is somehow staved off to a remarkable degree and often over long spans of years in the careers of many experts. Rigidity, indeed, is the mark of the failed expert. But explaining why experts don't get caught in their own ruts does present a puzzle, somewhat like the puzzle of why spiders don't get caught in their own webs.

When we have posed this problem to psychology students, their commonest answer is that experts are favored with a trait of flexibility. There may indeed be such a trait, perhaps even at the neural level, but there is no evidence or reason to suppose that experts have more of it than other people. Or even if they do, we still have to explain why, with increasing expertise, it does not become more and more difficult to adapt flexibly.

Rather than looking for something special in the make-up of experts, we do better to look for something in the process of expertise itself that keeps it from rigidifying. Getting out and tackling new problems has a rejuvenating effect. That much has been demonstrated in many ways through work with the elderly. Old people who have started to shut down and vegetate can change dramatically by getting re-engaged in problem solving of almost any sort. From work with monkeys (who show similar effects of aging), there is evidence that the effects are physiological, not just psychological. Hormone levels and sperm counts rise. The biological clock truly gets set back.[14]

Problem solving, it appears, is good for your health. There are dramatic data showing how closely longevity is related to occupational level. This holds even with the civil service, where all enjoy incomes adequate to meet physical needs and work under similar physical conditions. Careful analyses have indicated that the effect has much to do with autonomy and power. High-level managers, despite working under more stress, markedly outlive civil servants in lower-echelon jobs and indeed show less evidence of stress-related symptoms.[15] One of the things autonomy gives is ability to set the level at which one addresses problems, so that there is an appropriate match of problem complexity to ability to deal with that complexity. Flow experience may be only the more dramatic manifestation of a generally healthier state of affairs that occurs when this match is achieved. The alternatives—boredom if complexity is too low, anxiety and frustration if it is too high—are likely among other things to lead to rigidity and getting into a rut.

The puzzle of why automaticity does not inevitably lead to rigidity disappears if we think of automated skills as building blocks of new skills that are not automated. The experienced chess player learns many patterns. But for the expert these do not become patterns that restrict thinking and result in stereotyped, predictable play. Instead, they are used as building blocks for increasingly sophisticated analyses and strategies of play.

Similarly, the experienced writer learns to recognize many familiar rhetorical patterns—ways of organizing, of putting across points, of making transitions. These *could* be used to produce facile, unoriginal, and tiresome prose, which is what hack writers do. But expert writers are always constructing more challenging writing problems for themselves, both at the level of larger purposes and at the sentence-to-sentence level. In trying to do justice to their content, they raise more difficult writing problems for themselves, and in trying to produce a good piece of writing, they raise problems that force themselves to reconsider content. Thus writing becomes a process of discovery in which knowledge is transformed through the writing process and the writing itself ends up developing in ways they could not have anticipated.[16] It is the inexpert writers who get into ruts, whose writing is predictable and often much like that of their peers. We know of writing teachers who forbid their students to write science fiction, because they cannot stand the sameness of it—story after story patterned after whatever televised science fiction series happens to be popular at the time. For inexpert writers learned patterns direct performance. For more expert writers learned patterns provide a kind of vocabulary out of which to produce original constructions.

One often hears it suggested that knowing too much is dangerous because it provides prepackaged ways of thinking and acting and thus stands in the way of fresh ideas and new ways of seeing things. We will examine this notion a little more closely in the next chapter, in discussing creative expertise. But as an explanation for why people get into ruts, this notion is useless. Having a repertoire of learned patterns and procedures is not what causes people to get into ruts. Given enough experience, everybody acquires the repertoire. What gets people into ruts is reducing problems to levels that can be handled by those learned patterns and procedures. The anti-dote to this is progressive problem solving. Getting into a rut is proof that you are not carrying on the process of expertise.

Broader Implications of the Process View

Engaging in the process of expertise by no means guarantees expertise that will be recognized in the world at large. That may additionally require special talents and opportunities. It also, of course, requires a society prepared to recognize one's accomplishments. Expert moose callers will go unheralded in most parts of the world. And a common reaction to new movements in art has been to judge the practitioners as lacking in skill. To what extent the process of expertise is *necessary* for achieving recognized expert status is an open question. Evidence linking the process to experts is mostly anecdotal or based on samples too small for generalizing to whole populations. It seems a fair guess, however, that in many fields the category of recognized experts will include some who were so talented that they achieved expert status without putting effort into progressive problem solving and perhaps others whose superior training enables them to function on a par with those more fully engaged in the process of expertise.

If the process of expertise is neither necessary nor sufficient to achieve what is generally recognized as expert status, then why make so much of it? An analogy may serve in place of a full response: Aerobic exercise is a process that has been found to play a significant and many-faceted role in health, yet it is obviously not sufficient to ensure good health and it is not necessary, either, as demonstrated by the existence of people who enjoy good health despite total abstinence from aerobic exercise. For most favorable states of affairs in the world it is impossible to specify necessary and sufficient conditions. Rather, one looks for things that make a difference and that it is possible to do something about. Heredity probably has more to do with health than exercise ever could, but we cannot do anything about our heredity, whereas we can do something about exercise. Similarly, it may be that, at least in some fields, native talent has more to do with determining who will achieve an expert level of performance than does any process potentially under the control of the learner. But that does not detract from the value of examining processes.

Pursuing the analogy a little further, aerobic exercise and related ideas of fitness have contributed to changing the concept of health. The claim that there are healthy people who do not get aerobic exercise, and that therefore aerobic exercise is not necessary for health, starts to be weakened because we begin to have doubts about calling people healthy just because they are free of disease. Similarly, we believe that with advances in understanding the process of expertise, the concept of expertise will begin to be altered and sharpened so that it picks out something that is more clearly distinguishable from talent, routine skill, and advantages of training.

A refined concept of expertise would not only exclude some of what was previously in, but would include some of what was previously out. The implications in this direction are more interesting and promising. There are areas where it seems profitable to think in terms of a process of expertise, but where conventional notions of expertise do not apply. Examples of such areas are childhood, the handicapped, groups, and society.

Early Forms of Expertise

Although it may take years to achieve expert levels of performance, the process of expertise could in principle begin very early. Therefore, instead of looking only for potential or precursors of expertise in children and beginners, we could look for the real thing—that is, for evidences of reinvesting mental resources in progressive problem solving—and could try to support those early manifestations of the process of expertise.

Although people who work with children seldom apply notions of expertise, cognitive-developmental theories provide ideas that come close to defining a process of expertise. Piaget offered a very general conception of intelligence as the complexity of "the pathways between the subject and the objects on which it acts."[17] In his well-known stage theory of development, each stage represents a more complexly structured interaction between person and environment. Whereas Piaget dealt with the logical structure of stages, neo-Piagetians such as Pascual-Leone, Case, Fischer, and Siegler have formalized and extended the idea of growth in complexity and have been able to apply it to growth within particular domains of skill. Case has mapped developmental sequences according to the number of task or problem constraints that people are able to incorporate into an action plan. There is an increase within developmental stages in the number of constraints that can be handled and transition to a higher stage occurs when constraints that had previously been handled singly are chunked into larger structures that can be handled as single units, thus making possible a major advance in the complexity of mental tasks that can be managed. Intellectual growth according to such a scheme is essentially identical to what we describe as the process of expertise—growth that consists of addressing problems at increasingly complex levels, taking advantage of pattern learning and automaticity to free up mental resources that can be applied to taking more problem variables into account.[18]

Lev Vygotsky, a psychologist whose brief but illustrious career in the early years of the USSR has lately begun to influence developmental and educational psychologists worldwide, provides another perspective on child development that fits well with a process of expertise. The relevance of Vygotsky's ideas can be conveyed most directly if we translate them immediately into terms of expertise: Expertise, Vygotsky might have said, exists already in the culture. The learner's first contact with it comes through participating in activities along with people who already have the expertise (helping mother bake a cake, for instance). Gradually more responsibility is handed over to the learner, and in the process the learner 'internalizes' the expertise.[19] Vygotsky could be said to describe a process of expertise that is not carried on by the child alone—at least not at first—but that rather is carried on by child and parent acting jointly. Research by Benjamin Bloom and his students on the early beginnings of outstanding achievement in fields like music and sport indicates that such joint participation of parent and child in what amounts to progressive problem solving is vital for getting the child off to the early start that is necessary in such fields. In Chapter 6 we will explore in more detail the process of expertise among learners.

Expert Process without Expert Performance

The fact that the process of expertise need not necessarily result in what is socially recognized as expert performance has a positive side to it. It means that the benefits of pursuing this process can be experienced by people who have no prospect of achieving expert status. This is already obvious in the realm of amateur sport. One does not have to be an internationally ranked tennis professional to enjoy the flow experience that comes from being totally into one's game. All that is required, besides the right disposition, is to be matched with opponents at the right level, so that one is challenged but not badly overmatched. Amateur sport is generally organized so as to make this possible, and thus to provide possibilities for continual reinvestment and progress for that huge majority of people who have no prospect whatever of becoming world class athletes. Sports for handicapped people provide a particularly heartening example, one that has been handled so successfully that people who excel in some categories of 'special olympics' sports do in fact gain public recognition as experts.

There are other areas of life where the same principle could apply but usually does not. The wheelchair-bound people who learn to play competitive basketball get recognition and support, we suggest, not because the public recognizes the arduous process they have gone through to attain such skill but because their performance exceeds that of most people who are not wheelchair-bound. But what about the more severely handicapped person whose achievement is limited to navigating in a motorized wheelchair or to speaking just articulately enough to carry on a conversation with tolerant listeners—in short, someone whose visible achievement in no way exceeds the general norm? The *process* by which these seemingly limited achievements were made may have been just as expert-like as that of the wheelchair basketball star or the world-class tennis player.

This is not simply a matter of getting credit for trying. The world is not very generous in giving such credit in any circumstance. The practical point is that there are many areas of human endeavor where the process of expertise could produce significant gains for people, but where the process needs fostering and encouragement. Overcoming reading handicaps is an example. Although reading is a very complex skill, it is easily mastered by most people and so the ability to read a magazine article at the rate of a few hundred words a minute and understand it gains no recognition as expertise. But for some substantial minority of people—perhaps 10 or 15 percent of students undergoing conventional instruction in North America—such an achievement is problematic and likely never to be realized. Such people are categorized as learning disabled. The ordinary ways of dealing with them are as far as one could imagine from supporting a process of expertise. They are regarded as people with ailments that need to be diagnosed and treated. They may be coddled and given unchallenging tasks or they may be subjected to a regimen of exercises intended to improve their brains, but in any event they are shielded from any suggestion that there are problems to be solved and that they might be the ones to solve them. Although some may be helped in reading (the effectiveness of most treatments is abysmally low) nothing is done to provide them with either the motivation or the knowledge that would enable them to go on in an expertlike manner addressing problems of reading at progressively higher levels of complexity. With adults receiving treatment for reading problems, in fact, there are indications that they become so dependent on the therapist that they are sometimes reluctant to learn to read and thereby end the relationship.

Yet reading disabilities typically present conditions that are classic for the process of expertise. Poor readers, experiments have shown, have to invest more mental resources than good readers do in just figuring out what the words are. Consequently they have fewer resources available for understanding what they read. If they are to progress they need not only to build up efficient pattern recognition and procedures so as to free more mental resources, but they also need to reinvest those resources effectively back into the task of reading. We at one time worked with a child who exhibited the classical symptoms, but who was otherwise a bright child who took an expertlike approach to intellectual tasks as long as they did not involve reading. Clare Brett, who worked most directly with him, essentially instituted a process of progressive problem solving in which both of them participated, with increasing amounts of the initiative being turned over to the child. He began doing his own analyses of what he was doing in reading and devising strategies for doing it better. Not only did his reading skills improve to above-average levels, but he was able to go on improving on his own, despite being in a learning disabilities class where all his earlier, self-defeating strategies were reinforced. (Backsliding is a well-recognized problem in all kinds of educational remediation with children.) He soon earned release from the learning disabilities class and has been doing well since in regular classrooms. To our minds, this is an instance of someone becoming an expert—a competent performer in an area that does not require a process of expertise for most people but that did for him. In this case the child already had some expertlike dispositions to build on. However, Valerie Anderson has been helping teachers to take this same basic approach—getting the student as well as the teacher engaged in progressive problem solving—and impressive results are being obtained even with very low-achieving students who show no signs of expertise in any academic area.[20]

Once the process of expertise is unhinged from the idea of expert status, we can probably discover many other areas where the process would be worth trying to understand and to support. Some of these will be discussed in the final chapter, on prospects for an expert society.

Expertise not Confined to the Individual

When we view expertise as a process, there is no *a priori* reason for stipulating that the process must go on within an individual mind. One kind of joint process of expertise has already been mentioned—the kind that involves an adult and a child, where the child is not yet competent to carry on the process single-handedly, but can do so with an adult, who may gradually turn initiative over to the child. Other instances involve groups that function as units: sports teams, surgical teams, teams of air traffic controllers, and so on. Studies of such groups indicate that they show many of the same processes as individuals. They learn, solve problems, get into ruts, get out of ruts, display expertlike or nonexpertlike characteristics.

Viewing groups in terms of expert or nonexpert processes is a sharp departure from the way that has become entrenched in Western thinking since the Industrial Revolution. Industrial rationality called for a view of people working together as consisting of discrete individuals each performing a specified function—the gears in a machine metaphor. The industrial process depended on how skillfully and reliably the individual functions were performed. That proved to be a powerful notion, and it has spread to military and athletic organizations as well. The 'team player' is often thought of as one who unstintingly performs his or her designated function without trying to go beyond it.

Expert teams, or 'high-performance' teams as they are called by people who study them, turn out to be quite different from this. Although there may be assigned jobs, everyone on the team knows more or less how to do everything and thus they are able to trade off functions in a highly flexible manner as events require. The group progressively develops ways as a unit to achieve higher goals or to achieve goals more success-fully. Thus it makes sense to speak of a single process of expertise that is carried out by the team functioning as a unit. The expert team does not just do its work well, it *gets somewhere*. This is obvious in a scientific research team. It has a trajectory much like that of an individual research career except that it involves a group, whose membership may change from time to time even though the process remains coherent and continuous. The same is true of musical groups and improvisational comedy groups.

There have also been studies of groups that we see as following a nonexpert course of development. Deborah Gladstein studied sales teams and found a number that got on very well together, where problems were few and agitations minimal, and where everyone felt that things were going nicely—except that in comparison to other groups they weren't selling much. These would seem to be groups that followed the course of problem reduction, evolving routines that made life increasingly pleasant and effortless but at the expense of no longer addressing the problems that constituted their reason for being in the first place.[21]

At still higher levels of aggregation, we can imagine whole societies that could be characterized by expert or nonexpert processes. Even though the members would not be functioning in the coherent manner of a team, and so there would be no entity that you could call an expert, there may be much to gain by considering the social process as a whole from the standpoint of how surplus mental resources are invested, to what extent they are reinvested in progressive problem solving as against being dissipated in other ways. This is an idea we will explore in the final chapter.

Summary

In the normal process of becoming good at something, operations that once took thought and planning come to be done with little or no mental effort. Situations that once had to be analyzed come to be recognized instantly and effortlessly, like a familiar face. Behavior that once had to be thought through step by step becomes organized into efficient packets, nicely suited to the situations that call for action. Formal knowledge comes to be incorporated into the procedures themselves and no longer needs to be recalled. Actions become increasingly streamlined and precisely adapted to circumstances.

This normal process of learning is the foundation of expertise, but it is not what makes expertise distinctive. Expertise is distinguished by what people do over and above this normal process. While the normal process leads to efficiency, it also leads to rigidity and to a tapering off of learning as it reaches a level that suffices for ordinary needs.

In domains where expertise flourishes, problems tend not to have ceilings on them. There is always a higher level at which a problem can be approached, taking more variables into account, reaching a higher standard of result, or meeting a larger and more subtle range of requirements. The process of expertise is the process of tackling problems at higher and higher levels—what we refer to here as 'progressive problem solving'. This process builds on normal learning, because it is through normal pattern learning and proceduralization that mental resources become freed to reinvest in these higher-level efforts. But by continually incorporating already-mastered skills into more advanced procedures, the expert avoids the rut that normal learning can produce. The process is greatly aided by expert subcultures, where individual advances have a cumulative effect, progressively changing the conditions that members of the subculture adapt to. There remains, however, a heroic element to exceptional expertise, for it involves effort over and above what the surrounding society recognizes or rewards.

Chapter Five
Creative Expertise

In the first chapter we went to some lengths to defend the value of expertise against those who blame it for social ills. No such defense is needed for creativity, despite the fact that highly creative people produced the atom bomb, PCBs, cosmetic surgery, the junk bond market, and most of the other things that are routinely cited as examples of expertise run amok. Creativity remains one of the most revered of human characteristics. In some ways it is more like a virtue than an ability. But it is a virtue that one may believe in wholeheartedly and yet find oneself unable to practice successfully.

A New Way to Think About Creativity

We need a better way to think about creativity. Commonsense psychology does not do a good job, tending to mystify it as a 'gift'. But systematic psychology does not do much better. Psychoanalysts make it out to be a variety of neurosis. Behaviorists show us that by rewarding people for giving creative responses to test items you can get people to emit such responses at a higher rate. Cognitive psychologists treat it simply as problem solving. There is merit in all these views, but they do not combine into anything that feels like understanding creativity or knowing what to do about it. That has left the field open for a host of pop psychologists and quacks who present creativity as a matter of getting both sides of your brain working in concert or as a few tricks that can be learned in an afternoon spent at a creativity workshop.

Dissatisfied with what psychologists had to offer on the subject, Arthur Koestler, a literary intellectual, devoted ten years to his own investigations, culminating in a monumental book, *The Act of Creation*. Koestler was trying to explain how the mind is able to produce original ideas. It is now becoming increasingly apparent that Koestler and many others like him were barking up the wrong tree. The problem is not to explain originality. On close examination, practically everything we do from minute to minute is original. The problem is to explain how some people become expert at it, so that they can fairly regularly, almost on demand, produce work that stands out from that of their peers as not only good but original. Put more briefly, the problem is to explain creative expertise.

The popular view of creativity is a romantic one and is quite likely a survival from the Romantic Age. Creativity is equated with freedom of the imagination, which children possess by nature, but which schooling and the daily grind act to stifle. According to this view, the creative expert would be one who had managed to preserve some of this childish mental freedom despite the rigors of training, work, and the accumulation of habit. The process of becoming an expert is thus seen as a threat to creativity, one that only a fortunate few are able to overcome. It follows that to foster creativity, one needs to counteract the negative effects of specialist training. Although we call this view romantic, it is assumed by many people who would not otherwise qualify as romantics. American industries spend large sums of money every year subjecting engineers and other hapless specialists to creativity training based on the premise that something must be done to break these people free from the mindsets imposed on them by training and practice. One desperate electronics firm is reportedly putting its sophisticated engineers through a training program originally designed for backward school children. The implication is obvious: Experts are damaged goods, in need of repair.

The view that we shall propose, and which we believe is supported by the bulk of research, is almost the exact opposite of the romantic one. Everything that we have said about expertise applies equally to creative expertise. The process of expertise, the continual reinvestment of mental resources into the constitutive problems of one's field, is an inherently creative process. Compare experts to experienced nonexperts in terms of creative productivity and the experts will win hands down. It could hardly be otherwise. The experienced nonexperts have been devoting their efforts to reducing everything to routines. They are the ones clattering along in well-worn ruts, while the experts are out there breaking new ground in their efforts to address problems at increasingly complex levels.

If we are right, American industries are making a monumental mistake in their pursuit of creative innovation. They think they have a lot of noncreative experts who need to become creative, when their real problem is that they have a lot of experienced nonexperts who need to start acting like experts. Instead of sending them off to workshops to learn how to get in touch with their inner child or how to do clever tricks with matchsticks and beer glasses, they should be thinking about how to create a second-order environment in their firm that will support the process of expertise, replacing the first-order environment that encourages the reduction of everything to routine.

The fact remains, however, that there are some experts who are much more creative than others. Pinning down the nature of this difference has been the object of most of the research on adult creativity. One line of research has looked at personality traits that distinguish more creative from less creative people in various fields.[1] This research has tended to validate popular stereotypes: The more creative people are found to be more unconventional, flamboyant, willing to take risks. Efforts to identify creative mental abilities have been less successful. Numerous tests have been developed, but they do not correlate highly with one another. Lump them all together and you get a measure that is not much different from general intelligence. J. P. Guilford and his co-workers were able to tease out distinguishable ability factors that they identified as creative, but these have never proved very useful for distinguishing people who are creative in the real world. On quite a different track, Simonton has shown that a distinguishing characteristic of the most creative people in many different fields is the sheer volume of their productivity. This is as true of scientists as it is of painters and composers: The highly creative ones produce an enormous number of works compared to the average. Simonton's plausible explanation is that there is no reliable way to produce a creative result. It is always a chancy business, and so it takes a lot of attempts in order to get the occasional happy combination that results in a creative achievement.[2]

We are not concerned here with accounting for all the determinants of creative achievement, just as we have not been concerned with accounting for all the determinants of expert performance. There are surely personality traits, abilities, and motivational factors that contribute to creative performance, and some of these may be general across different fields. As before, we want to look at knowledge and process. Are there things that creative experts know that less creative ones do not? Is there something creative experts do that distinguishes them from less creative ones?

The question of process tends to get distorted when it is asked about creativity. Koestler was looking for a distinctive process that would explain how creative ideas are generated, and every creativity workshop leader is promoting some kind of process. But the process they are concerned with is what goes on in the actual production of a creative something. Pursuing the question of process at this level has proved remarkably unprofitable. In the next section we will try to show why. As we have been doing with expertise in general, we will address the question of process at the level of a career rather than at the level of the particular achievement: *Do creative experts do something different in their careers that separates them from less creative experts?*

The answer we shall offer is very simple, but the reason it is simple is that most of what distinguishes creative experts from the common herd is the same as what distinguishes all experts from the common herd—reinvestment in progressive problem solving. Progressive problem solving always involves some risk, some venture beyond what one already knows how to handle. What distinguishes creative experts is that they take bigger risks. Of course, they not only take big risks but they also succeed, some of the time, and through this experience they develop a kind of knowledge that increases their likelihood of success. This is what we will call knowledge of *promisingness*.

Let's be clear that we are not suggesting any mediocre dauber could become a Picasso simply by taking bigger risks and developing a knowledge of promisingness. We don't know what all is involved in being a Picasso, and neither does anyone else. All we are suggesting is that, as with expertise in general, there is something to be learned from looking at process and that by so doing we begin to get hold of ideas that may be helpful in fostering and supporting creative expertise. Picasso did take big risks and was extremely alert to promising directions. The same was true of Mozart, Einstein, and all the other darlings of creativity name-droppers. Researchers have long recognized risk-taking as an important aspect of creative work. The hard part has been to explain successful risk-taking. We believe that by building on an understanding of the process of expertise, it is possible to make headway on this problem. The process of expertise generates the knowledge that makes expert performance possible. *Creative experts are experts at taking successful risks in their domains.* It is through the same general process of expertise, we propose, that they generate the knowledge that makes this possible.

Creativity and Ordinary Thought

Almost everything that is wrong with how people generally think about creativity arises from a mistaken idea of what ordinary thought is like. The traditional view in Western culture, held by psychologists and lay people alike, is that ordinary thought processes are inferential. A implies B, B implies C, and so on. The inferences may not always be rigorous or correct, but it is assumed that some such step-by-step process describes how the brain plods through life. The ideas we call creative are good ideas that seemingly could not have been arrived at through inference. Creative thought is presented as a different kind of thinking, perhaps carried out by a different part of the brain, a kind of thinking that is 'lateral' rather than 'vertical', intuitive rather than logical, dealing with whole patterns rather than with a linear sequence of propositions. Therefore we conclude that creativity must arise through some mysterious process different from ordinary thinking.

Modern cognitive psychologists are rapidly abandoning the belief that the mind works by step-wise inferential processes. Much of our thinking can *after the fact* be justified by logical inference. In science that is pretty much a requirement. But it does not follow that the ideas were arrived at by such a process. Everyone agrees that the big breakthrough ideas of Newton, Darwin, Einstein, and their ilk were not arrived at by the same orderly processes that are used in explicating and defending those ideas. If they were, then there would no longer be any mystery to creativity. But why, then, is it assumed that our decision to stock up on canned pineapple when the local discount house is running a special on it results from an inferential process that corresponds to the logical justification that can be given for this decision (and that accordingly it reflects ordinary thinking and is not creative)? The difference seems to be only one of degree of plausibility. If you have seen a formal proof of the Pythagorean theorem, which goes on for 20 or more steps with nothing to suggest why each step is being taken, you know that it is utterly implausible that Pythagoras or anyone else would have hit upon the theorem by such a tendentious line of thought. You clearly have to know the theorem already in order to construct the proof. Therefore we assume some other process was involved. But on such mundane and simple intellectual achievements as saving money on groceries, the argument that justifies the conclusion is simple and straightforward enough that we can imagine it as describing how the conclusion was actually reached. You will even hear pet owners ascribing inferential reasoning to their pets, just because the animal has done something that can be justified by some simple logical argument which the proud owner believes to be within the intellectual capabilities of the brute.

Perhaps the best explanation for the persistence of this belief that the mind works through step-by-step inference is that there has not seemed to be any alternative. Give that belief up and then *all* thinking becomes as mysterious as creative thinking. Connectionist programs now provide us with observable evidence that nonmysterious alternatives exist. For less than the price of a Nintendo game, PC and Macintosh owners can now buy demonstration programs that make rationally defensible judgments without using any inferential processes.[3] They work by pattern learning and recognition. How seriously these should be taken as models of human cognition is not important in the present context. What is important is to recognize that once the traditional conception of ordinary thought is abandoned, there is no longer any need to conceive of creative thought as a different process.

Howard Margolis, in *Patterns, Thinking, and Cognition,*[4] gives one of the most elaborated and readable explanations of thinking as pattern recognition. This is how Margolis describes ordinary thinking:

> What appears to happen when we think is akin to tuning a radio. There is a rapid scanning, then a tuning in on some pattern. If the scanning takes a short enough time (for example, because we are already tuned to the right part of the dial), we may have no sense of this step at all; and if the scanning and

tuning together take a short enough time, the whole process seems immediate and processless. We just switch on the radio, and there we are. Open the mouth and (in routine situations) words flow out.[5]

According to the commonsense view, this sort of thing does not count as thinking at all. When people just open their mouths and let the words pour out, we call this speaking without thinking. But obviously something like thought is going on. The words make sense. Utterances frequently follow a logical order. Yet trying to account for casual speech by an inferential process would prove as difficult as accounting for recognized creative thought. It has the same properties of intuitiveness and nonderivability. And examined closely enough, at the level of word choice and intonation, ordinary speech shows continuous improvisation and originality. It is a far cry from piecing together prerecorded messages. All voluntary behavior is that way. People who design robots have come to appreciate this. If you design a robot that processes information in the step-by-step inferential way that commonsense and earlier cognitive theories suggest, it is too clumsy, inflexible, and dull-witted to find its way about and do things in a normal environment.[6]

Real creativity, though—the kind that society honors—isn't like tuning into a radio station that is already there. It is like creating a new station. Margolis devotes a substantial part of his book to how new patterns originate, using Copernicus and Darwin as case studies. His main argument is that there is an unbroken continuum ranging from tuning in to already familiar patterns to learning to recognize existing but unfamiliar ones and on to discovering new patterns. These are not different processes, just variations on the same process. New patterns are created through a sometimes lengthy process in which existing patterns that have some slight fit to the problem situation serve to suggest the kind of pattern that is needed and eventually the 'right' pattern clicks into place. It is much like the perception of puzzle pictures where the initially meaningless patches of dark and light gradually acquire meaning or else suddening click into a recognizable picture when a clue is given. Connectionist AI networks function in this very way, quickly and reliably recognizing familiar patterns but sometimes doing interesting and unpredictable things when presented with an atypical configuration.

This new view of thinking does not solve any problems about creativity. It merely eliminates an obstacle to solving them. As long as we believe that ordinary thought consists of step-by-step inference, we will keep looking for that special thing that happens when creative ideas occur. We will try to understand that flash of illumination, that sudden clicking into place of the jigsaw pieces that wouldn't fit, that idea that seems to come from nowhere. But if we recognize that these are just earthquake-sized versions of seismic events that are rumbling away all the time, we can turn our attention from the immediate phenomenon and try to understand what causes the differences in magnitude. If all our thinking is creative thinking, then what remains to be explained is how some people manage to be original in big ways while others are only original in little ways.

Creativity and Problem Solving

The link between creativity and expertise is problem solving. Progressive problem solving of daring kinds generates the knowledge that makes such daring ventures successful—or so our argument goes. But, it may be objected, there is surely more to creativity than solving problems. There are instances in the history of science where solving a problem was an important creative achievement. Pasteur was asked to solve the problem of bad molds in beer fermentation and through his ingenious experiments he demolished the doctrine of spontaneous generation. On a grander scale, Darwin was also solving a problem—the "mystery of mysteries", as he called it in his introduction to *The Origin of Species*. But what about Beethoven? Isn't it a gross simplification to represent composing a symphony as 'solving a problem'?

According to the expanded concept of problem solving that cognitive psychologists use, composing a symphony does count as problem solving. It is goal-directed activity in which a path to the goal is not known in advance and has to be discovered. But does that way of looking at it do justice to the creative aspect of composing a symphony? Problem solving sounds like what a hack composer might do in grinding out background music for a movie.

Let us work our way up to Beethoven by degrees. The simplest way that creativity may enter into problem solving is as a constraint. If you are arranging furniture in a room, there are constraints of comfort, convenience, traffic flow, and so on that may be imposed. The more constraints that are added, the more complex the problem becomes, as was discussed in the preceding chapter. An additional constraint that might be added is that the furniture arrangement must be creative. That constraint may make the problem more difficult—perhaps so difficult that you are driven to seek the services of an interior decorator who is expert enough to be able to handle that constraint along with the others. On the other hand, the creativity constraint may cause you to consider novel and unconventional arrangements that you would not have considered otherwise, and among these you may discover a furniture arrangement that is not only imaginative but that also meets the practical constraints better than the more conventional arrangements.

In furniture arrangement problems, creativity is an optional constraint. Usually it is only when creativity is optional that it is explicitly noted as a constraint—as in creative cookery or creative dance. In many graduate programs, students are not expected to do anything very original in their masters' theses. One may then hear an ambitious student say, 'I don't want to just do a minor variation on somebody else's study. I want to do something creative.'

Creativity is not optional in the arts. The painter, sketching out a painting, does not say, 'Oh, yes, I must remember to make it creative.' But the constraint is surely there. This becomes evident if a painting falls short of the artist's creative standard. The artist will attempt to modify the piece until it succeeds or, failing that, may destroy it or reclassify it as an exercise or an experiment.

In many other cases, however, creativity is not a constraint. These are cases in which the problem itself is difficult enough that any solution will be recognized as creative. For the Wright brothers, just getting a heavier-than-air machine to fly would constitute a creative achievement, no matter how they did it. Therefore they did not need to think about doing it creatively. Most scientific work is of this sort. Discoveries, theories, proofs and demonstrations that advance the field are assumed to require creative thinking, and so creativity is a superfluous constraint. Faced with the problem of extending a house foundation into an inaccessible back yard, an experienced builder will immediately recognize that no conventional solution will work. At that point, many builders will declare the problem unsolvable and will want to start tearing things down. The one who comes up with a solution will have accomplished something creative.

With tasks like these it seems all right to regard creativity as just problem solving, no different from other problem solving except for the difficulty and significance of the problems. That is what led Newell, Shaw, and Simon to conclude that "creativity appears simply to be a special class of problem solving characterized by novelty, unconventionality, persistence, and difficulty in problem formulation."[7] In such problems, creativity is not a *constraint* but an *entailment*.

In many fields the best way to achieve creative results is probably to forget about creativity altogether and focus on solving significant problems, which automatically entails creativity. That should be the advice to the graduate student who wants to 'do something creative' as a master's thesis. Similar advice might apply to industrialists worried about the creativity of their engineering and design staffs. But this advice is not easy to follow. It is often pointed out that *finding* the difficult and significant problem is itself a creative achievement, in many cases more so than solving the problem once it has been identified.[8] That is true, but unfortunately the point has often been used to reintroduce an element of obscurantism into discussions of creativity, the implication being that problem solving may be an understandable process but that problem finding involves that mysterious essence that marks the creative act.

Problem finding, as previously noted, is part of virtually all real-world problem solving. Seldom except in school do problems come to us ready-made. Real-world problems are what Newell and Simon call "ill-structured", which means that one does not know in advance or knows only vaguely what would constitute a solution. In the course of problem solving the goal itself takes shape. In many cases this means that the distinction between identifying a problem and solving it virtually disappears.

This is true of a very large class of problems that may be called *design* problems. Design problems predominate in the visual arts, architecture, musical composition, literature, planning of all kinds, and theory construction.[9] There are design problems even within the performing arts, as when an actor creates a role or a soloist creates an interpretation of a piece of music. In all these problems, what one is after does not become fully specified until the task is finished. The goal, we may say, is emergent—it emerges from the work itself.

This brings us to Beethoven. Keeping in mind the nature of design problems and their emergent goals, it is not such an absurd simplification to suggest that Beethoven began with the problem of composing a fifth symphony and then solved the problem, with his actual Fifth Symphony as the solution. In the process, Beethoven made many decisions large and small, and solved a great many problems. These problems were not treated in isolation, however. Each one had to be treated as a subproblem of the larger problem of composing the complete symphony. Every problem of chord progression had to be solved in such a way that it contributed to the development of the passage, the passage to the movement, the movement to the symphony as a whole. But how could this be done when the ultimate goal was vague? That is where the concept of *promisingness* comes in, which we will explore in later sections.

After the fact, a musicologist can study Beethoven's symphony and construct a plausible account of all the problems that had to be solved in its composition and can show how the resolution of each problem was constrained by the character of the whole. With the aid of thinking-aloud protocols from Beethoven, this analysis could be more accurate and complete. But before the fact, no one could have done such a problem analysis, not even Beethoven. The point is, however, that solving all those problems and subproblems fully accounts for composing the Fifth Symphony. We do not need to add some other kind of activity on Beethoven's part that amounts to 'being creative'.

Knowledge of Promisingness as the Guide to Creative Effort

Design problems, such as composing a symphony or inventing new electronic circuitry, cover a large part of creativity— perhaps all of the creative activity worth considering in connection with expertise. In all of them there is the overriding problem of how to get from the initially vague top-level goal to a succession of definite problems, the solving of which both satisfies and gives substance to the top-level goal. Being able to do that is the core of creative expertise in a domain.

The graduate student who wants to 'do something creative' ends up immobilized because she has no way of identifying sub-problems that will result in progress toward this vague goal. She may hit on a novel topic, but then she must narrow it down to a feasible project, and she has no basis for doing so. Or she may have a novel idea but no way of developing it into a creative study. Lacking any general direction or any general way of ensuring a creative result, she may resort to applying the creativity constraint at every step. She must have a novel topic and the theoretical ideas and the methodology must in all details be her own. This virtually guarantees failure. Students we have known who tried to do this ended up with a mishmash and 'creative' is one of the last words one would think of applying to it. We have also seen a thinking-aloud protocol from an amateur writer who tried to produce a creative story in this way. Every thought about setting, character, plot action, and even minor details was judged for creativity and used or abandoned on that basis. The result was a patchwork of oddities, more like a bad dream than a good story.

In trying to achieve a creative goal, one can work from the top down, trying to reduce the top-level goal to more specific problems that can be tackled, or one can work from the bottom up, starting with something specific and trying to build up from it to attainment of the creative goal. More likely, one will try to work both ways. That is what happens in solving any novel problem. It is the means-end analysis that we discussed in Chapter 2 in connection with missionary-and-cannibal problems. In creative design tasks, however, there is no assurance that the path leading down and the path leading up will ever meet. In very large part, it is this very uncertainty that identifies a problem as one calling for creativity.

Despite the occasional efforts to describe an ideal path for creative thinking,[11] we can be fairly confident that expertise does not lie in some particular way of going about the solving of problems. Katchadourian used biographical data to identify the starting points for artistic activity used by major artists. He identified six different ones. Starting by building particular idea on particular idea—the bottom-up approach—was one such way. He also found instances of top-down design, starting with an abstract purpose that was gradually made more concrete. Other starting points included starting with an existing work which was then modified, starting with a set of given elements, and starting with the requirements of some established genre.[12] There seem to be other possibilities as well. For instance, Agatha Christie reported that most of her novels started in her mind with a place that seemed like a good setting for a mystery, so that planning consisted principally of thinking of a crime to fit the setting. That would seem to be an intermediate starting point, being neither an initial creative idea nor a high-level purpose but rather an initial constraint that she somehow found helpful in generating creative ideas.

David Perkins[13] has taken a bold step toward making sense of the creative process in proposing that what it all comes down to is narrowing the space of possibilities by adding constraints.

To the creativity buffs who conduct workshops this must surely be a horrible idea, because their whole message is usually the removal of constraints. Where they are right is in regard to unfortunate constraints. Regardless of what path is followed in planning, one makes decisions that constrain the eventual result without adequate knowledge at the time as to whether the constraints are good ones. But constraints there must be. The painter's every brush stroke is a constraint on the form that the final painting may take. Even though the brush stroke can be eradicated, while it exists it places constraints on what the painter can *imagine* the painting to be. In the end (this is the emergent goals phenomenon again) the constraints become so elaborate that there is only one painting that could possibly satisfy them, and that is the painting that actually exists. On this view, then, creative expertise is purely a matter of selecting good constraints and avoiding ones that are not so good.

Our analysis so far would suggest, however, that only dumb luck could result in selecting good constraints over bad ones, since whether one is proceeding top-down or bottom-up, one is having to select constraints with inadequate information. No doubt there is an element of luck involved.[14] Creative people usually have their share of failures, and they probably do the same thing in failing that they do in succeeding; it just doesn't work all the time. But it is also obvious that people who pursue careers of high creative productivity must have some way of improving on dumb luck.

What we understand about expertise in general would suggest that if there is an explanation of creative expertise it should lie in *what creative experts know that noncreative experts do not know.*

In a word, creative experts can recognize *promisingness.* Let us go back to the naive graduate student trying to plan a creative thesis. Short of giving the student a research problem to solve, the most helpful thing the thesis supervisor can do is react to the student's ideas according to how promising they are. For promisingness is the very thing that the student, because of inexperience, is least able to judge. Whether an idea is reasonable, original, practical—these are questions that with sufficient industry a talented student can be expected to answer. But whether it is promising, whether it will lead anywhere—that is something that without a broader background of experience even the brightest students cannot be expected to judge adequately. Promisingness judgments apply at all levels of the top-to-bottom continuum. Is the topic itself promising, or the research tradition in which it is embedded? Or is a particular small twist on a familiar type of experiment promising? These, and many questions in between, require a kind of informal knowledge that is unlikely to be found except in people who are themselves experts of some creative accomplishment in their fields.

It would be easy to turn the evaluation of promisingness into something just as mysterious as creativity itself, and so gain nothing. For a start at seeing how promisingness might actually work, let us consider how a really expert creative writer handles the initial stages of planning. Dostoyevsky, in his notebooks, produced discourse much like that obtained from thinking-aloud protocols. At the opening of his *Notebooks for A Raw Youth*,[15] we find him rambling over a variety of ideas, developing each of them a bit but with no evident enthusiasm. It is bottom-up planning, with nothing being recognized as particularly promising. Then a magazine item gets him to thinking about "the predatory type" of person who, he remarks, the public does not understand. Immediately he enters a note to himself to keep the predatory type in mind for his forthcoming novel.

Subsequent notes offer clues as to why this idea struck him as promising:

> This will be already a genuine heroic type, above the public and its everyday life, and for this very reason will please it without fail. . . . Passion and immense *breadth of character*. The meanest coarseness along with the most refined generosity. And meanwhile, *the very strength* of this character *lies in the fact* that he can easily support this infinite breadth, so much so that, finally, he is looking in vain for a burden heavy enough for him. Both charming and repulsive. . . .

N.B. THINK ABOUT THIS TYPE.

At least three varieties of promisingness can be inferred from Dostoyevsky's remarks:

1. Direct match to goal. He sees the envisioned character as having audience appeal, one of the implicit goals of his composing effort.

2. Match to capabilities. One senses a bolder tone as soon as Dostoyevsky starts discussing the predatory type, as if he immediately feels, "Aha! This is the kind of character I know how to write about." Indeed, in just the few lines quoted above one can see a Dostoyevskian type of character starting to emerge.

3. Pointers to further possibilities. The very description of the character contains pointers to story themes that could be developed—the juxtaposition of coarse and generous acts, the search for a burden heavy enough for him. Assuming that these ideas also have some promise, there is a *propagation of promisingness* along lines that can be at least vaguely foreseen.[16]

Notice that each of these recognitions of promisingness depends on prior knowledge and experience. Recognizing direct matches to goals depends on a background of means-end knowledge in the domain. Recognizing matches to capabilities requires quite refined knowledge of one's relevant capabilities, which could only come from extensive experience. And recognizing pointers to other promising ideas requires richly interconnected knowledge about the promisingness of different courses of action, models, etc.

Generalizing from this one example, we may attribute to Dostoyevsky a *promising character* schema that contains knowledge about a. what makes a character appealing to readers, b. what makes a character easy and rewarding to write about (for Dostoyevsky himself), and c. what constitute pointers to other promisingness schemas such as *promising plot* and *promising theme* schemas. Agatha Christie, to judge from her own report, relied on a *promising setting* schema, which probably had much the same properties as the *promising character* schema attributed to Dostoyevsky. By extension, creative scientists would be expected to have a *promising question* schema, or perhaps a system of such schemas, which contain knowledge useful for matching questions to high-level goals, for evaluating questions according to the scientist's own abilities and passions, and for recognizing pointers leading from one promising question to another, or from the question to promising methods, promising data sources, and the like.

We can often recognize in our colleagues some who have a particular talent for identifying promising directions, and perhaps others who are notably unfortunate in this regard. The talent often appears unaccountable, a certain kind of blessedness that one could not hope to achieve by study. Let us try, however, to domesticate the idea somewhat.

A first thing to note is that people who do creative work are very much concerned about promisingness, and so if there is relevant knowledge and skill that can be acquired, they are likely to acquire it. Creative achievements, unlike the trivial tasks of creativity tests, generally take extended effort, and no one likes to waste it on a project that proves, in retrospect, to have been ill-conceived. A second thing to note, however, is that judgments of promisingness remain chancy even for highly creative people. Simonton's exhaustive studies of the careers of geniuses in various fields indicate that they produce prodigious amounts of both successful and unsuccessful work.[17]

Judgments of promisingness are essentially predictions, hence their inherent chanciness. Although they are fallible, it is better to make them than not to make them. The amateur writer we mentioned earlier based decisions on immediate assessments of the 'creativity' of individual ideas. A more expert writer, as exemplified by Dostoyevsky, would have judged individual ideas instead on the basis of their promisingness as contributors to an emerging design. Both kinds of judgments undoubtedly have some validity. For a novice writer, immediate assessment of creativity might have greater validity, because the writer's judgments of promisingness would be so poor. But in the long run, promisingness is undeniably the better criterion, because one can bring increasing amounts of experience to bear on improving its validity.

Like other sorts of informal predictions, promisingness judgments are based on variable knowledge, unsystematically combined. Connectionist networks probably provide better models of such judgments than do systems of rules. And so there is probably no point in trying to formulate a theory of promisingness. As people try repeatedly to judge whether something will lead to a desired outcome, and as they experience the results, they acquire a repertoire of indicators that gradually increase their ability to predict. The indicators may be so subtle and they may combine in such an unsystematic way that the only thing that comes to consciousness is an impression or 'gut feeling'. A promisingness *schema,* in this case, is nothing more than a collection of indicators that has begun to coalesce into a pattern, so that when one indicator is activated the person becomes alerted to watch for the others. Even though it may be difficult to pin down what the coalition of indicators is, the feeling associated with it can be intense. A creative person who has just caught the scent of a promising idea acts in many ways like a bird dog that has just caught the scent of a pheasant. Frozen in motion, ears pricked up, nose turned toward the wind. . . .

Sometimes knowledge of promisingness can be consolidated into rules. The rules are more likely to identify unpromisingness, but that is important. A rule we find worth passing on to students is that all research questions which begin 'What is the relative contribution . . .' are unpromising. No doubt there are exceptions to the rule, but the role of promisingness knowledge is not to achieve certainty, only to improve on chance. The role of promisingness is most obvious in the case of lengthy design projects, like writing a novel, planning a building, or developing a theory, but it is also involved in the kinds of problems requiring split-second decisions—like the quarterback's decision of what to do with the football or the jazz musician's choice of a musical line to pursue during an improvisational episode. Quarterbacks and jazz players who develop skill in judging promisingness earn the label *creative* just as deservedly as the person whose promisingness judgments apply over weeks or years.

Judgments of promisingness play a part in ordinary cognition as well, although it only becomes evident when they are missing. In reading comprehension, it has been found that unskilled readers tend to judge the importance of each statement on its individual merits as they encounter it, much as the bottom-up story-teller judges the creativeness of ideas. The resulting 'copy-delete' strategy works reasonably well for clear and easy passages, but not for ones in which higher-level ideas have to be inferred. The more skillful reader builds up a more structured mental representation of the text and in the process also deletes some propositions as unimportant—but the judgments take into account the predicted contribution of propositions to overall meaning of the text, which is not yet fully developed. Hence propositions are retained or deleted on the basis of promisingness.[18] Promisingness is also relevant to the grasping of new concepts and ideas. As we will argue in the next chapter, expertise in learning involves being able to make good predictions about what will eventually prove meaningful, given that at the time one does not understand things well enough to make direct judgments of significance.

In short, we use promisingness knowledge all the time, but the extent to which we use it depends on the extent to which we are trying to achieve something beyond our current knowledge. Hence its close connection to the process of expertise, which is a process for overcoming the limits of competence. This brings us back to considering creativity as a form of expertise.

Creative versus Noncreative Expertise

If creativity is found in ordinary cognition and if judgments of promisingness are important in the process of expertise across the board, then what distinguishes creative expertise from any other kind of expertise? The short answer is that the difference between creative expertise and, if you will, noncreative expertise is a matter of degree. All that our inquiry has enabled us to do is to be clearer about what it is a degree of.

The process of expertise is inherently venturesome. In continually redefining problems at higher and usually more complex levels, experts face the risk of setting themselves tasks that are too difficult to perform. This is not an imaginary risk. Usually it doesn't lead to catastrophe, because the expert can quietly back off to a simpler task. But its reality is demonstrated in those cases where the field itself is progressing to such levels that people who back off to more manageable levels of complexity lose contact with it. This seems to have been true in the field of artificial intelligence, where people of considerable talent and the right intentions have found that their rate of progressive problem solving was not sufficient to keep them in the march. Crudely put, they discovered that problems that were simple enough for them to solve were not problems that the field considered worth solving. The cause is not necessarily a lack of talent; it could be a dispersal of effort over a wider range of goals—in principle a good thing, but with the result that one falls behind more single-minded people, which in a rapidly progressing field may mean that one's wider-ranging efforts are merely old hat. Another way that the inherent riskiness of the process of expertise shows itself is in the effects of aging. In rapidly progressing sciences it is commonplace for aging scientists to withdraw from active research and to become administrators (there are outstanding exceptions, of course).[19] These are fields in which the historical record shows that creative contributions are mostly made by people under the age of 40. It is not that scientists over 40 have lost their wits or that they have ceased to pursue a process of expertise. Rather, it is that the field is progressing so rapidly that, in order to make a recognizably creative contribution, the elder scientist would have to attack a problem that would most likely prove too difficult to solve, because of the combined encumbrances of old habits, dying neurons, and a decreased ability to work late hours.

Creative experts, according to this view, are simply people who take greater risks than other experts—and succeed. This sounds too pat, and it does demand some qualifications, but on the whole we think it covers known cases surprisingly well. One part of the proposition is easy to accept: The great creative leaps in thought have been bold ones that involved risks of failure, disapprobation, and the like.[20] The obvious objection to our formula, however, runs along this line: It isn't true that nineteenth-century biologists all thought of trying to give a mechanistic explanation of the origin of species and only Darwin and a couple of others were brave enough to try. The idea never occurred to most of them, and that is where the issue of creativity lies. (Besides which, Darwin was rather a chicken about it, if one accepts Howard Gruber's biographical analysis.[21])

Saying that the difference between creative and noncreative expertise is in the extent of risk is equivalent, from the standpoint of process, to saying that the difference is in how far one ventures beyond what can be easily handled by existing competence. Trying to accomplish things that really stretch one's competence means striving to do kinds of things that are often counted as creative achievements.

This is true of everything from mountain climbing to theory building. If you are attempting a harder climb than you have accomplished before, you will encounter problems that your procedural skills have not fully equipped you to handle. You will thus be involved in progressive problem solving, the essence of the process of expertise. But only if the climb is a great deal harder than previous ones will the project be considered to demand creativity. You will have to create a plan, a design, that will achieve the objective with the resources you have available. You will be faced with serious judgments of *promisingness*: Not knowing with certainty what the alternative courses of events will be, you are literally faced with alternative paths that can only be chosen on the basis of chancy judgments about how promising they seem. Like Dostoyevsky planning a novel, you will have to assess promisingness on several bases: promisingness with respect to the goal, promisingness with respect to your own abilities, and promisingness with respect to other aspects of the task.

In theoretical work, any effort to take account of more facts or variables than your current theory can handle is an instance of progressive problem solving and thus an exercise of the process of expertise. How creative the effort is will again depend on how large a step beyond your existing knowledge is required. The larger the step, the less you will know about where you are heading and how to proceed and the more you will have to rely on judgments of promisingness.

This notion of creative expertise as a matter of step size most clearly fits revolutionary sorts of creative achievements— radical new theories, designs, and the like. But what about the steady creativity of the productive artist? Are we to say that each of Mozart's 41 symphonies represented a large step upward in complexity beyond its predecessor? No. But that is not the point. The step-size notion does not imply that Symphony number 28 must be a large advance over Symphony number 27. It implies that Symphony number 28 is a new design problem which, as it evolves, forces the composer into untrodden paths where risky judgments of promisingness must take the place of well-informed calculation. The resulting symphony may be less successful, less 'advanced' than its predecessor, but to the extent that it is a serious artistic effort and not an easy exercising of existing skills, it constitutes a large step outward from what could be accomplished with the composer's available stock of symphonic routines. It is the size of steps within the mind of the expert that we are talking about, not the size of steps as manifested in the resulting object.

How is Creativity Acquired?

Two ideas, if combined, provide a hypothesis about how creative expertise is acquired. One is the idea that the special knowledge involved in creative expertise is knowledge of promisingness. The other is the idea that the process of creative expertise is distinguished from that of noncreative expertise by step size—by how far successive steps in progressive problem solving venture beyond what the person already has the knowledge to accomplish. Combined, they suggest that by taking larger, riskier steps, one is forced to make greater use of judgments of promisingness. From the resulting successes and failures, one acquires a greater fund of informal knowledge with which to improve judgments of promisingness. This makes it possible to take still larger steps with confidence, resulting in more extensive knowledge, and so on in an ascending spiral of creative expertise.

If your process of expertise consists of many small ventures beyond existing competence, you should steadily increase your competence—this may, in fact, be the best way to build solid expertise in most fields—but you will not have had to worry very much about promisingness. It is as if you were camped in a desolate region and were venturing forth without a compass to explore the terrain. If each trip extends but a short distance beyond where you have gone before, you can rely on an accumulating knowledge of landmarks to find your way. Only if you make larger ventures, beyond the range of already known landmarks, will you have need to learn how to read the stars, the moss on tree trunks, and the like, in order to find your directions. Otherwise, you may master the vicinity very well, qualifying as an expert in its geography, but you will not have acquired the abilities of an explorer. Only by venturing more, by employing a larger step size, would you acquire those skills.

This analogy leads to a commonsense conclusion about creative expertise. It is acquired, like all expertise, through progressive problem solving. What distinguishes it is problem solving directed toward creative goals. The essential characteristic of such goals is that they are sufficiently beyond the reach of well-learned procedures that one has to rely heavily on judgments of promisingness in order to proceed.

Why don't all experts become creative? To a degree they do, to the extent that they keep solving problems at higher levels. But it should not be surprising if most experts prefer a cautious approach to problems that does not confront them with continual gambles on promisingness. Without sufficient talent and perhaps a considerable amount of spontaneous creativity and luck thrown in, one's initial creative ventures may all fail. This is not only discouraging, it also prevents acquiring the vital informal knowledge of promisingness. As a result, future creative ventures are also likely to fail. A reasonable person will soon learn to pursue less creative goals.

Automaticity and creativity. There is no reason to doubt that automaticity operates in creative activities just as it does in others. The reason it doesn't show, the reason creative achievement doesn't become easy, is that the automated parts keep being assimilated into new creative efforts that venture beyond what the expert is already able to do. But it must surely be the case that creative experts in all fields accumulate a repertoire of well-practiced routines that produce results the world counts as creative. If they rely entirely on such routines, of course, they are liable to be accused of imitating themselves, of having lost the creative spark.

Internal versus external referents of creativity. It may sound anomalous to suggest that experts can produce creative results by rote.[22] The anomaly is trivial, however; it merely reflects the discrepancy between internal and external referents in discussions of creativity. What is regarded externally as a creative achievement may usually depend on an internal creative process, but not always. It could occasionally arise by chance or, as we suggest, by a routine procedure that generates sufficient novelty. There is much of sociological interest in the external side of creativity—what society chooses to count as a creative achievement—but none of it is very relevant to understanding creative expertise. As far as expertise is concerned, creative people are not doing anything different when they are following a promising line of effort that will produce results honored by society from what they are doing when following an unpromising line that will produce results which society will ignore or ridicule. (And, of course, society's judgment may be reversed by a later generation.) All that we have been trying to understand is how people get better at choosing promising directions—both on the grand scale of major life choices and on the small scale of deciding where to make the next brush stroke or which parameter to fiddle with in trying to make a computer simulation work.

Fostering Creativity

So long as creativity continues to be thought of as separate from expertise, there will be a market for various brands of creativity-enhancing snake oil. Some of it may actually do good. Some people may profit from being told that when they are stuck they should try thinking about things a different way. Others may benefit from encouragement not to be so quick in criticizing their own ideas. And to the extent that creativity training promotes a more light-hearted approach to problems it is probably good for high achievers of all sorts. Another worthwhile characteristic of many creativity programs is that they urge teachers and employers to provide a secure environment in which people are not afraid to be different and to take risks. As we have argued, taking risks is essential to produce the knowledge of promisingness that makes creative expertise possible—but they do not have to be risks that put your diploma or your job at stake. All of these good points of creativity training having been acknowledged, it remains that a rather different perspective on fostering creativity is afforded by considering it as an aspect of expertise.

There is little point in trying to promote creativity outside of expertise. This does not mean you cannot do anything creative until you have achieved expert competence in a field. On the contrary, people who become creative experts probably strive to achieve creative goals throughout their development as experts. That is how they build up the knowledge of promisingness that gradually increases their ability to succeed in risky creative ventures.

Knowledge for judging promisingness, we have argued, is the kind of knowledge that distinguishes creative from non-creative experts. Such knowledge cannot be acquired in the abstract. Creativity seminars will never give it to you. You can only gain it through experience of solving problems within a particular domain, so that you come to recognize the signs of promising and unpromising paths within that domain. The process of developing creativity is simply the process of expertise directed toward creative goals. Conditions that are good for developing expertise will be conducive to developing creative expertise as well—opportunities for learning and experimentation, suitable levels of challenge, a secure and supportive environment that encourages the progressive tackling of higher-level problems, and a good match between talents and demands. Even at best, however, only a minority of the people who develop expertise may develop creative expertise. That may simply reflect its greater riskiness, the likelihood that some intrinsic or accidental factor may doom creative efforts to failure.

The requirements for developing creative expertise are deceptively simple. They reduce to two: You must pursue creative goals and you must occasionally succeed. The latter requirement is not trivial. An unbroken series of failures will not provide you with the knowledge of promisingness required for eventual success. For that reason, coaches or mentors can play a vital role in the early stages of a creative career, because they can start you along promising paths, using knowledge acquired through their own creative efforts. Notice that mentors who have not achieved a measure of creative success themselves are in no position to offer such guidance, even though they may be valuable in other ways.

It is the steadfast pursuit of creative goals, however, that ultimately produces a creative expert. Is there any help outsiders can give, other than encouragement to try harder? A few suggestions can be made:

> 1. Conceptual understanding of creativity may help. Even among graduate students, who ought already to be some distance along the road, we find some who hold the most naive and unproductive notions about creativity. To them the essence of creativity is doing something different. If you suggest a good idea to them, they resent it,

because you have deprived them of the possibility of thinking of it themselves. They get caught in an oscillation between grandiose creative goals and low-level ideas that they can only evaluate according to a crude criterion of originality. Often their notions can be traced to pop psychological treatments of creativity, which confuse it with free-spiritedness. Understanding creativity as a part of expertise would seem to be essential for freeing them to pursue more productive efforts.

2.   Promisingness can be studied explicitly. Although the ability to judge promisingness depends on informal knowledge gained through experience, the construction of such knowledge ought to be aided by conscious attention to questions of promisingness. We are told that among graduate students in theoretical physics the issue of promisingness is an obsession. If they do their thesis in a line of research that is on its way up, they believe a bright future awaits them, whereas if they do it in a line of research that is headed toward a dead end or a decline (even though it may be very hot at the moment), they will graduate into obsolescence. Obviously this kind of concern can degenerate into contemptible trendiness. But we find, in our own somewhat slower-moving field of cognitive psychology, that many students give no thought to where lines of research are heading. Teachers in any field could do a service by bringing issues of promisingness out for discussion. What is the likelihood that a particular theory will eventually be able to account for such-and-such phenomena? What is there in this student's design that has the potential for further development? Which approach to solving this problem holds most promise?

3.   Teach design. As we noted, most creative work is design, broadly conceived. Schools of design are among the few kinds that actually incorporate the pursuit of creative goals into the development of expertise.[23] But design is involved in practically every field where creative

expertise can thrive. Good teaching of design is deeply enmeshed in the issue of promisingness. Designs typically emerge through a series of drafts or versions. Bad teaching focuses on the merits and shortcomings of the present version, whereas good design teaching focuses on what the present version might eventually *become*. Teachers of creative writing split dramatically on this point, with teachers who are creative writers themselves tending much more to focus on discovering elements of promise in a composition and helping the student develop those into something. This 'writing process approach', as it is now called, originally developed with aspiring adult writers, has turned out to work well even with young children.[24] Children get involved in a very natural way in trying to make their compositions evolve into something rather than simply trying to do their best in the present instant—although much of the judgment of promisingness comes from the teacher. Design-oriented teaching is to be contrasted with the sort of thing that typically goes on in the behavioral sciences in courses on research design. These are usually not courses in design at all, but courses which teach certain logical constraints on research design and conventional forms which meet those constraints. But there is no reason that research design could not be handled the same way that engineering design schools handle product design and good creative writing teachers handle the development of students' stories. That would be fostering creative expertise along lines in which promisingness plays a natural and integral part.

4. Promote cooperative creativity. The mythology of creativity, which sees it as a strange event taking place in the mind of an unusual person, has created a strong bias toward treating creativity as an individual affair. There is obviously historical warrant for this. Few creative achievements have been attributed to committees. But this may be partly a matter of grain size. Large-scale innovations like the Impressionist movement, the

Russian Revolution, and the rise of medical science have tremendous complexity, originality, and coherence, but it is impossible to attribute them to an individual or to the uncoordinated activity of a multitude of different individuals. Were it not for our individualistic prejudices we would probably count them as creative achievements as much as Shakespeare's plays or Freud's theory of the unconscious. Certainly, in each case, the principal actors were deliberately pursuing a creative goal—a shared goal, to which they variously contributed, an emergent goal that changed its shape (for better or worse) as a result of their contributions. Apparently there are some creative goals that can be shared and pursued jointly and others that cannot, but we do not know of any analyses that would allow us to distinguish them systematically. Cooperative pursuit of creative goals is commonplace in science and industry, and the fact that some individual usually emerges as the genius behind a major achievement should not detract from recognizing the value of cooperation. It can make up for individual gaps in talent, and it can also achieve important advantages through the pooling of knowledge about promisingness. Assemble a team to pursue a creative goal and the first thing you will hear is a great deal of discussion about promisingness; often, in fact, the group will dissolve because they cannot agree on that matter. We suspect there are many people who could participate in creative achievements but who do not do so because of a mistaken notion that the creativity has to come out of their own brain.

Summary

We began this chapter by noting two points that are difficult to reconcile. One is that nothing special can be identified that goes on in the mind during creative activity that does not go on in ordinary cognition. The other is the fact that there are people who stand out from their peers because they regularly produce creative results. In short, creativity appears to be both common and uncommon. In our discussion we have tried to honor both truths.

The first step in reconciling these truths is to bracket off the spontaneous, effortless creativity found often in children and in the kind of adults who get labeled 'originals'. This kind of creativity depends on being different in a fortunate way. It is, if you will, a common kind of uncommonness—a factor in creative careers, perhaps, but not fundamental.

The fundamental fact about people who maintain creative careers is that they are experts. Everything that is true of expertise in general is true of creative expertise. But what, then, distinguishes the creative from the noncreative expert? It is being expert at attaining creative goals, of course. The more pointed question to ask, therefore, is what is it about creative goals that makes them attainable only by the select few?

The difficulty with creative goals is the great qualitative gap between the goal and current situations. Ordinary means-end analysis does not work, because there is so little likelihood that the path generated by reasoning backward from the goal will ever join up with the path generated by reasoning forward. One has to proceed by adding constraints on the goal and constraints on solution paths, but one cannot know for certain whether these constraints are good ones. Creative experts are distinguished by their ability to identify promising constraints, which offer promising paths of action. They are able to do this by having built up a large body of informal and impressionistic knowledge about promisingness within their domains. It is not perfectly valid knowledge—creative experts often make unfortunate choices—but it is vastly superior to the more arbitrary or local criteria that nonexperts are obliged to use.

Knowledge of promisingness is built up in the normal way—by making decisions about promisingness and learning from one's successes and failures. This leads to the unexciting conclusion that people develop creative expertise through practice, just like any other kind of expertise. Indeed, we concluded that the *process* of creative expertise differs from the normal process of expertise only in degree. Progressive problem solving is its essence; what makes it creative is the progressive tackling of problems that lie far enough beyond what already-learned routines can handle that one is forced to make decisions on the basis of promisingness.

The main practical implication of this view is that there is not much value in trying to teach creativity outside the context of expertise. Conditions that are conducive to the process of expertise will be conducive to the development of creative expertise. If outsiders can do anything special to help in the development of creative expertise it is likely to be through helping novices choose promising directions and devote attention to learning to recognize promising directions themselves. That is already done to some extent in schools of design and in the teaching of creative writing, but it is often neglected in the sciences, even though the progress of science itself depends crucially on the ability of its practitioners to make keen judgments of promisingness.

Chapter Six
Expertlike Learners

People are always learning, whether they are experts or not. For some professionals learning undoubtedly becomes a matter of routine. They develop quick and relatively effortless ways to make additions to their repertoires of facts, techniques, cases, or whatever. But the ideas developed in the preceding chapters, about reinvestment of mental resources into progressive problem solving, would suggest that learning ought to have a more dynamic character in experts. In this chapter we examine what it might mean to learn like an expert. We will start with two studies carried out by students of ours, in which experts are compared with novices in how they approach novel and challenging tasks.

Expert and Nonexpert Approaches to Learning

One field in which learning plays an obvious and continuing role is music, where performers have to keep learning new pieces. Pam'la Ghent recorded a concert pianist, who agreed to 'think aloud' into the microphone during the first two hours of learning a new piece of music. She did the same with two advanced piano students in a university music department, giving them the same piece to learn as the expert was working on. One student went about the task in essentially the same way as the expert. The other student, although regarded by his teachers as highly talented, did not resemble the expert at all in his approach to mastering a new piece of music.[1]

Naomi Tal did a similar study with four medical students, except that instead of observing them on one task, she followed them through an entire year of medical training. On a variety of tasks, two of the students behaved in a consistently expert-like way and two did not. For one task, she gave the students a difficult diagnostic problem in neurology both before and after a period of intensive training in neurology. She also gave the problem to two recognized experts. Although both groups of students handled the problem more competently after training, the two expertlike students were closer to the experts even *before* their neurology training than the other students were *after* it.[2]

Before elaborating on these findings, we want to point out why they are important, even though based on few cases. The ten years or so of training and experience that typically go into the making of an expert pose a serious obstacle to research on the acquisition of expertise. The obvious kind of research to do is longitudinal and prospective: Follow a large group of medical students, for instance, through their early years of practice, collecting data that could later be analyzed for clues as to why some achieve high levels of expertise while others become experienced nonexperts. But no one funds research of that duration any more. And it would have to be intensive research, tracking people in the course of their work. Merely giving batteries of tests and correlating scores with later performance might yield findings useful for screening candidates, but it could not be expected to add much to our understanding or to offer leads for improving the education and nurturance of experts.

Lacking long-term research that follows the same people from novicehood to mature status, we are left having to look for plausible resemblances or parallels between what may be observed among students and what is known about experts. It is therefore a matter of considerable note that students can be found who already resemble experts in important respects. Case studies provide no basis for estimating how numerous such students are, but the fact that they exist at all should give us something to ponder.

It is tempting to infer that today's expertlike students are tomorrow's experts and that the others are tomorrow's experienced nonexperts. But we ought to resist that inference, plausible as it may be. There is no evidence for or against it. Expertlike students are of interest for what they can tell us about the nature of expertise and for giving us a different angle from which to look at it. According to the conventional view, there should not be such a thing as expertlike students. On this view, expertise is a final state reached by going through one or more prior states. There is no more reason to expect students to resemble experts than there is to expect caterpillars to resemble butterflies. So the existence of expertlike students gives us reason to question the conventional view. Perhaps there is a reasonable sense in which one can be an expert even in the early stages of a career, even though it may take years to reach the level of performance that the public will recognize as expertise.

How far down the age scale is it possible to find expertlike learners? That depends, of course, on what one is willing to credit. In this chapter we will start by examining in more detail the findings of Ghent and Tal in their case studies of piano and medical students. There it will be apparent that the expertlike students resemble the experts not so much in what they are able to accomplish but in what they are *trying* to do and in how they approach challenging problems. Having developed a notion of what constitutes an expertlike approach, we can then apply the notion at successively lower levels of schooling, with the result that even in the nursery school we can discover some children who are more expertlike than others.

Progressive Problem Solving versus the 'Best-Fit' Strategy

It was not a coincidence that in the studies by Ghent and Tal half the students resembled experts and half did not. The students were selected with that distinction in view. Faculty in the schools of music and medicine were asked to nominate students whom they considered already to be functioning in ways that resembled experts in those fields and also to nominate what they considered to be typical students. It is interesting that faculty members, asked to pick out students who resembled experts, did not find this a strange or foolish task. So it could be presumed that the students would differ in some way. The question was how, and whether the differences would make sense from the standpoint of psychological ideas about expertise.

The concert pianist's approach to an unfamiliar piece of music, in Ghent's study, typifies what we have been referring to as progressive problem solving. The music was a transcription for piano of Indonesian wayang music, which is normally played on drumlike instruments and serves as accompaniment to puppet shows. Like experts in other fields, the pianist devoted considerable time at the outset to characterizing the problem before him—in this case, to forming a conception of the effect he wanted to achieve in performing the piece and of what needed to be done to achieve it. He wanted to capture the character of the original music, and to do this he saw that he would, on one hand, need to suppress some of his Western ideas and techniques and, on the other, to work out a different way of striking the keys, so as to create a more strongly percussive effect. He also saw that there was a problem in making the music interesting, since, as background music, it was not originally intended to be the center of interest.

Within the limits of his knowledge, the expertlike student tried to do essentially the same thing. Ghent had provided the students with a tape recording of authentic wayang music and some descriptive text. The expertlike student made use of this in trying, like the expert, to form a conception of what the piano performance should sound like. He too recognized that the mindset instilled by training in Western classical music stood in the way and would have to be overcome. By contrast, the other student's approach to the music was to decide what musical style that he was already familiar with most closely resembled the wayang music. He concluded that French impressionism provided the best fit, and so proceeded to rehearse the piece in that style. As a follow-up, Ghent had a musicologist listen to tapes of the two students' performances. He credited the first student with trying to capture the character of wayang music. Of the second, he remarked that it sounded like French impressionism.

We see these two piano students as not just different but opposite in their approach. The second student's approach to an unfamiliar kind of music was to find the best fit between it and what he already knew, and to be satisfied with that. The expertlike student approached the new piece of music as a problem to be formulated at the highest possible level. This meant that, instead of fitting the task to existing competence, the expertlike student had to extend existing competence in order to fit the requirements of the task. In the present instance, it is arguable which is the better approach. (If the music was judged not to be worth much effort, for instance, then the best-fit strategy would make sense, conserving resources for more important purposes.) But as a general approach to music, the expertlike approach is clearly the route to excellence. The best-fit strategy deals with the immediate problem, perhaps quite effectively, but it does so in a way that minimizes new learning. The expertlike approach results in new technical skills and new musical concepts. In future encounters with unfamiliar music, these will make it possible to approach problems of performance at still higher levels, resulting in further gains in competence—and so on in the spiral of progressive problem solving.

The best-fit strategy takes on a special significance in the context of medical diagnosis. Most of the cases a physician sees are readily diagnosed by recognizing a match between the patient's symptoms and some classic pattern of indicators. One of the expert neurologists in Tal's study estimated that 95 percent of the cases he saw were diagnosable in this way. This is an example of effective use of a best-fit strategy—diagnosis on the basis of finding the best fit between the patient's symptoms and the symptom patterns of known diseases. Of course, the ability to use this strategy effectively depends on having accumulated a vast store of learned patterns, much like the thousands of chessboard patterns learned by a chess master. An inexperienced diagnostician could not be expected to have this repertoire of patterns to draw on, and so would have to depend on more laborious processes of analyzing evidence. That, in fact, is what interns are found to do.[3]

The diagnostic problems used in Tal's study were, however, among the five percent that defy best-fit diagnosis, even for an expert. With such cases, the experts go into a kind of *theory-building* mode. They try to construct an explanation that accounts for all the symptoms.[4] That, essentially, is what the expertlike students in Tal's study also did. They lacked the knowledge required to be highly successful in their theory-building efforts, but, then, the experts were not always successful either.

What did the nonexpertlike medical students do when faced with a difficult diagnostic problem? They tended to use a best-fit strategy—in other words, to treat the difficult problem as if it were an easy one that could be solved by matching symptoms with known patterns. Even though they knew relatively few patterns—just some of the classical ones presented in textbooks—they tended to choose whichever one of those few provided the best fit. One thing about the best-fit strategy is that it always yields an answer. Even if the symptoms do not fit any known pattern very well, one can always select a pattern that fits better than the others. As with learning a new piece of music, one might argue in particular instances that a best-fit strategy is the better strategy. In a medical emergency, for instance, acting on the basis of best fit might well be preferable to theorizing about puzzling symptoms. But as a general approach, it is severely limiting. It avoids the reasoning that draws connections between formal knowledge and actual cases, and thus fails to generate the body of intermediate, informal knowledge which, as we have argued in Chapter 3, is the basis for expert performance. Instead, it would seem to lead to developing stereotypes that simplify the disease world—making life easier for the doctor and more precarious for the patient.

The similarity of pattern in two such dissimilar fields as music and medicine is quite striking. To take a different slant on it, let us ignore for a moment the expertlike students and compare the experts with the typical students. The fact that the experts approached their respective problems at a higher level than the typical students comes as no surprise. What is ironic is that, in spite of having much more relevant knowledge to begin with, the experts seemed to *learn* more from the experience than the typical students. This is obvious with the concert pianist. He set himself an ambitious learning agenda, whereas the typical student reduced the task to learning to play the notes in an already familiar style. This is not so obvious with the medical experts and must be inferred by reading between the lines of their protocols. They seemed to relish the diagnostic puzzles (which were drawn from real cases), and it seems unlikely that they would so willingly have given time to them if they did not feel that they were getting something out of it. To the extent that they relied on a best-fit strategy, the typical students gained little from the experience except for a chance to rehearse what they already knew.

A reasonable speculation, therefore, is that the experts gained their superior knowledge (superior, we must assume, to many other practitioners of equal experience) through the kinds of progressive problem-solving efforts they exhibited in these studies. Those same efforts were exhibited by the expertlike students, and notably absent in the typical students.

A Question of Goals

The expertlike students in music and medicine resembled experts and differed from nonexpertlike students primarily in what they were trying to do. A substantial body of research indicates that goals are a major factor in differences among students. It doesn't require research, of course, to establish that there are students whose goals are quite at odds with those of the schools. Where research has been more useful is in sorting out differences among students who are all trying to do well in their studies. Students who are all trying hard to be good students may nevertheless be pursuing quite different goals— different notions of what it is to be a good student. Out of the research that has been done on student beliefs and student studying behavior, we can distill three different types of goals. Successful pursuit of any of the three could result in being judged a good student (according to grades, test scores, or teacher ratings); but of the three types, one is much more closely linked than the others to expertise as it is recognized in mature careers.[5]

In brief overview, the three kinds of goals are these:

1. Task accomplishment goals. In one way of looking at it, school is a job like any other. There are bosses (teachers) who assign you jobs to do, and if you are a dedicated student you try to do them well. The teacher supposedly has ulterior educational goals in mind for the various tasks and activities, but the students are not necessarily guided by or even aware of these educational goals. They may simply be engaged with the tasks or activities, with learning occurring more-or-less as a by-product.

2. Instructional goals. These are the things that the teacher or the instructional materials are manifestly aiming to teach. Sometimes explicit, sometimes inferable, often taken for granted, they are what a curriculum is supposed to be about. Students engaged in pursuing these instructional goals would be doing more than trying to accomplish the expected tasks; they would be aiming to achieve the knowledge and skills that the tasks were intended to cultivate.

3. Knowledge-building goals. These are goals held by the student, which may include instructional goals but which are not limited to them. They constitute a larger, more personal agenda of things one is trying to understand, of gaps one is trying to fill, of puzzlements one is trying to resolve, of connections one is trying to make between one chunk of knowledge and another.

These goals are not mutually exclusive, although they may at times compete with one another. Goal conflicts occur most often when there is a mismatch between the student's level of knowledge and the level presumed by the instructional goals. Both mathematically gifted and mathematically backward students typically have a bad time with the instructional regimen of school mathematics. The mathematically gifted are occupied with knowledge-building goals so far in advance of the curriculum that the instructional goals and tasks are irrelevant, while backward students, failing to grasp the conceptual content of the curriculum, devise unmathematical procedures for coping with the assigned problems.[6] In more comfortable circumstances, however, the three types of goals are nested one inside another: Pursuing one's private knowledge-building agenda will often entail pursuing established instructional goals, which in turn may entail accomplishing the assigned tasks.

These three levels of goals can be illustrated from a study by Evelyn Ng, in which adult volunteers studied BASIC programming for the computer. Learning was self-directed, with the learners thinking aloud as they selected goals, studied text material, worked on programming examples and problems, and evaluated their progress.[7] Here are some thinking-aloud statements that reflect goals at each of three levels:

1. Statements oriented toward task-completion goals.

—Yes, I'm just copying the example. . . . So, that's enough of example one. We'll go on to example two, where I'm going to use the *PRINT* to do a computation, and to do that I just—according to this, I don't use brackets.

—I'll give myself a *4,* because I figured out a lot, but I didn't figure it all out.

2. Statements oriented toward instructional goals.

—I'm just going to combine together the ideas of the two examples, and do a computation which follows logically from both the examples. So, if I say *PRINT N1 times N2,* it should automatically give me the multiplication of those two—I think. I'll find out.

—I'll give myself 5, because I tried out the *GOTO* and I used it on my own to expand—amplify—an example, and it worked as I thought it would work, *so I feel I mastered that concept.* It was quite easy to master, so . . . it was very straightforward.

3. Statements oriented toward knowledge-building goals.

—I think I get the idea without trying to find an example . . . but I will put . . . You see, what's interesting to me is you're programming, but you're also using values. . . . Because I'm thinking that for a program you'd want to have it open. I'm thinking that programming in this instance means having the computer do certain arithmetic calculations where the data isn't actually known yet. . . . Yes, I would like to have a program which accepts numbers unknown to me right now and then does a certain calculation.

—I understand what programming is about and what it is for, I feel, at a very superficial level. But I'm not sure how to access any more information, beyond talking to you [the experimenter]. I want to just think about what other questions I have.

The students in this study presumably all wanted to learn about BASIC programming, and all of them would seem to have been trying to do well. But what they were trying to do well differed, at least in emphasis. Those whose emphasis was on task-completion were trying to do well on the exercises and problems presented in the text material. They studied the text in order to learn how to do these tasks, and they evaluated themselves according to how successful they were on the tasks and to what extent they were able to solve the problems without help. The difference that enters with an orientation toward instructional goals is that the student is now focusing on the concepts that the tasks are meant to teach rather than on the tasks themselves. And so we find students at this level evaluating themselves according to how well they feel they have grasped those concepts. With knowledge-building goals, however, the focus shifts from what the materials are trying to teach to what the student is trying to learn. In the examples given, we see in one case a student trying to work out how a certain capability of computers (the capability of doing pre-determined computations on new data) can be realized with the program statements that have been provided. In the other case the student is making an overall assessment of the state of her knowledge and is expressing uncertainty about how to advance it beyond its superficial level.

Notice that we have been inferring learners' goals from the kinds of things they say in the course of working on lessons. Seldom are learning goals stated directly. In Ng's study one of the things participants had to do was select goals from a fixed set. Those who were rated high in knowledge-building or instructional goals also tended to choose more learning goals and fewer task goals when forced to make an overt choice. This adds a modicum of plausibility to the classification of learners according to goals, but it does not imply that somewhere in their minds students carry around explicit statements of the form, 'My goal is such-and-such'.

Task goals and instructional goals may be quite explicit. Young students, firmly in the grip of task goals, can often tell investigators precisely what job they are trying to finish. Knowledge-building, on the other hand, tends to be carried out according to vaguer goals of the kind that may be called *emergent*.[8] You start out often with a general intent to under-stand or learn more about something, and as you pick up knowledge it becomes clearer what it is you are trying to understand and what kind of knowledge it is you are construct-ing. The knowledge-building goals may never be very explicitly formulated in your mind, but if you look back you will see that what you were doing made sense in relation to the knowledge you eventually ended up with. You persisted and engaged in various sorts of strategic moves until you managed to achieve the desired state of learning or until you put the enterprise on hold, to be taken up when a further opportunity presented itself. That is really all it means to have a knowledge-building goal. Whether people's goals are explicit or not, the fact remains that behavior in learning situations always shows evidence of being directed toward goals of some kind, but only in a minority of cases can those be identified as knowledge-building goals.

Goal Orientations and Expertise

Although there is an obvious pecking order among the three kinds of goals, it would be a mistake to equate task-completion goals with poor students, instructional goals with mediocre students, and knowledge-building goals with good students. We shouldn't turn our noses up at task-completion goals. Most of what we learn in everyday life is learned through pursuit of them. We pursue tasks such as making a sale, cultivating the asparagus, or reading the newspaper, and in the process we learn things—but not by pursuing learning as a goal in its own right. In school it is possible to develop high levels of skill, to do well, and to keep moving to higher and higher levels of learning through concentrating on any of the three types of goals.

Goals do make a difference, however. In Ng's study, the students who ended up with the best knowledge of BASIC programming were not the ones who started out with the most computer experience but the ones who pursued the highest level goals during the course. They were the kind who were not limited to the progression of tasks and instructional goals built into the program but who were directing efforts toward prob-lems of understanding that they formulated for themselves as they went along. This doesn't mean they ignored what the course was trying to get them to do. They were beginners, after all, and weren't in a position to decide independently what it was they needed to know. But at the same time they were capable of skipping over a task if they thought they had already mastered what it could teach and of being dissatisfied with their knowledge even though it was sufficient to handle the assigned tasks.

Let us consider how these different goal orientations fit within the conception of expertise as progressive problem solving. Knowledge-building goals are inherently progressive. Advances in knowledge permit one to formulate still higher goals, to aim at deeper understanding, to pursue more complex questions, and so on. Thus, in the last example given above, we see a student in effect saying that she has pretty much understood what the program has to teach, but that she must now consider what further questions she can pursue, so as to take advantage of the experimenter's knowledge and thereby move beyond her own superficial level of understanding. Such an approach to learning has the progressive character that distinguishes the process of expertise. Neither task-completion nor instructional goal orientations, on the other hand, are progressive. Once one such goal is achieved, the student has nowhere to go unless guided by the curriculum. Otherwise, the expected result is diminishing returns from experience and a tapering off of learning, just as we observe with nonexpert development in the out-of-school world.

Are There All-Round Expert Learners?

Margaret Ogilvie has analyzed the behavior of the same elementary school students as they were engaged in learning a motor skill (juggling), an academic subject (human biology), and a computerized pattern-detection game. Of the measures she took on these students, one was a measure of the extent to which they regarded learning as problem solving versus regarding it as a routine. She also interviewed the students periodically during their weeks of learning, and from these she

derived measures of motivation for learning the several subjects and of how deep the planning was that went into their
work. Then she correlated all of these with each other and with
measures of performance in the three areas. All of the measures correlated substantially with one another, but there was
an especially strong consistency in the extent to which students
applied 'deep planning' to learning. Those who were deep
planners in juggling were deep planners in biology and the
computer game as well.[9] Furthermore, the deeper the planning, the better the performance in all areas.

Is Expertise in Learning Just Intelligence?

Clearly, in Ogilvie's study, some students were more expert
learners regardless of whether they were learning a motor skill,
an academic subject, or an intellectual game. A commonsense
explanation for this consistency would be that the more expertlike students were simply brighter. The same might be said of
the more expertlike students in any of the other research we
have described. There is a complex issue here, which we can
only touch lightly upon. What it comes down to is this: You
cannot put intelligence on one side of the balance and expertlike learning processes and knowledge on the other and ask
which weighs more in determining performance. They are too
interwoven for such a separation to be possible.

What we call intelligence is not some simple power rating,
such as one might find on an electric motor. It is an overall
estimate of mental proficiency, which undoubtedly is affected
by organic factors, hereditary and acquired, but also to a great
extent it reflects what one has learned—especially what one
has learned in the way of skills and strategies that apply to a
broad range of unfamiliar tasks. And so the attributes of
expertlike learners are an important part of their intelligence,
which cannot be separated off and compared to it.

There are statistical techniques for teasing apart the effects
of complex variables, but when these are applied to data like
Ogilvie's, they tend to lead us in a circle. Ogilvie did not have
IQ scores for the students in her study (IQ testing is outlawed
in many schools these days, except for special students). Total

scores on a general achievement test can serve fairly well as a stand-in, however, and those were available. A statistical technique called 'step-wise regression' can be used to test whether one variable has an effect over and above the effects of other, related variables. In this case, we used scores on general achievement and motivation to predict learning. Then we added in the 'deep planning' scores to see if they significantly improved the prediction. They did so in the case of juggling and the computer game, but they did not improve the prediction of learning in the biology sequence. This perhaps seems strange, in that one might expect expertise in learning to have its strongest effect in academic areas. Our explanation is that what expertise contributes to learning in academic subjects is already reflected in the general achievement scores (which correlated highly with learning in the academic subject but not in the other two areas), and so adding in scores on deep planning does not add much relevant information in that case. In other words, in academic areas, once you have measured academic achievement you have already measured expertise in learning, and it does not help much to measure it again. The same would probably be true, to a lesser extent, with measures of intelligence.

Asking to what extent expertise in learning depends on intelligence or on motivation or on background knowledge amounts to expressing a perfectly reasonable concern in the form of an unanswerable question. A more profitable question, which gets at more or less the same concern, is to what extent expertise in learning can itself be learned. We will take up that question toward the end of this chapter. But before that question can be pursued, it is necessary to probe more deeply into what expertise in learning consists of.

The Role of Knowledge-Building Schemas

A persistent fact of life for beginners, and especially for students in school, is that much of the time they are required to learn things in areas where their prior knowledge is scanty, providing no coherent structure to relate new information to. And it is often the case that knowledge has to be built up over a long period of time, sometimes years, before it can start to be functional in solving problems—even problems within the knowledge domain itself. (Historical knowledge is a good case in point; until you have a considerable amount of it, what you do know is of little help in making sense of new historical information or in solving problems of historical knowledge, such as figuring out causes or making comparisons between one historical circumstance and another.)

The axiom that you need knowledge in order to acquire knowledge has led some thinkers to doubt whether it is even possible to learn something more complex than what you already know.[10] A more commonsense view is that advances in the complexity of skill and understanding do surely occur but that they are inherently problematic. Prior knowledge is necessarily inadequate as a basis for advances in complexity. Although a solid mastery of whole numbers, for instance, may be valuable for understanding fractions, you can't derive an understanding of rational numbers from it. Some kind of intellectual 'bootstrapping' is needed.[11]

If there is such a thing as generalized expertise in learning, it ought to show up in the way people deal with this pervasive problem of how to acquire new knowledge in the absence of sufficient prior knowledge. In the case studies of students in music and medicine, we saw examples of expert and nonexpert approaches to learning—a progressive problem-solving approach contrasted with a best-fit approach. In this section we examine these approaches more closely as alternative ways of acquiring new knowledge when prior knowledge is deficient.

The 'Best-Fit' Approach to New Knowledge: Direct Assimilation

If it always takes a great deal of prior knowledge in order to grasp new information, then children ought to live in a state of constant bewilderment. But of course they do no such thing. School children are seldom at a loss for an interpretation of what they encounter. They find some knowledge to relate it to, some schema that they incorporate the new information into. Thus the problem, from a teacher's point of view, is not that students are sitting mystified by what they have heard or read, but rather that they have quickly settled on some interpretation that is likely to stand in the way of further learning.

We will call this immediate best-fit matching of new information to old knowledge *direct assimilation.* We all do it constantly and would be helpless making it through an ordinary day if we did not. Direct assimilation works because most of the time new information does fit nicely within our existing knowledge. The differences between expert and inexpert learners show up when information comes along that does not fit. Here the inexpert approach is to find the best fit and go with it, even if the fit is not very good. That is what the music student did who *directly assimilated* an exotic piece of Oriental music to whatever familiar style of music he judged to provide the best fit. As we noted, the strategy always works after a fashion, but it minimizes learning.

The Expert Approach to New Knowledge: Knowledge-Building Schemas

If you were to undertake the study of some field almost wholly foreign to you—let's say metallurgy, just to have an example—you would nevertheless have a significant advantage over the typical ten-year-old. Through experience in tackling other disciplines, you would know some important things about disciplines in general. For instance:

• There is probably more to be learned than you can imagine at the outset.

• You may often be unable to tell what is important from what isn't, and so you had better err on the side of assuming things are important.

• Words that you think you already know may turn out to have different meanings in the new discipline.

• Your initial understanding is likely to be simplistic, and so you had better be on the watch for complicating factors.

- No matter how unappealing the field might at first seem to you, there are intelligent people who find it fascinating, and so you should be on the watch for what it is that arouses the intellectual passions of people in the new discipline.

In addition to this very general knowledge, you also have some knowledge about metals, however slight, and some small or large amount of relevant background knowledge from fields such as physics and chemistry. By putting these several kinds of knowledge together, you would have something that is not just a *metallurgy* schema. It is, rather, a *learning-about-metallurgy* schema, or, as we shall put it, a *knowledge-building* schema for metallurgy.

Nonexpert learners tend to deal with new information in ways that suggest they either don't have or else don't consider the sorts of general 'knowledge about knowledge' itemized above. Thus, they will do things like the following:

- Give no thought to how much more there is to learn, and jump to conclusions on the basis of the little they have already learned.

- Make subjective judgments of importance, ignoring events or statements that do not stand out as important in their own right.

- Assume words mean what they are used to having them mean.

- Quickly construct simplistic interpretations, which are then retained in the face of contraindications.

- Dismiss whole topics as boring, without attempting to discover what might be interesting in them, while allowing themselves to be captivated by items of tangential interest.

The result is that nonexpert learners suffer all the consequences of inadequate prior knowledge—faulty concepts, oversimplification, disconnectedness, dysfunctionality. Knowledge-building schemas provide a means of at least partly overcoming these handicaps. Instead of relying on a best-fit match to whatever you happen already to know or believe, the knowledge-building schema lends itself to provisional inter-pretations, to keeping questions open, and to actively pursuing fuller understanding. New information is thus interpreted against a background of recognized uncertainties about just what it means, what its importance is, what significance it will prove to have in light of other information not yet acquired. Thus a knowledge-building schema serves as a framework for progressive solving of knowledge problems.

Some Examples of Knowledge-Building Schemas

Evidence that there is a distinction between direct assimilation and use of knowledge-building schemas has appeared even in preschool children. Susan Carey studied nursery school chil-dren who had been casually introduced to a new color, olive.[12] Some children connected olive to its neighboring color, green, and treated the two as equivalent. This is *direct assimilation* of new information to old knowledge. Others adopted what Carey called the 'odd color, odd name' strategy. In various ways they showed that they knew there was something different about olive-colored objects and about the color name, but they were some weeks in getting the lexical relationships worked out. As Carey explains, there is quite a bit to learning a new color term. The child has to work out how it relates to already known terms—is it a synonym, does it refer to a subclass, or does it refer to a larger class that includes other known colors, or is it a new color term on a par with other color names? Over a period of weeks, these matters were worked out by the chil-dren, but they were worked out faster and more reliably by children who used the 'odd color, odd name' approach.

In our terms, 'odd color, odd name' refers to a knowledge-building schema in which information about the newly-named color is accumulated and processed until it is ready to take its place in the child's existing structure of color knowledge.

Essentially the same distinction appears in experiments in which adults learned new word meanings. In these experiments, van Daalen-Kapteijns and Elshout-Mohr[13] used invented words for realistic concepts that did not already have labels in the language. An example is *kolper,* referring to 'a window that transmits little light because of something in front of it'. Students were presented a list of sentences using the neologism. No single sentence was sufficient to establish the meaning of the term; rather, each sentence implied some important feature of its definition. Students read the sentences in order and thought aloud as they tried to work out the meaning of the term. The sequential nature of the task enabled the experimenters to code the thinking-aloud protocols according to the type of approach taken toward knowledge building. They identified two basic approaches, which appear to correspond to direct assimilation and use of a knowledge-building schema. In the former, the students immediately assimilate the neologism to a known term—for instance, *kolper* means *window.* Subsequent information causes them to modify the meaning—for example, *kolper* means *small window* or *shaded window.* In the knowledge-building approach, the students successively identify components of the new term, finally arriving at a definition that integrates these components. The experimenters' characterization of this approach refers specifically to the kind of structure we are calling a knowledge-building schema: "One might say the subject reserves an empty model for the new word meaning and fills this with components from local models" (390). Van Daalen-Kapteijns and Elshout-Mohr found that students of high verbal ability tended to use the knowledge-building schema approach, while students of relatively lower verbal ability used the direct-assimilation approach.

The fact that this same contrast between approaches to learning appears among preschoolers and among university students suggests that what we have here is not a difference between experienced and inexperienced learners, but rather a more fundamental difference that can be observed at all stages of development.

Building Knowledge in Complex Domains

Although differences in approaches to learning show up even with such simple tasks as learning a new color term or learning a single new concept in an already familiar domain, the magnitude of the difference between expert and nonexpert learning becomes much more striking when some advance in the complexity of knowledge is involved. To about one hundred children ranging from first through sixth grade, we presented series of statements about germs or dinosaurs and asked children to think aloud after each statement. Carol Chan scaled these relatively free responses according to five levels.[14] The first two levels are ones at which the child did not show evidence of having assimilated the new information at all. Instead, the child responded to an isolated word or proposition by recalling old information that was cued by it. One of the text statements that proved most provocative of differences in response was the following:

> Harmful germs are not trying to be bad when they settle down in your body. They just want to live quietly, eat, and make more germs.

A Level 1 or 2 response might merely consist of associations to a word or phrase—for instance, a discourse about parts of your body that germs can settle into—without evidence of having grasped what the text said. At Level 3, however, one might get a comment or restatement that would make it clear the passage had been taken in. For instance,

> That means they don't want to really hurt you, but they just want to live quietly and eat the food you digest and all the things that could go in your stomach and they just want to get more bacteria.

What is remarkable here, though, is that the child shows no recognition that the text's message flies in the face of the whole popular image of germs, as conveyed by television commercials, cartoons, and often by teaching, in which germs are depicted as aggressors. Thus the new information is assimilated with no apparent concern about its relation to prior knowledge. In other Level 3 responses, children might recognize the contradiction and dismiss the new information as wrong or stupid. That, too, is a direct-assimilation way of dealing with the new information. It stands in sharp contrast to Level 4 responses, in which children would recognize that there was a problem about what to do with the new information. For example,

> That's hard to believe. Let's see. Then I always thought [of] germs moving around or fighting us. I didn't think that they would just settle down and raise a family. That's not exactly my idea of a germ.

Here the child recognizes that there is more at issue than a solitary matter of fact. "That's not exactly my idea of a germ" suggests a dawning awareness that germs are more complex than the child had thought and that a knowledge-building schema may be set up to develop this enlarged conception of germ behavior. At Level 5 we see enough new thinking to be confident that, in fact, the child has started work on a new knowledge structure. Here are two instances:

> Well, I guess they don't know they are hurting you. . . . Well, I'm not sure. They are killed by other cells in your body. I wonder what they think, if they knew that they were doing something so they could prevent it or something, or if scientists could find a way that bacteria or viruses could live in your body without hurting you.

> I wonder if germs are intelligent. I guess not. Maybe there's a whole new world, like . . . there is fighting going on between the good and the bad. . . . It's kind of neat when you think about it, 'cause to think of a whole new world inside your body.

In this scoring scheme, then, Levels 1 and 2 may be thought of as sub-assimilative levels, Level 3 as corresponding to direct assimilation, and Levels 4 and 5 as showing increasing indications of use of knowledge-building schemas. That these are also increasing levels of progressive problem solving is shown by the examples. As might be expected, the level of response to new information was significantly correlated with both age and extent of prior knowledge about the topic, and these were also correlated with the amount that children learned from the texts. However, statistical path analyses showed that level of response exerted the only significant direct effect on learning, and mediated the effects of age and prior knowledge.[15]

An adequate account of how complex knowledge is built up from scant beginnings remains to be worked out. Our current research program is mainly concerned with this question. Knowledge-building schemas, in at least some embryonic form, must themselves be acquired through learning, and this adds a further layer of obscurity to the question of accounting for complex learning. A student might have effective schemas for building knowledge in one domain but not in another, but we suspect that the expert learner has some basic forms of knowledge-building schemas that are applicable across many domains,[16] and that this helps to account for the high correlations across domains that are found in studies of school achievement.

People on an expert track of development are continually striving against the limits of their competence. For beginners, this means striving against the limitations that insufficient prior knowledge places on their ability to learn. For experts, the problems of insufficient prior knowledge never go away, however. The expert track of development keeps rising toward levels of increasing complexity of performance and understanding. This means that present knowledge is always superficial, simplistic, and fragmented relative to the knowledge the expert is trying to achieve. Accordingly, to understand how expert learners deal with new information that they cannot yet fully comprehend is really to understand expertise itself at a deeper level.

School and Family Influences on Approaches to Learning

We suspect that the conditions of schooling are antagonistic to the knowledge-building schemas discussed previously. These schemas serve the expert learner's need to incorporate new information into more complex structures than present knowledge is able to support. They are thus structures for long-term accumulation of information, reflective thinking, and laborious constructive activity. School conditions would tend to favor schemas specialized for rapid pickup and retrieval of knowledge, so as to keep pace with the frequent topic shifts in schooling and with the perpetual need to be able to respond very quickly to demands for knowledge recall. Knowledge-building schemas are poorly adapted to these demands. A more efficient type of schema from the standpoint of school demands is one that links new information to scholastically important topics and that involves the minimum of interpretation and reconstruction of information.[17]

There is some evidence that students favor rapid, super-ficial uptake of information over more constructive approaches. Studies of summarization find that students tend to retain or reject text information on the basis of superficial indicators of its importance rather than on the basis of its interrelation-ships. Thinking-aloud studies of readers show that the less able ones attend mainly to topics and details rather than to overarching propositions. Several studies of notetaking show that students do better the less interpretation they put into their notes, and one study found students actively resisting efforts to get them to write interpretive rather than verbatim notes during lectures.[18]

Conventional wisdom already recognizes that being a good student can interfere with getting an education. Yet studies of highly talented experts indicate that they do not on the whole fare badly in school. In the studies by Bloom and his col-leagues,[19] it was found that highly ranked mathematicians had generally been at odds with their teachers in school, but this seems to have been a consequence of their mathematical precocity putting them so far in advance of their teachers. Distinguished medical neuroscientists, on the other hand, seemed to have gotten along well and been all-round high achievers in school. It seems unjustified, therefore, to treat adaptation to schooling and the development of expertise as being inherently at odds.

Under favorable circumstances expert learners can use the school curriculum to advance their own knowledge-building agenda. Good courses of study can spare them a great deal of floundering about in ignorance. Good teachers can help them in many ways, including serving as models of learning expertise itself. Since students have the whole world to learn, they can afford to be flexible in adapting their knowledge-building ambitions to what the school happens to provide. With reasonable luck they will be able to do well in school and develop as expert learners without conflict. Under less favorable circumstances they may have to compromise, developing some of the adaptive strategies required for school success while continuing to pursue their own goals as well. These goals involve continually extending their competence and moving to higher levels of understanding; and ultimately whatever they get out of school—even if, at worst, it is nothing but a few academic skills and a basket of facts—they can manage to make use of it somehow in building their own knowledge.

What we have just said applies to students who are already expert learners, however. The danger is that students in a school environment may never get started at active knowledge building. To young children school is just tasks and activities.[20] No matter how worthy those activities may be, the young child cannot be expected to intuit the educational purposes behind them. By continuing to do well on the activities served by the curriculum, the child moves ahead without ever having to pursue knowledge itself as a goal. And it cannot be supposed that the situation is any different in more open or child-centered schools, where children's own interests dictate more of the curriculum. Initially, at least, the children's interests are likely to be in activities, and it is not obvious what there is in the school environment to make this change.

This is evidently true even of highly talented children. In a wide-ranging study of the educational histories of eminent people, Bloom and his coworkers uncovered an astonishingly consistent pattern in the development of pianists and tennis champions, all of whom began specialized training by about the age of six. According to reports of parents and teachers, these people were not what could be called expert learners at that age. Mainly they were just having fun and trying to please their elders. Nevertheless, a course of progressive problem solving was going on. As skills were learned, freed-up resources were being reinvested in higher-level goals. But executive control of this process of expertise was not in the hands of the child.

Generally, it was in the hands of the child's parents. In many cases the parents virtually gave their lives over to advancing the child's development.[21]

It would be inaccurate to say that the parents' role was that of mentor. (Mentors were important, but at a later age.) Rather, the way we see it is that a single expert learning process was going on but it was a joint production of child and parents. The child supplied talent and a willingness to comply;[22] the parents provided the executive structure for progressive problem-solving, moving the child on to higher challenges as the child acquired resources to meet them. Eventually, of course, the child came to take on executive control of the process. Having mentors or role-models was important at that point, whereas at an earlier stage they would not have had much impact.

There seems to be hardly any way that conventional mass education can provide this sort of cooperative sustaining of an expert learning process. And without it, getting started on an expert course of development must be a very chancy business. In Chapter 7 we will consider some possibilities for modifying schools to make them more supportive of expertise in learning. With only general sorts of encouragement, however, its seems that some children are able to acquire the ingredients of a progressive problem-solving approach to learning through informal experience. Several studies have shown that prior experiences of independent intellectual achievement (in science fair projects, ambitious hobbies, artistic or literary pursuits, and the like) are an important predictor of above average performance. A questionnaire tapping such independent activities has, in fact, been an important part of the National Merit Scholarship competition, and there is evidence that it predicts career productivity better than do academic grades.[23]

Given the inherent limitations of schooling, it seems essential for a child to have an intellectual life outside of school. It gives the child a chance to develop personal knowledge-building goals and schemas for incorporating new information in ways that advance toward those goals. Thus equipped, the child is in a position to *use* schooling as a source of learning opportunities without being drawn into short-cut strategies that work well for handling school tasks but that lead nowhere in the lifelong development of expertise.

Keeping Learning Expertise in Perspective

Research on students gives us good reason to believe that there is such a thing as expertise in learning, that it is something over and above expertise in handling academic tasks, and that it is probably important in advancing other kinds of expertise. However, we need to be careful not to exaggerate its scope on one hand or take too narrow a view of learning expertise on the other.

Expertise does not depend wholly on expert learning. Most of what we learn from day to day is picked up incidentally and effortlessly; or if effort is involved, it is likely to be directed toward achieving some result and not toward the learning that accompanies the process. The same is surely true of most of the learning experts do in their domains. The part of learning that is deliberately pursued, however, that is the object of effort over and above that devoted to achieving other results, may be extremely important even if it accounts for only a small fraction of the learning an expert does.

Some experts may not be expert learners at all. Exceptional natural talent in performance, combined with exceptional learning opportunities, may compensate for a lack of expertise in learning. Schools, however, need to focus on promoting expertise in learning because it is something they may be able to influence. Whatever natural talent is, schools are in the business of helping people make the most of it, and that entails becoming expert in learning to the limits of one's talents.

All this talk about goals, effort, and the like, can lead to an oversimplified idea of the nature of learning expertise. Critics of the notion will bring up 'inner skiing' and 'superlearning' as supposed counterexamples.[24] Both of these advocate a sort of passive going with the flow. The idea with 'inner skiing' and similar 'inner' approaches to motor skills is that your body can do the learning better if your mind doesn't get in the way with its analyses and rules. 'Superlearning' has been mostly applied in foreign language learning and features mental relaxation intended to allow information to go straight to the unconscious mind without being interpreted and fussed over by the conscious intellect.

How valid the specific claims made for these approaches are need not concern us here. It is sufficient to grant the general point that rational analysis and control can interfere with some kinds of learning. Most notably, they can interfere with impressionistic learning, which—as we discussed in Chapter 3—depends on emotional response. But they may also interfere with learning skills that require rapid coordinations in real time, too rapid and complex to be effectively guided by consciously formulated rules. In all such situations, expert learning would entail using alternatives to rational analysis and control. It might involve mental relaxation, use of imagery, or other more esoteric tinkering with attention, moods, and mental states.

Most likely expert learning always involves some balance or alternation between relatively controlled, problem-solving processes in learning and more spontaneous, playful, or passively receptive processes. Expertise in learning would then include finding the right balance or way of moving between modes of learning. The right blend will vary both with the subject being learned and with the person. It is probably true that adults trying to learn foreign languages tend to get it wrong and to adopt an approach that is more suitable to learning conceptual subject matter than to learning an idiom. In foreign language learning, as well as in performing arts and sports, coaches play a valuable role. Part of their value may be in helping the learner find the right personal balance between control and spontaneity. They may also provide such balance directly, supplying analysis while the learner attends to the whole and paying attention to the whole when the learner is caught up in detail. Such considerations remind us that expertise is not necessarily situated within the individual. Some kinds of learning may be so complex and multifaceted that an expert learning process can only be maintained by having it distributed over more than one person.[25]

Summary

Everyone learns, which is to say that everyone continually encounters new information and assimilates it into what they already know. Most of the time learning goes on effortlessly and without need for thought, but occasionally it is problematic. The expertlike learner carries on a program of progressive solving of learning problems. Inconsistencies between existing beliefs and new knowledge are not resolved by problem-reducing changes but by efforts to construct new knowledge structures that can deal with the newly recognized complexities. The nonexpert learner, by contrast, tends to minimize new learning by immediately making a best-fit match between new information and whatever is already known. The nonexpert learner is likely to treat formal education as a series of tasks to be performed and to find effort- and risk-reducing ways of accomplishing them. The expert learner, by contrast, pursues a personal learning agenda and develops ways of making opportunistic use of school tasks and resources to advance on this agenda.

Chapter Seven
Schools as Nonexpert Societies

Expertise, as we have been representing it since Chapter 1, is an advance over what comes naturally. So is formal education. If everyone became sophisticated and proficient at fixing automobiles, just by growing up in an automobile-driving society, we would not recognize auto mechanics as experts. We might still employ them to fix our cars, because of the dirt and grease, but they could expect to earn car-wash wages. Similarly, if everyone learned to read just by growing up in a literate society, one of the main reasons that children are required to go to school would disappear. Schools and experts owe their existence to the same condition—that some of the competencies required by human societies, unlike those required by nonhuman societies, depend on learning that goes beyond what comes naturally.

Thus there ought to be a strong bond between schooling and expertise. Instead, we find an education system designed as if its purpose were to produce nonexperts.

Mass education is not very old. It took shape in the nine-teenth century. But that was long enough ago that it predates the information explosion, the need for highly specialized exper-tise, and any modern conceptions of the nature of expert knowledge and of expertlike approaches to learning. Although there have been substantial changes in schooling during the twentieth century, for better or for worse, these changes have not done anything to remedy a fundamental mismatch between the training and knowledge-propagating functions of the public school and the needs of a modern society.

Children enter school at the age of five or six, but it is usually not until they are close to 20 that they encounter any serious effort to develop them into experts. Many, of course, will have left the system by that age. Those who have persisted will be in a technical college or in their third year of university, and their first encounters with education for expertise will coincide with their entry into specialized courses. Most discus-sions of education for expertise deal with what happens from that point onward, but that is not what we are going to deal with here. Instead, we want to focus on the decade and a half of schooling that goes before.

There are several reasons for focusing on earlier schooling. For one thing, advanced education in North America seems to be in relatively good shape. Other countries are sending their students here for finishing. It is education up through the early years of university that is in bad shape and that almost all other industrialized parts of the world seem to be managing better. Another reason for focusing on the earlier stages of education is that they are, as is commonly said, 'general'. To say anything worthwhile about improving the education of electrical engi-neers or accountants or dentists, one needs to enter in some depth into the particulars of these specialties. There is a solid body of research on medical expertise that has implications for education in that profession,[1] most of it done by psychologists who have close ties with medicine. There is another body of research on expertise in computer programming.[2] In time there should be research bases for improving expertise in many other specialized fields. To the extent that there are general principles of education for expertise, however, they ought to apply to earlier, more general education as well.

The urgent concern in North American society is with increasing the number of students who are ready, by the time they reach the age of 20, to profit from specialized education in ways that will lead them to expertise. Recall Naomi Tal's study of expertlike and typical medical students. It is possible that medical schools could do something about helping typical students to become more expertlike. But medical educators we have talked to seem not very hopeful. They think it is too late. However that may be, it seems clear that it would be desirable to start earlier, possibly much earlier, in developing in students the dispositions that would make them expertlike learners in whatever field they chose to enter. Medical schools are not short of qualified applicants, which is to say applicants who can be expected to make the grade. But apparently only a tiny minority of those have expertlike characteristics. Some may acquire them during the course of their training—we don't know; but many more might have done so if their earlier schooling experience had been different. And then there are the great numbers of students, especially from disadvantaged minority backgrounds, who might have had the potential to be great doctors but who never make it to the door—who are defeated by science and mathematics or perhaps do not even learn to read at an academically functional level. Their fate, too, might have been different in an education system that was geared to fostering expertise from an early age.

The preceding remarks might be interpreted as endorsing an elitist model of education—one that has the whole education system geared to the elite minority that emerges at the upper end. Quite the contrary is true. Our notion is of an education system that promotes expertise for everyone. This is to be compared with the sort of democratic elitism that

Thomas Jefferson proposed and that (although his proposal was never explicitly adopted) our schools have tended to shape themselves toward. Jefferson's idea was that everyone (he actually had in mind only males) should receive a basic schooling that would equip them to function competently as citizens and voters. Out of each school class, officials would rake out the "four boys of best talent" and send them on to the next higher level of schooling, at the end of which there would be another raking out of the select few, and so on until the elite remainder reached the pinnacle, which was to be admission to the University of Virginia.[3] Those who were eliminated at earlier levels would not have wasted their time, however, for each level would prepare students for the station in society to which their capacities were appropriate. The result would thus be a society stratified according to talent, with education appropriate to the stratum, but—this is where Jefferson's democratic principles came in—there would be no *a priori* stratification according to birth; all would have an equal chance.

Ever since the 1960s, however, evidence has been accumulating to show that in any realistic sense children do not in fact start out with an equal chance. This is a complex issue. All sorts of sociopolitical cant have been layered on it and the facts are often distorted.[4] We can deal with only one corner of the issue here, which has to do with the making of expertlike students.

One thing all the research on student differences points to is that if children are to become expertlike learners, they must at present acquire the dispositions outside of school. Schools do not foster expertlike learning and do not even provide an environment in which it is easy for it to survive. The deficiencies of schooling run very deep. We are not talking about a problem that could be solved by installing a more capable teaching force or by switching from a traditional to a child-centered classroom or *vice versa,* by instituting an effective testing scheme or by irradiating the schools with multicultural values. We are talking about something that is wrong with the very process of schooling in all its extant forms.

What is Wrong with Our Schools versus
What is Wrong with All Schools

School-bashing is a popular sport, and when intellectuals do it it often takes the form of caricature. Schools are depicted as places where students spend their time memorizing dull facts and where any show of critical or imaginative thought is suppressed. Alternatively, they are caricatured as playrooms where nothing at all is taught but students spend their days making anti-drug posters or something equally innocuous but unedifying. There is, of course, some truth in the caricatures, and classrooms can even be found where the reality is more extreme than the caricature. But these simplistic descriptions suggest equally simplistic remedies, and that is where trouble starts.

We will turn later to the question of why schools tend to take on the surface forms that are represented in these caricatures. But it is important to look beneath the surface forms to see what is wrong with schooling even when it is at its apparent best—even when capable teachers are teaching lively and significant content and engaging students in activities that are challenging and relevant to educational objectives. As regards the development of expertise, we can identify three serious defects in schooling:

1. Schooling deals with only the visible parts of knowledge: formal knowledge and demonstrable skills. Informal knowledge—both the kind that students bring in with them and the kind that they will need in order to function expertly—is generally ignored in school curricula.

2. The knowledge objectives that are pursued, limited as they may be, tend to be made invisible to the students. The objectives are translated into tasks and activities. The students' attention, and often that of the teachers as well, is concentrated on the activities and not on the objectives that gave rise to them.

3. Scope for the exercise of expertise—for progressive problem solving, in other words—is generally available

only to the teacher, and schooling provides no mechanisms (such as those that exist in trade apprenticeships)
for the teacher's expertise to be passed on to the students.

These are not the defects usually noted in critiques of
American schools. Instead one hears about declining standards,
poorly qualified teachers, drop-outs, declining enrollments in
science and mathematics, and—on another plane—violence,
drugs, poor discipline, and functional illiteracy. We do not wish
to minimize any of these problems, but rather to look beyond
them. Suppose all these widely noted problems were eliminated. Would this achieve the *America 2000* goal of making the
United States first in the world in mathematics and science
achievement? At best it would put the United States somewhere in the middle of the pack, given that the leading nations
(Japan and the nations of northern Europe) are already ahead
in those regards and are not resting on the oars.

What could conceivably give us a competitive edge? It
would have to consist of overcoming limitations that are shared
by the educational systems of other nations. Otherwise we are
only playing catch-up. Those limitations, we shall argue, are
problems like the three enumerated above. These characterize
schools in general. Schools have never been designed with a
conception of expertise as a process that can be fostered at all
levels of development. They have all been built on a primitive
conception of knowledge that leaves out most of what is
required to become an expert. And so there is an opportunity
to leapfrog over the school systems of more complacent nations
and to create a form of schooling that would more effectively
promote expertise of all kinds.

How Commonsense Epistemology Limits Schooling

One of the ways schools are caricatured is by attributing to
teachers an 'empty bucket' theory of learning. According to this
purported theory, children's minds are regarded as empty
buckets which it is the teacher's duty to fill up by pouring

knowledge into them. In fact no such theory is propounded anywhere in educational circles, and anyone found espousing it would be mercilessly ridiculed. But as usual there is some truth behind the caricature.

It is the fact that, even in the most intellectually barren of schools, students are expected to leave with more knowledge than when they arrived. But what schools do to bring this about has never been guided by theories of knowledge and knowledge acquisition, even bad theories. Instead, it seems fair to say that at all levels, from kindergarten to university, education has been based on commonsense beliefs about knowledge. We discussed the limitations of commonsense epistemology in Chapter 3—how it recognizes only the visible kinds of knowledge—formal knowledge and demonstrable skills—and ignores the informal, impressionistic, and self-regulatory kinds of knowledge that actually make up the bulk of what experts know. These limitations have serious implications for educational practice, which extend beyond the fact that a great deal of knowledge gets left out.

The closest education systems usually come to declaring themselves on epistemological matters is in curriculum guides that set forth what schools are supposed to teach and how. Look at almost any curriculum guide, and you will find that it contains some or all of the following, but little more of substance:

1. A list of the facts and principles to be taught or of topics to be covered.

2. A list of skills to be developed (often labeled 'processes' because 'skill' is a bad word in some quarters): measuring, comparing, observing, punctuating dialogue, multiplying three-digit numbers, and so forth.

3. A catalogue of suggested activities—games, experiments, projects of various sorts.

Sometimes, especially for lower school grades, a curriculum guide is nothing but a catalogue of activities, with the other components reduced to labels attached to the activities. A curriculum guide may state aspirations of kinds that could be construed as referring to impressionistic or self-regulatory knowledge. Some are of an attitudinal sort: love of literature, spirit of inquiry, respect for people of different cultures, and so on. Others may refer to good study skills, habits of careful observation, and such. But almost always they are expressed as wishful thinking. They are hoped-for by-products of the suggested activities rather than knowledge that can in some fashion be taught.

In order for anything new to enter the school curriculum, it has to undergo a series of transformations that tend to defeat the original purpose for introducing it. First it has to be transformed into formal knowledge and/or demonstrable skills—the sorts of itemizable, visible, testable things already found in curriculum guides. Then these knowledge items have to be translated into activities or tasks intended to produce the desired learning. Since there is no theory or science to guide either of these steps, the transformations are generally carried out on the basis of custom and surface resemblances. It would perhaps be more accurate to say that they are carried out unconsciously. In any event, the result is that what may sound like a substantial enrichment of school practice gets reduced to familiar-looking content and activities that bear only a superficial relation to the high-sounding educational objectives that supposedly motivate them.

Mathematical problem solving provides a contemporary illustration with obvious implications for the development of expertise. Commonly, mathematics education in elementary and high schools has consisted of the teacher showing the students how to carry out an operation (such as long division) and the students doing pages of exercises practicing it. Until recently, the largest selling textbooks supported this mindless approach. Then, national and international testing programs began to dramatize the fact that American school students were miserable at solving mathematical word problems. The first response was merely to include more word problems in the exercises related to algorithms. Since there was nothing but custom and surface appearance to guide the creation of these problems, they tended to be, as Janine Remillard has observed, "dressed-up algorithms":

> Key words or phrases, such as 'in all', 'left', 'all together' pervade most of the problems so that the student can select the correct operation without necessarily understanding the question. The chapter organization also makes the necessary operation or procedure to solve a problem obvious. Division problems with 1-digit divisors, for example, are grouped together in one chapter and each lesson is grouped by the number of digits in the quotient.[5]

More recently, as part of a thrust toward 'teaching thinking', there has been pressure to teach strategies of mathematical problem solving, rather than depend wholly on exercises. This is something new to school mathematics, and it provides a striking instance of the process of degradation we have been describing. In the popular mathematics texts, the old lessons with their mindless pseudo-problems remained, and problem-solving strategies became a separate topic, in separate sections of the book. The content consisted of strategy rules (formal knowledge) accompanied by exercises for practicing the use of them. Commonly, the rules specify a set of steps; for instance:

1. Understand the question.

2. Find the needed data.

3. Plan what to do.

4. Find the answer.

5. Check back.[6]

Although this routine might help some students organize their efforts, it seems obvious that students who were already able to perform these feats would have little need of lessons on problem-solving strategies. Far from teaching students how to think, these lessons reduce that ambitious objective to bits of formal content and procedure, which in turn are reduced to tasks that the students must carry out. Also noteworthy is the fact that solving word problems has now become an end in itself. It is put off in separate sections and unrelated to anything else in mathematics. Why students should be solving word problems at all, where any of this is supposed to lead, no one bothers to ask.

In every area of the school curriculum, the activity replaces the objective and eventually obliterates it. Anyone rash enough to put forward a mathematics program that did not contain word problems would be accused of neglecting thinking and problem solving, even if the whole program centered around thinking and solving problems of mathematical understanding and application. In the case of reading, 'comprehension questions' (questions asked by the teacher or workbook to test comprehension of a reader selection) have obliterated the objective of teaching students to wrestle themselves with text meaning.[7]

What we have been describing is the conventional, textbook-based instruction that continues to be the prevalent mode in American schools. Things are not fundamentally different, however, in those schools that practice some version of progressive or child-centered education. These schools resist the reduction of educational goals to testable items of formal knowledge and skill, but what this tends to amount to in practice is that they by-pass this step and reduce educational objectives directly to activities. So, instead of doing word problems, children may be measuring the playground or each other's shoes. The activities may be more lively, and may allow more scope for student initiative, but it remains the case that the relation between activities and objectives is based on custom and surface resemblance and that in time the activities take the place of the goals. Thus, teachers' instructional planning is found to consist mainly of planning activities and selecting materials.[8]

Of course, learning goes on in both traditional and progressive schools, and with the right teacher and with ready students schooling can be an intellectually lively experience. But even at its best, schooling as we know it is designed so that the only person who is likely to gain expertise through the process is the teacher (and even that is questionable). It is the teacher who knows what the top-level goals are and who recognizes and tries to solve problems on the way to those goals. It is the teacher who exerts the efforts that we have identified with the expertlike learner: setting goals of understanding and competence, identifying with the values of a discipline or profession, monitoring knowledge, formulating problems. The skillful teacher renders all this expertlike activity invisible to the students, who busy themselves with their tasks and activities.

Thus the comparison of schools to factories is an apt one. The students are the workers; learning is the product. But the workers have little identification with the product, may not even be aware of it, and do not participate in its design or improvement. It is for the engineers and managers to do that. And no matter how zealously the workers perform their tasks, they will never get any closer to being engineers or managers. In modern industries, of course, efforts are being made to change. The workers are now being brought into the engineering and management aspects of production, and are expected to grasp the nature of the product and to take a problem-solving approach to improving its quality. This is requiring a radical restructuring of the industrial process, however.

The factories that schools resemble are the factories of the old-fashioned type. A characteristic of such factories is a sharp separation between experts and workers. Workers are referred to as 'semi-skilled', which means that they must master certain procedures—sometimes quite complex ones—but that once these procedures have been mastered, work continues as a routine. The expertise that goes into improving the product or its manufacture is invisible to the workers and is brought down to them only in the form of job changes, which require a further stint of learning before work settles back into a routine. That seems to be precisely how schools are run as well. Being a student is a semi-skilled occupation. Learn a procedure and then practice it as a routine. The only difference is that the jobs change more frequently—too frequently for some students, who can't keep up or won't.

Pursuing the factory metaphor, we could argue that most of the reforms being called for in American education are aimed at changing students from semi-skilled to skilled workers. Give them jobs that require higher levels of skill and give them adequate training for those jobs, with licensing tests to make sure they have qualified. What is needed if education is really to address twenty-first-century needs, however, is a restructuring of the whole process, as is going on in some industrial plants, so that the workers are brought into the expert processes by which the product and its manufacture are continually improved. If this is proving important in automobile manufacture, how much more important ought it to be in schools, where the product is the students' own knowledge.

The Poverty of Current Efforts at Educational Reform
How can schooling be modified so that more students will develop into experts? This question *per se* has not been posed to educators or the public, but from the discussions that have taken place on such themes as 'achieving excellence', 'meeting the global challenge', or 'preparing students for the twenty-first-century', it is easy to infer what the responses would be. The main responses to calls for upgrading and reform of education are of three kinds. One response, heard mainly from school officials and teachers, is denial: Things are not as bad as they have been painted, and they would be better if more money were appropriated for schools. We will ignore that one and focus on two more positive responses, which may be labeled the *didactic* response and the *child-centered* response. Each has some merit, but each fails gravely to address the need to promote expertise from an early age.

The Didactic Response
One line of response to calls for educational upgrading would simply extend the conventional curriculum that we have been criticizing. It would add or update the formal knowledge content. (California, for instance, is now calling for the schools

to teach discrete functions in mathematics, believing this to be important in electronic technology.) It would add skills, most likely more thinking skills. Educators swayed by the arguments we have presented might also call for the teaching of informal knowledge, or for activities believed to foster informal knowledge, and for the teaching of progressive problem solving. Especially when it comes from outside the school system, the didactic response also usually entails testing aimed at ensuring that what is purportedly taught is actually learned.

These might all be helpful moves. Formal knowledge is important and does need occasional updating. Cognitive strategies have been taught with a measure of success, and it is reasonable to expect some increment in expertlike behavior through teaching students the idea of progressive problem solving, showing them examples of it, and providing them with reminders to do it. More doubtful, however, would be activities intended to promote informal knowledge. These would be in constant danger of deteriorating into idle amusements or busywork. And even more doubtful, yet highly predictable, would be activities designed to exercise students' 'progressive problem-solving skills'. Lacking in all of this is anything that would encourage students to adopt for themselves an expertlike approach to knowledge or that would sustain them in working at the edge of their competence and trying to extend it to problems of increasing complexity. Without that, it is foolish to speak of 'teaching progressive problem solving' or 'teaching students to be like experts'.

Superficially, it makes sense to specify what students should learn rather than what the schools should teach—hence, set standards and use a testing program to enforce them. Schools are then free to use whatever means they think best to get their students up to standard. By now even the most optimistic advocates of higher standards recognize that testing programs can have the opposite effect. They can induce teachers to abandon educational efforts in favor of grinding rehearsal for tests.[9] Currently there are ambitious efforts afoot to design new tests, testing higher-level skills and deeper understanding. The idea is to design tests such that 'teaching for the test' will be a good thing to do. We do not know how this idea will fare. If the tests are used coercively, they will create a situation in which the teachers and the test-makers are trying to outsmart each other. Even if the tests are used to good effect, however, they cannot be expected to make schools more conducive to expertise. They will encourage schools to focus even more strongly on formal knowledge and testable skills, and at best will only succeed in broadening the range of skills that are tested. More worrisome, however, is that testing reinforces what is most detrimental in didactic schooling to the development of expertise in learning: In didactic schooling the setting of goals, the monitoring of progress toward goals, and the solving of problems blocking progress toward goals are all kept out of the hands of the students. In that kind of situation, becoming an expertlike learner is something that can only be accomplished *despite* the school system.

The Child-Centered Response

A different response to the challenge of promoting expertise can be expected from child-centered educators. It will stress creating a school environment that encourages students' taking responsibility for their own learning and that provides scope for creativity, thoughtfulness, efforts to gain competence and to make sense of the world. There is nothing new in this, however. It is the same message that has been spread for almost a century. It is not altered by predictions concerning the next century or by new understanding of the nature of expertise. The child-centered educator's answer tends to be the same, regardless of the question. There is reason behind this monotony, however. It rests on a belief that natural human development in a healthy, nurturant, and stimulating environment will produce people who readily acquire the knowledge and skills needed for the world in which they find themselves. Therefore we do not need to train up a special kind of person for the twenty-first century. We need to raise the kind of healthy, confident, intellectually and emotionally alive child who would fare well in any century. If anything is changing, it is only that the stress and flux of the postmodern world make optimal development increasingly difficult and at the same time increasingly important.

It is easy to dismiss the child-centered educator's claims on purely empirical grounds. There are, after all, a number of schools strongly committed to this kind of education, under any of its modern labels, such as 'open education' or 'whole language'. It may be debatable whether these schools are more or less successful than the more didactic schools,[10] but there is nothing at all to suggest that they are turning out students more likely to develop as experts. The only schools that could conceivably make such claims are the occasional science high school or university-based high school that can point to a list of Nobel laureates among their graduates. These are usually schools that follow fairly traditional methods, but with very high standards and dedication—supported, of course, by high entrance requirements.

Yet we should not lightly dismiss the child-centered viewpoint, which looks on schools as environments in which children develop in certain ways. If we are to reform schools so that they foster expertise, we are going to have to view them in just that way. We cannot simply convert our aspirations into things to be taught and then require the schools to teach them. An institution that converts all such aspirations into schoolwork routines will inevitably subvert any efforts to instill a spirit of expertise. The essential insight that we ought to preserve from child-centered education is that children will naturally grow into and acquire the competencies needed to function in their social environment. Therefore design of the social environment of the school becomes crucial.

The trouble with child-centered education is that it is not progressive and offers no conception of a school environment that encourages progress rather than static adaptation. (This is ironic, inasmuch as child-centered education came to prominence through the Progressive Education movement.) If results are poor or mediocre, child-centered education has no way to improve, except by trying harder to do what it was already trying to do.[11] Excessive faith gets invested in children's natural goodness, curiosity, and desire to grow, because child-centered educators recognize nothing beyond. There is no room in the child-centered philosophy for a concept of expertise as going beyond what comes naturally. Child-centered education just is nurturing what comes naturally.

Practicing educators will typically deny this, and will point to all sorts of positive things that child-centered teachers do to promote learning. But these turn out to be commonsensical kinds of teaching that grow out of the same commonsense epistemology we have been criticizing. There are, however, places where child-centered education appears to produce outstanding results. One that has received much attention is a school in New Hampshire where, under the guiding influence of Donald Graves, a school culture has evolved in which children get passionately interested in writing and begin at an early age to develop a professional approach to it. They often rewrite pieces many times, the way expert writers do, often in response to reactions from other students. Graves and his associates have documented what we would call progressive problem solving on the part of children struggling with the complexities of punctuation or organization or searching for the *mot juste.*[12]

Under the label of 'process approach' or 'whole language', Graves's methods have been widely imitated, but usually with mediocre results. The methods are based on the child-centered premise that children want to express themselves in writing and, given opportunity and encouragement, will progress in their ability to do so. That much appears to be well-founded, and the premise seems to be sufficient to support an approach to writing in which children enjoy what they are doing and acquire about as much skill as those who are taught writing by didactic means. But to get the expertlike behavior that Graves obtains, something more is required, and child-centered philosophy is not of much help in identifying that something more. What Graves and the teachers working with him have managed to achieve is an expert literary subculture in the school. It is a kind of miniature Bloomsbury. It is what we have referred to previously as a *second-order* environment. Adaptation to that social environment does not mean just writing what you feel like or something that will satisfy one's classmates. It means writing something that goes beyond what you have been able to accomplish before. Rewriting is not just honing the style; it is reformulating the original purpose at a higher level and trying to achieve that higher purpose. The result is an environment that does not merely support natural development of ability to express oneself in writing. It supports development beyond what comes naturally.

The secret of producing a school environment that supports development beyond what comes naturally is what we must discover if we are to educate for expertise. If it can be discovered and somehow made merchantable, we could have a kind of schooling that would perhaps leapfrog over the best of existing school systems and produce a nation of prospective experts.

The Idea of a Knowledge-Building Community

The educational pendulum swings, inevitably although not always regularly, between conventional, didactic instruction and child-centered education. There ought to be a third alternative, but what could it be? Not some compromise between the other two, for that is what already exists in most schools.

From time to time in recent decades it has occurred to educational thinkers that the learned disciplines themselves might serve as models for the redesign of schools. This is an especially attractive notion when considered in light of the ideas we have been trying to advance about expertise—conceiving of it as a process of progressive problem solving and advancement beyond present limits of competence. The sciences, especially, whether viewed at the abstract level of disciplines or at the local level of individual laboratories and research centers, have epitomized this expert process. They have been astonishingly successful at producing continual advances to higher levels of knowledge, gathering strength as they go. Although knowledge creation depends on chancy processes of discovery and invention, we have come to take it for granted that good research groups will be able to do it with some regularity. This is what Whitehead referred to as the "method of invention". The "method" is in large part a method of social organization that allows both individual and group expertise—especially creative expertise—to flourish in ways that lead to collective advances in knowledge.

So successful have research groups been that they have begun to be used as models for many other kinds of enterprises—for management teams, sales teams, even secretarial staffs.[13] The restructuring of manufacturing processes that we mentioned earlier also owes something to the research team as a model. Why, then, should the research group not also be a model for restructuring schooling? Could knowledge-building, carried out in the progressive manner of scientific research groups, provide the missing third way to conduct education?

In an earlier era it was possible to dismiss this idea as romantic. Researchers are discovering or creating new knowledge; students are only learning what is already known. By now, however, it is generally recognized that students construct their knowledge. This is as true if they are learning from books and lectures as it is if they are acquiring knowledge through inquiry. This is not an article of faith (although it is treated as such by some educators). It is an obvious implication that falls out of any plausible theory of knowledge acquisition. A further implication is that creating new knowledge and learning existing knowledge are not very different, as far as psychological processes are concerned. Thus there is no patent reason why schooling cannot have the dynamic character of scientific knowledge building. If there are insurmountable obstacles, they are more likely to be of a social or attitudinal than of a cognitive kind.

The contrast between the excitement of real research and the dreariness of school routines has struck many an educational thinker. 'Learning by discovery', which flourished for a while around 1960, was one effort to inject the spirit of research into school curricula. 'Cognitive apprenticeship' is a more recent notion, which adds a social dimension to modeling schooling after real research enterprises. Here the idea is that students are apprentice scientists and scholars, who are not expected to play the mature role but rather to work their ways gradually into more responsible roles as their competence increases. Both these approaches have a 'let's pretend' character to them, however. In learning by discovery, the students are expected to act like scientists who are making new discoveries, even though the facts they are attempting to establish could be obtained more readily by looking in a book. In cognitive apprenticeship it is the teacher who pretends. Since few teachers actually practice science or original scholarship, their role as master to a roomful of apprentices necessarily has a bogus character to it.[14]

One of the weaknesses of past attempts to make schooling more like scientific inquiry has been that they focused on the individual student's abilities, dispositions, and prospects. The focal question has been: *To what extent can a child be expected to act like a physicist, biologist, historian, literary scholar, anthropologist, or whatever?* This question does not yield useful answers. Of course children are curious about the world and they can in some fashion collect and evaluate evidence, venture explanations, test conjectures, and so on. Thus they can be said to act like researchers. But that only suggests to didactic educators that research skills and laboratory activities should be incorporated into the curriculum and confirms for child-centered educators the claim they have been making all along, that children's curiosity should be allowed to guide their activities. It does not suggest any new structure for schooling.

The question needs to be reformulated at the level of the group rather than the individual: *Can a classroom function as a knowledge-building community, similar to the knowledge-building communities that make up the learned disciplines?* To this question there is no facile answer. We need to try it and see; and before that we need to determine what it would mean for a classroom to function in this way.

We have used the term 'knowledge-building community' so as to avoid some of the unwanted connotations of more familiar terms. 'Research' and its related terms suggest science. While science provides us with the cleanest examples of collective knowledge building, we would not want knowledge building in schools limited to science or to those aspects of the humanities that emulate scientific research (that would be deadly). There are film societies and literary cliques that qualify as knowledge-building communities insofar as they keep advancing toward a fuller, deeper knowledge of their subject matter. Some industrial firms, most notably in high-technology fields, function as knowledge-building communities. These are companies whose major asset is expertise and whose survival in the face of competition depends on continually advancing the company's collective knowledge and skill.

Finally, some families function as knowledge-building communities. They are not simply collections of people who individually pursue knowledge, even though their individual interests may be diverse. They are a community in the sense that they share their knowledge, support one another in knowledge construction, and thus develop a kind of collective expertise that is distinguishable from that of the individual family members. We suspect that the students described in the preceding chapter as 'expertlike learners' must come from families that function at least to some extent as knowledge-building communities. Otherwise it seems impossible to account for the characteristics of these students.

In order to arrive at a preliminary idea of what it would mean for a school classroom to function as a knowledge-building community, let us draw some contrasts from other institutions that may be helpful as analogies. Most university departments are not knowledge-building communities, even though many of the faculty members may also belong to research centers, which are. Much of the attraction of research centers seems indeed to be that they are places where knowledge-building becomes a community endeavor. Departments are usually held together by their teaching functions. Research is an individual matter, although frequently obligatory—much like studying in school. People may pursue individual projects in research centers as well, but there are questions or objectives common to the individual efforts. What one person finds out matters to the others in a way that it usually does not in a department. Schools, clearly, are more like departments. What one student learns does not matter much to the others, even though everyone benefits from belonging to a class full of good learners.

Among industries, there are many that provide a relatively stable product or service. Maintaining quality and productivity are accordingly the major concerns of people on the operational side of the business. Although expert knowledge of many kinds may be involved, advancement of knowledge is likely to be incidental, not a collective goal that is pursued strategically and with deliberate investment of resources. It is quite a different matter in high-tech industries, where advancing the state of the art is essential for survival. Concerns for quality and productivity are high in these industries, too, but these concerns apply not only to the product but also to the activity that is generating advances in technology. Those involved may not think of what they are doing as building knowledge, but some of the more mature technology firms are finding it profitable to think of it in those terms. The engineers and scientists are not simply devising new products. They are also building up the knowledge that makes it possible to stay in the lead technologically. This knowledge may include design principles, strategies for tackling new problems, and deep understanding of the strengths and limitations of available technology. 'Corporate memory' is a term coming into use to refer to this collective, frequently unrecorded body of knowledge. Schools resemble stable industries, where there is a job to be done and the concern is with doing it well and efficiently. A notion such as 'corporate memory'—that this year's class should profit from and build upon what last year's class learned—would seem very odd in a school setting. But perhaps it is the setting that is odd, not the idea.

For families to function as knowledge-building communities is probably far from common. In fact, there is only anecdotal and inferential evidence that any at all do so. It is not enough that the parents themselves be active learners and that they encourage learning in their children. Little John Stuart Mill being quizzed on Latin by his father does not exemplify a knowledge-building family. The family that William and Henry James grew up in might do so. It is described by R. W. B. Lewis in *The Jameses*.[15] Such a family has a mental life. It need not be a mental life on the grand scale of the James household. The essential thing is that there is a collective pursuit of meaning and understanding, in which the children participate to the limits of their competence. A colleague who claims to have such a family said he realized it was working when, after a family discussion, his seven-year-old daughter said, "Let's summarize what we've figured out about this." One might hear an utterance like this at school, coming from a teacher. It would be a sign of intellectually above-par education going on. But even at best, one would not expect to hear such an utterance coming from a student.

In all three of these comparisons—with university units, with industries, and with families—what sets those that are knowledge-building communities apart is the investment of resources into the advancement of the group's knowledge. Thus they carry on an expert process at the group level that is engaged in progressively solving problems of knowledge. Organizations may be excellent and progressive in other ways, of course. We are not simply drawing a distinction between effective and ineffective enterprises. But a knowledge-building community develops expertise in that very activity. Thus, for a school to be a knowledge-building community would mean that expertise in the construction of knowledge characterized the school as a whole, the functioning entity that includes staff, students, and their joint activity.

What Makes Knowledge-Building Communities Work?
The Role of Progressive Discourse

When we talk to people about the idea of schools as knowledge-building communities, and even present evidence suggesting that it is possible, a common response is 'That's all right for students who are highly motivated' or 'It might work with children who come from intellectually stimulating homes. But what about . . . ?' And there follows some allusion to the great masses who have other things on their minds than the pursuit of knowledge. Behind these objections lies the quite valid recognition that there has to be an abundant source of energy to make a knowledge-building community work. The fallacy is to assume that this energy must come from the individual student's thirst for knowledge. Other people will buy the idea immediately, yet entertain the same fallacy, the difference being that they have extraordinary faith in children's natural curiosity.

It is safe to say that few research laboratories or technology firms would thrive if they had to depend solely on the natural curiosity of their research personnel. It is perhaps equally true that they could not thrive without it. But the point is that no successful organization, even when it is free to be highly selective in its recruitment, can afford to bank everything on its members' dedication to the selfless pursuit of knowledge. So why should we expect that of a school, which has to make do with whatever children arrive at the door?

Any community has to provide sufficient satisfactions of people's diverse motives that they will want to belong. Belonging means adapting, and in the case of a knowledge-building community, adaptation entails continual investment of personal resources in the advancement of knowledge. The last point is the tricky one. Social psychology, along with common knowledge, can tell us a great deal about what it takes for a group to be satisfying to its members, but what it takes for a group to be both satisfying and dynamic is problematic. In her study of sales teams, Gladstein found that familiar psychological principles (having to do with democratic leadership, open communication, and the like) did a good job of predicting how satisfied members were with their teams, but they were somewhat negatively related to how effective the teams were in selling.[16]

In all the learned disciplines, journal publications play a significant role in defining, guiding, and motivating work in the field. They are worth examining as a source of clues to how knowledge-building communities succeed in marshaling people's energies in ways that produce continual advancement of knowledge. The almost universal criterion for publication in a learned journal is that an article must represent an advancement in the field's knowledge. Thus, it is not enough to have done an experiment that honors all the methodological canons of the discipline. It must additionally be perceived by editors and reviewers as contributing somehow to progress.

People outside the academic world who are aware of the amount of effort academicians put into journal articles are sometimes amazed or even outraged to learn that the journals do not pay their contributors anything. How can they expect authors to do all that work for nothing? And how can the authors be so foolish as to allow their vanity to be exploited to that extent?

Of course, the editors are not paid either, nor the reviewers, who are the jurors of the publication process. They, along with the authors they deal with, are all voluntary collaborators in a time-consuming and laborious process which has as its main function to keep a discipline progressing along lines that the discipline collectively endorses. The journal system is full of imperfections, which are frequently pointed out and sometimes demonstrated empirically.[17] Peer review, generally regarded as superior to any other kind of selection procedure, is nevertheless a conservative force that can stifle progress; however, when a group of rebels feels that this is happening, their frequent recourse is to start a new journal. Discipline-based journals, despite their drawbacks, manage to harness an enormous amount of energy and get it working toward collective advance in knowledge, and so they surely hold a key to what makes knowledge-building communities work.

Cynics will quickly point out that a reason academicians put so much energy into journal publication is that all kinds of material benefits—hiring, promotion, tenure, merit pay, grants, and awards—are tied to it. It is certainly true, and much to the point under discussion, that there are motives besides dedication to one's discipline that drive people in the pursuit of journal publication. Two things should be noted about material incentives to publish, however. One is that academicians themselves are responsible for the ascendancy of journal publication as a criterion of performance; although administrators and regents may now back it up, they didn't originate the notion, nor are they the ones who decide what counts and for how much. Therefore, the use of material incentives to encourage publication should be considered as part of the workings of the academic disciplines, not as something external to them. The second point to recognize is that there are many people who actively pursue journal publication without material incentives. These include tenured professors already at the tops of their pay scales, scientists working in industry, and faculty members in the many colleges and universities where incentives to produce research are slight or even negative.

Among the other motives that are easy to spot in the knowledge-building communities known as academic disciplines, perhaps the most elemental one is *desire for recognition and respect from the people one regards as peers.* Related to this are *desire to have impact* (at least locally, on one's peers, but the desire can range upward from there to wanting to have an impact on the course of history) and *desire to participate in significant discourse.* Journal publication signals recognition and respect from peers and at least creates the illusion of impact and participation in grand discourse. But these are fairly basic motives, not limited to people with intellectual ambitions. They are clearly evident in school children. The most electrifying thing that it lies within the power of teachers to bring about is to get a classroom discussion started on a topic that the children care about. Then you will see children jostling to make themselves heard, to have their ideas recognized and respected, to influence one another, and to establish some kind of collective 'truth' that they feel good about. These are all the same motives that, for a select few, will some day be channeled into the discourse that advances a science or a scholarly discipline. But in school these motives seldom get channeled into anything more significant than the occasional gabfest.

There is much more to knowledge building than discourse. This is true in schools just as it is in the research laboratory. There has to be new information, usually furnished by research of some kind. But disciplines do not progress through the mere accretion of research findings. As Karl Popper has argued, discourse is the medium through which "objective knowledge", as he calls it, is formed, criticized, and amended. ('Objective' in Popper's sense doesn't mean free of bias; rather, it refers to knowledge that is 'out there' constituting a science or discipline, belonging to the culture rather than to the individual mind. It is what we have been referring to as 'formal knowledge'.) Discourse can also serve to motivate the research and the individual reflection that lie behind the successful functioning of a knowledge-building community. There is a continual cycling of new research findings into the discourse, where new questions and hypotheses are raised, which give direction to further research. Discipline-based journals serve this process, as do other kinds of discourse that go on in the disciplines— conferences, seminars, informal discussions, sometimes even keynote addresses.

Knowledge-building discourse is progressive. Its goal is not consensus but a provisional synthesis that those involved will recognize as an advance over what they understood before. Like progressive problem solving in general, it has no ceiling. There is always a higher-level formulation of issues which the current version of truth does not fully address. Thus to participate in knowledge-building discourse is to participate in the process of expertise; to be initiated into an ongoing discourse is to begin learning how to function as an expert in the domain of that discourse. Accordingly, if we want to have schools that produce experts, we need to have schools that support progressive knowledge-building discourse. The point of our excursion into the world of discipline-based journals was to show that there is more to knowledge-building discourse than simply having a topic that appeals to curiosity. There has to be an institution, a stable way of organizing behavior, so that the discourse satisfies a sufficient range of human motives that it will be sustained, that people will keep putting energy into its advancement.

There is plenty of discourse in schools, but it is radically different from what would characterize a knowledge-building community. Classroom studies over many decades show that most of the oral discourse can be characterized as 'recitation'.[18] When there are discussions that could be construed as building knowledge, whatever progressive character they have is given by the teacher. Socratic dialogue is the model, which means that the teacher, playing Socrates, is the only one who functions as an expert, leading the discussion to deeper levels. Transcripts of classroom discussion indicate that the basic unit, a typical session consisting simply of a chain of such units, is *teacher initiates, student responds, teacher verifies.*[19] Whatever this formula may represent, it is surely not a formula for developing students into progressive problem solvers.

Among behavioral scientists working on educational reform, an increasing number are focusing on changing the form and character of classroom discourse. Many, like ourselves, started out focusing on the individual students, with the idea of teaching them strategies for expertlike reading, writing, and problem solving. But the limited effects that could be got from even the best strategy instruction soon became apparent. If the purpose of reading is to be able to answer questions asked by the teacher, if the purpose of writing is to produce something the teacher will label as 'Good work!' and the purpose of problem solving is to get already-established right answers, then there is no reason to function like an expert. The optimal strategies will be routines that reliably achieve these limited purposes. There is no working to extend the limits of competence, no reformulating problems at higher levels. And, as we noted at the beginning of this chapter, it is pointless to attempt to translate the process of expertise into strategies and teach them. Schooling needs to be reconstituted so that functioning like an expert becomes a more natural, adaptive thing to do. Changing the nature of school discourse, removing the straightjacket of *teacher initiates, student responds, teacher verifies,* seems the obvious place to start. But where do we go from there? Can we establish a kind of discourse that functions like discourse in the learned disciplines, where it serves to motivate inquiry and transform its results into knowledge?

A New Model for Schooling

There is much talk at present about 'restructuring' schools and the need for breaking the mould. Industries are being asked to contribute millions to the New American Schools Development Corporation, whose purpose is to demonstrate new models. Promising ideas are sprouting, and we may expect some of them to come to flower in these demonstrations. Still, it would be an exaggeration to say that a major search is on to discover a third form of schooling, a form that is not merely another variation on either didactic or child-centered education. Most people seem rooted in the conviction that one or the other of these familiar approaches is basically right, and they are looking for ways to enhance or promote it. And then there is a lot of technobabble about artificial intelligence, virtual reality, multimedia, and networking, expressing a vague conviction that new technology itself will produce a transformation.

Yet, we see evidence that a third model is beginning to take shape. There is no agreed-upon name as yet, no organized movement, only a rather loose consensus about general principles. However, the term we have been using, 'knowledge-building communities', captures much of what is common to the various experiments and proposals. Other terms in use are "communities of learners and thinkers" and "reflective communities".[20] In all these variations, the central idea carried by the term 'community' is that schooling should become a collective effort to understand the world. The idea sounds so innocent that it is easy to miss its quite revolutionary implications for the nature of schooling. That is why we have gone to such lengths in this chapter to show what is wrong with the way schools presently deal with knowledge and how different they are from real knowledge-building communities of the kinds found in research centers, modern industries, and some families.

Schooling according to the knowledge-building community model has the following distinguishing characteristics:

> 1.   There is sustained study of topics in depth, sometimes over a period of months, rather than superficial coverage.

2. The focus is on problems rather than on categories of knowledge: not 'the heart' but 'how does the heart work?'

3. Inquiry is driven by students' questions. The teacher helps students formulate better questions and encourages them to reformulate questions at higher levels as inquiry proceeds.

4. Explaining is the major challenge. Students are encouraged to produce their own theories to account for facts and to criticize one another's theories by confronting them with facts.

5. Although teachers pay close attention to how each student is doing, the day-to-day focus is progress toward collective goals of understanding and judgment rather than on individual learning and performance.

6. There is little schoolwork of the conventional kind, where the students are working individually but all doing the same thing. More typically, students work in small groups; each group has a different task related to the central topic and plans how to distribute work among its members.

7. Discourse is taken seriously. Students are expected to respond to one another's work and are taught how to do so in helpful, supportive ways.

8. The teacher's own knowledge does not curtail what is to be learned or investigated. Teachers can contribute what they know to the discourse, but there are other sources of information.

9. The teacher remains the leader, but the teacher's role shifts from standing outside the learning process and guiding it to participating actively in the learning process and leading by virtue of being a more expert learner.

Clearly, this approach to schooling is oriented toward expertlike learners. Students are expected to formulate their own problems of understanding and to pursue them in a progressive manner, formulating new higher-level problems as they go. Yet there are dramatic demonstrations of this process going on in a second-grade mathematics class composed of traditionally low-achieving students and in elementary social studies, with children who had been segregated because of behavior problems.[21] It isn't presupposed that students are expertlike learners to begin with. Considerable work may be required to get them there. The idea, however, is to create a classroom activity structure in which active knowledge-building is the natural, adaptive thing to do.

Although in principle the knowledge-building community model can function with ordinary classroom resources, most of the people experimenting with it have found computer-based technology important for maintaining the kind of information flow that the model requires. Computers can give each student access to what other students are doing and an opportunity to comment on it. They can provide access to new information through electronic knowledge bases, simulations of natural systems, and linkages to students and experts outside their immediate classroom. We have designed what is presently the only system specifically designed to perform all these functions in a school environment. Called CSILE (Computer Supported Intentional Learning Environment), it is built around a community database created by the students. Using networked microcomputers, a number of students can be simultaneously creating text or graphical notes to add to the database, searching existing notes, commenting on other students' notes, or organizing notes into more complex informational structures.[22]

The community database serves as an objectification of a group's advancing knowledge, much like the accumulating issues of a scholarly journal. In fact, the system supports a publication process similar to that of scholarly journals. Students produce notes of various kinds and frequently revise them. When they think they have a note that makes a solid contribution to the knowledge base in some area, they can mark it as a 'candidate for publication' and subsequently complete a form that indicates, among other things, what they believe the distinctive contribution of their note is. After a review process (typically by other students, with final clearance by the teacher), the note becomes identified as 'published'. It appears in a different font and students searching the database may, if they wish, restrict their search to published notes on the topic they designate. At the end of the school year, a class can decide on a selection of notes to remain in the database for the benefit of classes that come after them. Thus, as in the real world, each generation does not have to rediscover everything that the previous generation found out, but can instead attempt to go beyond it.

Two examples, both involving fifth- and sixth-grade children, will give an idea of the system in action. In a unit on ecology, one group worked on the topic of fossil fuels. In a conventional class one would expect a book-like production that contained sections on the various fossil fuels, with information about their sources, supply, properties, uses, and so on, mostly taken directly from an encyclopedia. This group started with a kitchen scene that one of the students had created as a CSILE note. They took as their challenge to identify the uses of fossil fuels represented in an ordinary kitchen. Different students tackled different parts of the kitchen, researching such matters as the composition of plastic wrap, the generation of electricity, the origin of natural gas, and the manufacture of Kitty Litter. This information was used in creating subsidiary notes consisting of pictures of the relevant kitchen object with text explaining how fossil fuels were involved. The system permits linking such notes in a hierarchical fashion, so that a reader could start with the kitchen scene and, for instance, click on the refrigerator. This would open a picture of the interior of the refrigerator; clicking on the various items in the refrigerator would bring up pictures and text presenting the fossil fuel information. The result was a museum-like demonstration that dramatized the extent to which virtually every detail of daily life involves some dependence on fossil fuels. This is by no means deep science, but the conventional treatment of such topics is even less so. What can be claimed is that the children were using scientific information to make more sense of their world, rather than simply reproducing the information, and that they were engaged in an effort to advance the state of knowledge in their group and class. That is the essential idea of a knowledge-building community.

The second example illustrates more clearly the progressive character of knowledge-building and thus points more directly toward the development of expertise. This incident occurred spontaneously and was not even known to the teacher until a researcher came upon it while exploring the student-produced database in CSILE. In the course of work on a biology unit, one student had entered a note reporting that sponges have three ways of reproducing. This fact caught the fancy of other students who came upon the note through database searches, and there followed a series of twelve notes and comments dealing with why nature would have contrived to provide sponges with such an array of options. Plausible conjectures were offered about the value of back-up systems and the survival of a species unable to defend itself. One student, however, kept raising the question in comments to others: If three ways of reproducing are better than one, why don't other animals have them too? This is an illustration of progressive problem solving in the construction of knowledge. The solution to the first problem—why three ways?—gives rise to a higher-level problem that raises deeper issues about evolution. The answer that was finally proposed to the second question drew upon an idea that has figured prominently in evolutionary theory of recent decades: structural constraints on evolutionary possibilities. By going deeper into the study of reproduction, a student came to the insight that it is because they are structurally so simple that sponges are able to reproduce by budding and regeneration in addition to sexual reproduction. Higher animals are too complex for this. As the student put it, "A stomach, lungs, a brain, and a heart, etc., could not grow on your finger if it was cut off."

Experimental versions of the knowledge-building community approach vary considerably in amount of structure and teacher direction but they are all committed to moving toward a self-maintaining knowledge-building community in the classroom. Evaluations to date indicate that individual achievement, as conventionally measured, does not suffer. In fact, these students do better on standardized tests in reading, language, and vocabulary. They greatly surpass students in ordinary classrooms on measures of depth of learning and reflection, awareness of what they have learned or need to learn, and in understanding of learning itself.[23] What most impresses teachers and observers alike, however, is what the students are able to do collectively. As the above examples suggest, they seem to be functioning beyond their years, tackling problems and constructing knowledge at levels that one simply does not find in ordinary schools, regardless of the calibre of students they enroll. Even though, in any given class, only a minority of the students will actually be functioning as expertlike learners, there is a genuine sense in which the group as a whole does so. That is really all one expects of a progressive science or discipline, and so it is perhaps all that should be expected of a knowledge-building community in the classroom.

It might still be objected that all this is pretend, that the students are not really advancing the frontiers of knowledge but spending a lot of time conjecturing about questions that could have been answered straight away by a knowledgeable teacher. Many educators would concede this point and try to justify the practice as improving the students' thinking skills. But that is a feeble rejoinder and one that misses the main point. The students are not absorbed in their pursuit of scientific questions because they enjoy the mental exercise. They think the questions really matter, and they are right.[24]

The fact that someone out there already knows the answer to the question that is puzzling you does not diminish the importance of the question; it only diminishes the importance of your achievement in answering it. Finding the answer will not advance the world's knowledge, but it may significantly advance the knowledge of your immediate community. If the answer is one that involves an unfamiliar concept, theory, or line of thought, then even if you are told the answer by an authority, you still do not have the answer. You do not have the answer until you have produced the mental construction within which the answer makes sense and coheres with what you already know. This is important work, the kind of work that builds expert knowledge. Conventional schooling, whether of the didactic or the child-centered variety, does not support students in doing this kind of work.

The computer technology that enables students to share knowledge with one another, as in CSILE, is rapidly being extended to give students access to the great bodies of information now being stored on compact discs, videodiscs, and the like, and also access to live experts. Much of this technology development, guided by a commonsense epistemology inadequate to the task, is proceeding without thought to deeper educational issues. In principle this greatly expanded access to knowledge resources should be all to the good, but unless schools can be restructured into communities that actually work to build their own knowledge from those resources, the technology will be largely wasted.

Prospects for Restructuring Education

The basic principles of a knowledge-building community model—as listed, for instance, in the preceding section—are already endorsed by most educators. The trouble is that the principles get attached to a didactic model or a child-centered educational model that proves inadequate for carrying them into practice. On paper, schools following the didactic model have long lists of cognitive and even spiritual objectives; it is just that in practice they end up focusing on working for grades. On paper, child-centered schools look much like the knowledge-building community model; it is just that in practice they tend to settle into a pattern of hobby-like pursuits in which academically unmotivated students spend their days on nonacademic things.

In short, the kind of schooling that educators favor in principle is quite congruent with the process of expertise. But the normal conditions of school life create a press toward types of schooling that are easily manageable under those conditions.

The didactic model and the child-centered model seem to have been the only two that fit those conditions. The only successful school reforms we are aware of have involved shifting from one model to the other. Efforts to introduce some model different from the basic two may succeed for a while under charismatic leadership, but eventually things subside to either a didactic or a child-centered model, like the ball in a pinball machine that is kept in action for a time by the skill and vigilance of the player but that eventually finds its way into a channel from which there is no return. The two basic models are self-maintaining systems. This means, broadly speaking, that they internally generate the fuel that keeps them going and the constraints that keep them stable. If a third model is to succeed, it will also have to be self-maintaining.

In a self-maintaining social system, continual effort does not have to be exerted to make the system function. People pursue their individual goals and yet the system as a whole works to make it possible for them to achieve their goals. That is how it is with the village market, so dear to libertarian economists. That is also how it is with a thriving science or scholarly discipline and with a well-functioning classroom. In an ill-functioning classroom the teacher is visibly laboring to maintain whatever order and productive activity exist. Burn-out and early retirement are in store. In a well-functioning classroom of the didactic variety, the teacher may be busy teaching, but the students are busy paying attention, doing their exercises, and so on. The impression is that everyone is doing what they want to be doing and it is working. It is the same in a well-functioning child-centered classroom, except that the teacher is less prominent and the activities are more diverse. In both cases, quite a bit of work may have gone into getting the social system up to the point where it is self-maintaining, and the teacher has to be continually alert to things going wrong (no system is perfectly self-maintaining as long as it is composed of imperfect human beings). But the effort required of the teacher is well within tolerable limits.

Any viable system of schooling has to be accommodated to such hard realities as the need to preserve order in a setting where children outnumber teachers by 25 or 40 to one. One way to do this is by regimentation, with routinized tasks for the student and a teacher in firm control. That is the traditional system, and from it follow the didactic role of the teacher, the cursory curriculum, in which a certain amount of time is allocated to a topic, students all performing the same work, and hence perennial difficulties of coping with individual differences in aptitudes and dispositions. Another way is to provide a range of activity options and a set of constraints, within which children may pretty much do as they wish. That is the framework within which child-centered education functions. Neither of these systems is as simple as these descriptions suggest. The motives and the rewards, the checks and balances that keep things going in an orderly, pleasant, and seemingly productive manner are extremely complex, and it requires skilled effort for teachers to manage them. But the two familiar models do work, insofar as they enable schooling to go on. The trouble is that they do not produce the kind of education we need.

We might say that the two familiar models of schooling are well adapted to their ecological niche. In order for a third model to flourish, the niche will have to change in some significant way, so that the old forms of adaptation do not work so well and the new form has a survival advantage. It appears to us that the big hope for advanced technology in education lies here. It does not lie in bringing new kinds of information and experience to the minds of students, desirable as that might be. It lies in altering the conditions to which the social structure of the classroom, particularly the structure of discourse, must be adapted.

When CSILE is put into use in a classroom, with one computer to every two to four students, certain changes take place immediately. The teacher at the front of the classroom no longer functions as the hub around which the whole educational dialogue rotates. A new channel of communication has opened, which runs concurrently with other kinds of discourse, and which the teacher may enter into but cannot regulate on a minute-to-minute basis. Communication is asynchronous, which means that one student's note or comment is received by others at a later time. This has two effects. For the students it means that they must express themselves in a more literate manner, because they do not have the immediate context to make clear what they are talking about. For the teacher it means that work cannot proceed in a lock-step manner and is generally harder to pace. As a result, it is actually easier to devote long stretches of time to treating a topic in depth rather than to move rapidly through a survey, as the traditional curriculum tends to do.

Of course, technology alone cannot turn a classroom into a knowledge-building community. That is a radical transformation. As we have argued, it requires a different epistemology from the commonsense one that has shaped schooling as we know it. But teachers' thinking is already tending in that direction, and it is not difficult to win converts. The hard part is to translate the notion of a knowledge-building community into a form of practice that does not downslide into one or the other conventional form. At present the most serious obstacles are at the top, with the government leaders, the educational bureaucracies, the activists from the business community, and many different pressure groups that try to influence educational policy. They all have a fair idea of what is wrong, but no vision of any real alternative to the forms of schooling now being judged as failures.

Conclusion

We have tried to show how the conventional approaches to education, both the didactic and the child-centered, are inadequate for fostering expertise. Neither one encourages progressive problem solving, the reinvestment of mental resources into tackling problems at higher levels, the working at the edge of one's competence, the continual effort to build more complete knowledge. We could now turn the argument around and say that an understanding of expertise would help a great deal in envisioning a new kind of education. The seemingly unresolvable conflict between didactic and child-centered approaches to education arises in large part from the difficulty of reconciling education as preparation for adult roles and education viewed as an aspect of young people's lives. An unenlightened concern with expertise only intensifies the dilemma. We must prepare students for their future roles, and therefore turn up the didactic burners, but at the same time we must produce people who are creative and willing to take responsibility for their own competence. But understanding expertise as a process that can go on at any age, in any situation that provides scope for progressive problem solving, removes the dilemma. It is possible to have schooling that encourages students to function as experts in the here and now—not in the sense of performing at the level society looks for in experts but in the sense of pursuing similar goals in similar ways. That is what the knowledge building community model of schooling offers. It is the best preparation we can currently imagine for future expert roles and it is at the same time simply a better way of living than schools have previously been able to provide for young people.

Chapter Eight
Toward an Expert Society

Through the preceding chapters there has been gradual movement from an inside, psychological view of expertise toward a
more social perspective. We began, as psychologists generally
do, by regarding expertise as something exceptional that needs
explaining, and we concurred with most recent investigators in
locating the explanation in what experts know that nonexperts
do not. We then pressed beyond that explanation to ask how
expert knowledge comes about. This led to the pivotal idea of
a *process* of expertise, a process that generates expert knowledge through the continual reinvestment of mental resources
into addressing problems at higher levels. But this is a very
general process, not necessarily confined to an individual. In
the case of a youthful musician or athlete, for instance, the

process may be sustained through the joint efforts of child and parent. No matter how it is carried out, it is an effortful process that typically depends for support on an expert subculture. But in an expert subculture, the process of expertise is not exceptional. It is what people normally do. This shift to a more social perspective became central to the approach we have taken to education. If schools are to become more effective in developing expertise, they need to become communities in which the process of expertise is normal rather than exceptional.

A logical next step is to consider the possibility of a whole society in which expertise is normal rather than exceptional. That is the purpose of this final chapter. We do this with some hesitancy. In moving from an inside-the-head to a social view of expertise, we move farther and farther away from what, as psychologists, we are best equipped to do. The idea of an expert society raises issues of social planning, social controls, economic growth, equity, labor relations and the nature of work, quality of life, and political questions as well. Each of these issues has its complexities, which, as relative novices, we can scarcely hope to do justice to separately, let alone work them all together into a coherent analysis. But of course social analysts suffer from their limitations as well. One of these limitations, as we have noted before, is a weak conception of expertise, which confuses it with specialization or treats it merely as a social status. The idea of an expert society makes no sense whatever in these terms. If there is promise in the notion of an expert society, it will require a great variety of scientific and practical expertise being brought together in a substantial rethinking of social issues. Obviously we cannot do that here. The most we can hope to do is clarify the idea and show that it does have promise.

The starting premise for exploring the idea of an expert society is a belief that the modern world sorely needs a better way of taking advantage of the human capacity for expertise. The present role of experts is nothing that has been planned or forced upon us. It is something that has been developing since the earliest days of civilization, moved along by the division of labor, the rise of crafts, the advance of technology.

Considered one at a time, the experts of today are not much different in their social roles from the coopers and cabinet-makers, the midwives and horse trainers of a pre-industrial town. But considered in the mass, they give an impression that things have gotten out of hand. Experts have penetrated too many societal functions; the technologies they manage are too powerful, too far-reaching in their effects. And so there are continual calls for restraints and for countercultural moves that will return more autonomy to ordinary folks.

About restraints we can say the same thing that was said about the role of experts. Looked at individually, each one may seem proper, but in the aggregate something is wrong. It makes sense to restrain surgeons by requirements of informed consent. It makes sense to restrain dam builders by requiring environmental impact assessments. But overall, it seems unfortunate that society's main way of dealing with its resources of expertise should be through the application of restraints. Surely there must be some more positive way. As for empowering the lay public, by putting them on boards of corporations, for instance, it is hard to see this as anything but another form of regulation, which may have merit but which has the same negative quality.

Obviously controls are necessary, and they have to extend beyond the traditional controls against doing direct harm to others. Indeed, the trouble seems to be that we are trying to struggle along with the common law principle that you can do anything you want with what you happen to own or control, subject only to the constraints necessary to protect the rights of others. The potential consequences of actions taken by a giant petrochemical company, for instance, are too vast and long-range to be managed by such a feeble principle. Yet the only recognized alternative, central governmental planning, has failed so dramatically in Eastern Europe that the very idea survives only in remnants.

The ideal is easy to name, hard to imagine. It is a society in which expertise flourishes and is naturally used for the common good. It is a society in which constraints serve to create opportunities rather than to diminish them. And where the hens lay soft-boiled eggs, you may say. We have reason to be cynical about any notion that depends on human nature being other than it is. However, in the last chapter we noted how it is possible to have successful sciences, and successful schools modeled after them, which do not depend on individual dedication to the selfless pursuit of knowledge. It is possible for a collective to make advances toward ideal goals, even though the goals of the individuals are various. Is it not conceivable that a whole society could function in this way, so that it advanced toward ideal societal goals, enlisting the varied expertise of its members in this effort, without depending either on central controls or on the ideals being replicated in every individual? That is the possibility we want to probe here, using as an instrument the notion of a process of expertise that can go on above the individual level.

The Nature of an Expert Society

The idea of an expert society is simply the idea of a process of expertise going on that involves the society as a whole. The kind of school envisaged in the preceding chapter, one that functions as a knowledge-building community, is a miniature version of an expert society. It is not a society dominated by experts, which is the image recent social criticism primes us to imagine. In an important sense it is the opposite. The teacher, who is the designated expert in the conventional classroom, becomes less dominant when a classroom is transformed into a knowledge-building community. This is not because the teacher's authority has been reduced or because the teacher's skill has been rendered less functional. It is because expertise now characterizes the whole schooling process, encompassing the students as well as the teacher. The teacher's expertise, whatever its strengths and limitations, is assimilated into the larger expertise of the classroom as a functioning social unit. That is the essential idea of an expert society.

The knowledge-building school community is a good model to keep in mind, because it makes it obvious that an expert society is not a society in which everybody is an expert. In an expert society one would expect individual expertise to flourish and thus to become less of a rarity, but there is no expectation that everyone would be an expert. For one thing, the norm would keep changing. Expecting everyone to be an expert is like expecting everyone to be above average.

It is not even necessary that everyone be engaged in the process of expertise. The idea, rather, is that this process should characterize the way the society itself functions. In this it is similar to democracy. We call a society democratic if it functions according to democratic processes. This it can do even if a number of its members are not personally inclined toward democracy. In the preceding chapter we discussed the workings of expert subcultures such as sciences and scholarly disciplines, laboratories and work groups, and classrooms that function as knowledge-building communities. In all of these, a process of progressive problem solving goes on, to which all or most people can contribute, without necessarily manifesting an expert process in their own work.

Generalizing from the characteristics of expert subcultures that already exist, the ideal characteristics of an expert society can be identified:

> **1. Ideal goals.** At every level of society there would be ideal goals that are not ultimately attainable but that permit demonstrable progress. Such goals are currently found in science and technology and in professions—goals such as understanding the formation of the earth, perfecting human-computer interface, and achieving a healthy populace. In an expert society, goals of the professions would be goals of the society, no longer the special province of the professions. There could be other goals, such as promoting civility and beautifying the environment, which are not currently the province of any particular profession and which are not so centrally dependent on specialized competence, but which nevertheless have ideal characteristics.

2.   Work as contribution. Individuals see their work as contributions to progress on these goals. Henry Adams, reflecting on the construction of the great gothic cathedrals, supposed that a stone mason, asked what he was doing, would not have replied, 'I am carving a stone.' He would have said, 'I am building a cathedral.' Considering that construction often went on for more than a century, building a cathedral was in practical terms an ideal goal. Adams was speculating, of course, but his intuition seems plausible: that progress toward ideal goals cannot be sustained by decomposing the task into discrete jobs that are performed with no sense of higher purpose.

3.   Intrinsic rewards. Rewards for contributions are intrinsic to the social process. This would be true of both material and psychic rewards. Subsistence agriculture has this character—work is rewarded both by the satisfaction of seeing things grow and by food in the belly. So does work in the arts (slight as the material rewards may often be). Contributing to the production of a play is rewarded by artistic satisfactions, esteem of fellow cast members, and, one hopes, by income from the box office that is a direct consequence of progress that has been made toward ideal goals of the production. This is in contrast to salary and wage labor, which as Marxists put it is purchased at a price, so that its role in the industrial drama is more like that of the nails and canvas than it is like that of the actors or set-builders.

4.   Emergent goals. Higher-level or more elaborated goals emerge naturally from contributions to progress. Ideally, goals would not be legislated from above nor thrashed out through a political process. Like the goals of the sciences, they would be emergents of progressive problem solving, only made explicit after they had appeared. Another way of saying this is that progress itself provides the higher-level goals or problems that guide further progress—as occurs now in the advance of scientific knowledge.

5. Sharing of expertise. Within professions and other expert subcultures, the norm is for expertise to be shared rather freely but to be withheld from outsiders. There are exceptions to both parts of this statement, of course, but the general expectation is that if you are consulted by a colleague or by a student in your field you will not only give them the benefit of your expert knowledge but will show a willingness to convey it to them.[1] Ideally, in an expert society everyone would be regarded as more or less of a colleague and thus would come under the sharing part of the norm rather than the withholding part.

One is immediately tempted to ask how, if at all, these characteristics can be achieved. Let us not rush into that question, however. It is worth taking time to consider how different these characteristics are from those that usually figure as goals in social planning. Social goals usually represent desirable stable states of affairs: an end to poverty and other social ills, domestic tranquility, meaningful work, world peace, sustainable consumption, and so on. The characteristics listed above are of quite a different order. They represent processes rather than end states. They suggest a dynamic society, a society that is going someplace, although where it is going is only vaguely specifiable. Values such as peace, prosperity, and equity may figure just as prominently in an expert society as in present-day societies; but extending beyond these values is a commitment to unforeseen goals that emerge from the social dynamics.

Most social goals are like traditional ideas of heaven; they project a state of unchanging bliss, an end to striving. Equity, the withering away of the state, a chicken in every microwave, satori—the goals differ, depending on one's philosophy, but they all have this terminal quality. No doubt this reflects a deep human need. Probably most of the workaholics and runners of the rat race imagine someday getting enough on top of things that they can settle down and experience bliss. A long-running advertisement tells us we can do this by age 55 if we invest in the right insurance policy. The closest thing to a dynamic social value is 'lifelong learning', but we suspect that in most people's minds this reduces to the image of settling down with a good book. To put it in the terms most relevant to our topic, human goals usually project an end to problem solving.

The major exception is science. No modern scientist would see as the goal a state of everything having been found out and there being no more problems to solve. Scientists are people, too, of course, and so in their own lives they may aspire to a state of problem-free bliss. But in their careers as scientists it is not that way. For most of the scientists we know, their idea of heaven on earth would be freedom from all impediments to getting on with their research—no more grant proposals to write, no more committees to serve on, just lots of time and money and eager graduate students. It is this more dynamic idea of heaven that we are proposing for society as a whole.

Quality of Life

One very natural response to the idea of an expert society is that it does not sound like much fun. One tends to think of expertise in connection with work, and so an expert society sounds as if it might be all business. But on several grounds, this is the wrong way to think about expertise in relation to quality of life. The topic is a very large one, with many different lines of thought worth pursuing. In the present context, where we are only trying to get some thinking started about the possibility of an expert society, it is premature to go very deeply into the quality of life issue, which is surely one of the most speculative. Instead, we will simply present a series of *aperçus* in list form.

> • Science fiction and utopian fiction alike fail miserably at the imaginative construction of ways of life. In science fiction of the 1950s, the attitudes and ways of life portrayed are those of the 1950s, regardless of what remote century the story is set in. Human beings are apparently quite incapable of imagining a way of life much different

from what has been experienced. Hence, we will not know what life is like in an expert society until it has come about.

• Of course people do not want to be solving problems all the time. They want problem-free leisure. But it takes progressive problem solving at the societal level in order to have safe parks to stroll in, carefree transportation, and all the other things that make such leisure possible. An expert society should be able to do that better.

• To keep the quality of life issue in perspective, one must keep in mind that the nonexpert life is not necessarily one of comfort and wholeness. In today's world, the experienced nonexpert is likely to be signing up for workshops on stress management. For everyone, changes due to new technology, new job demands, unemployment, break-ups of personal or work relationships, and so on threaten and sometimes shatter their established routines. For people who fashion their lives around progressive problem solving, such changes are less disruptive and they are often turned into opportunities. Changed conditions mean changed constraints, but the process of expertise is geared to incorporating new constraints into problem formulations.

• There are overworked and driven experts, but recall that the two we have used as exemplars in an earlier chapter—Willie the fixer and Margot the teacher—are both unhurried individuals, and Willie in particular shows a talent for getting people to slow down to his pace rather than his speeding up to theirs.

• In an expert society, where expertise is pervasively supported by the ordinary processes of social life, it should take less effort and strain to pursue expertise than it does in contemporary society—just as it takes less effort to maintain civility and charity in a community where those are normal than it does in a community where they are exceptional.

• The idea of taking a progressive problem-solving approach to living one's life is far from new. Oriental religions have represented it explicitly in a series of stages or levels that one must go through on the way to perfection.

• It might be objected that the eastern religions do not generally advocate rational problem solving—that Zen, for instance, calls for turning it off. But who said problem solving must be rational? Problem solving means finding a path toward a goal when none is known in advance. That description seems to fit the search for spiritual enlightenment as well as it does the search for the answer to a mathematical puzzle.

• Most people, however, would not want to give their whole life over to progressive problem solving, whether the problems are of a spiritual or a more earthly kind. There is a need for balance, which has been recognized in one way or other by practically everyone who has philosophized about the conduct of life. One part of this could be conceived of as a balance between striving for progress and enjoying or enduring things as they are.

• Attaining a balance between striving and letting things be is itself a problem that has taxed wisdom throughout the ages. Kitto, in *The Greeks*, argues that the reason the ancient Greeks put so much emphasis on balance was not that they excelled at it but that it was so difficult for them.[2]

Bringing Wisdom into Progress

The idea of an expert society is closely tied to the idea of progress. An expert society is going somewhere under its own steam. It is not merely trying to solve problems but is trying to build on its successes in order to address enduring problems at continually higher levels. Yet it is not a managed society, with a central authority deciding which way things should go. Progress *emerges* from the opportunities created by earlier progress—as it does in the sciences, which make disciplined and sometimes dramatic progress without centralized authority.

Such talk of progress is likely to sound naive to some, distasteful to others. It is indicative of the troubled nature of these times that progress has begun to be treated as a social problem itself rather than as a synonym for things getting better. Christopher Lasch[3] has provided the most apocalyptic treatment of the topic, but the idea has started to come up in otherwise quite moderate and optimistic discussions. There are two main concerns. One is that progress has come to be an article of dumb faith for the masses. People believe it is inevitable and will eventually solve all problems. Poverty? Progress will take care of it. Running out of energy sources? Progress will turn up new ones. And so on. Thus faith in progress acts as an opiate, dulling the urge actually to do anything about the world's evils.[4] The other concern is that progress is like a continually accelerating engine that will eventually destroy itself. Progress keeps demanding more goods, more materials, more energy, at an increasing rate such that all curves extrapolate out to disaster.

In circles where postmodernism flourishes, progress has come to be regarded as another of those Enlightenment ideas that ought to be buried, along with the conquest of nature and the pursuit of objective truth. There are suggestions that we should return to the more ancient idea that history goes in cycles and that we should begin dedicating ourselves to making do with what we have. In essence, we are being asked to give up the most powerful intellectual tool of Western civilization, the "method of invention", as Whitehead called it—the method of generating progress intentionally through organized problem-solving effort.

There is a comic-book simplicity to the way progress has been treated by culture critics from Jacques Ellul onward. Progress is an infernal machine running out of control and *experts are part of the machine.* Bringing the machine under control thus means controlling the experts, a view that has given rise to notions such as 'counterexpertise'—common folks organizing to oppose the amoral experts—and to the popular slogan that today's problems are too important to leave to the experts. Although there is some sense in this view, it is so radically unpromising that most critics who espouse it find themselves in despair.[5]

The alternative is not to paint a rosier picture of progress but rather to reconceptualize progress and its relation to expertise. If expertise is viewed as a process that may be carried out not only by individuals but by groups, the essence of the process being continual reinvestment in addressing problems at higher levels, then we can begin to see a way past the culture critics' despair. The relation between progress and expertise is even closer than the critics sense. They are different aspects of the same process. Progress, we might say, is simply the process of expertise viewed from the standpoint of overall result. Thus, experts are not the servants of some mythic force that is greater than they are. They are just people going about their work in a certain way that is highly productive of results which consumers typically view as progress but sometimes see as things running out of control. There is no suprapersonal engine of progress against which it is vain to struggle. Wisdom, far-sightedness, and human values can influence progress to the extent that these can be brought into the entirely human process of expertise.

To conclude that all we need are wiser experts into whose hands we may entrust the future would be even more simplistic than the infernal machine notion. Better education might give people more of a start toward wisdom, but effective wisdom is going to have to be acquired on the job. We need to consider how the process of expertise might be carried out so that it produces wisdom and not just further specialized expertise and how the social organization of expert processes might be changed so that the public interest is represented in the process itself rather than standing outside it as a watchdog. In short, we need *active wisdom*, which manifests itself in the way problems are framed and solved, rather than a passive wisdom that deals only in generalities and after-the-fact judgments.

One of today's profounder ironies is that the people who are telling us that we should make peace with nature and stop trying to control it are often the same ones who are telling us that we must control technology. The futility of controlling the one has much in common with the futility of trying to exert hierarchical control over the other.

It is not because technology has a mind of its own, any more than that there is a life force in nature that defies our efforts at mastery. Nature and technology share two characteristics that make both of them controllable only in the short term, frustrating long-term plans. Both of them are so complex in the interactions of their variables that they exceed rational control. The current uncertainties about global warming illustrate this on a large scale, but the same complexity exists on a small scale in such matters as nutrition. You can't be sure what will happen as a result of taking an iron supplement, for instance, because it depends on interactions with other substances in your diet, influenced by factors in your own constitution. In technology, robotics teaches us the lesson about complexity that exceeds rational control in two ways. The early assumption about robot servants was much as portrayed in Woody Allen's film, *Sleeper*— that it would be fairly easy to build robots that could shuffle around the house and handle things but difficult to get them to behave intelligently. It now appears that virtually the reverse is true. For an artificial system to exercise logic is within modern capabilities, but shuffling around the house and handling things without continual mishap has turned out to be forbiddingly complex and impossible for a machine that works by rational procedures. A machine that tries to follow a plan for accomplishing some simple chore and to revise the plan when things go amiss proves to be too slow-witted and inflexible to succeed. The secret for the robot, as well as for the human being trying to cope with the uncertainties and complexities of the real world, is not better long-range planning but an ability to respond to immediate circumstances in ways that achieve progress toward goals.[6]

The other characteristic shared by nature and technology is that they proceed in a bottom-up, opportunistic fashion. Every change creates new problems and opportunities, the response to which creates new problems and opportunities, with unpredictability mounting at each step. Thus, as biologists remind us, evolution cannot be predicted. Looking backward, evolution seems purposeful, giving rise to the Lamarkian notion that ducks grew webbed feet through the effort to swim. But looking forward, who can predict the evolutionary effect of global warming, which can create new opportunities for some organisms, new difficulties for others. Looking backward at computer technology, we can see what looks like rational, step-by-step progress toward such contemporary phenomena as virtual reality and desktop publishing. But in 1950, these would surely be among the last things that a computer engineer would have seen as objectives. This is what makes it seem as if technological progress has a mind of its own, but the only mind involved is in the brains of the participants, and they are busy taking advantage of the opportunities present to them.

How, then, can wisdom be brought to bear on such an uncontrollable, unpredictable process? How can there be wise progress when progress has no destination? These questions bring us back to consideration of expertise. The problem of wise progress is basically the same as the problem of creative expertise, except on a grander scale. Creativity, we argued in Chapter 5, is progressive problem solving under risky conditions. Whether it is painting a picture or pursuing a research program or playing a game of chess, one cannot be sure how things will end up or what effect immediate choices will have on the eventual outcome. Creative experts are ones who make choices that turn out in retrospect to have been good ones, in the light of outcomes that were not clearly foreseeable at the time the choices were made. No extrasensory gift is implied, however. Creative experts make their fortunate choices on the basis of knowledge of *promisingness,* largely impressionistic knowledge, accumulated through extensive experience in trying to achieve creative goals.

Choices that show wisdom are, by analogy, choices that turn out in retrospect to have been wise ones, in light of socially and culturally relevant outcomes that were not clearly foreseeable at the time the choices were made. That may seem like a strange way to define wisdom, but try defining it some other way that takes realistic account of the uncertainties of progress. As with creativity, promisingness is the pivotal consideration. A wise choice is one that shows promise of outcomes that are socially desirable, consonant with humane values, and so on. Knowledge of promisingness is all that can distinguish wisdom from good intentions. Such knowledge, we must assume, is acquired like other knowledge of promisingness, through continual efforts to make wise choices and learning the indicators through successes and failures.

If this conception of wisdom is correct, then wisdom is not separable from expertise. Active wisdom, indeed, is a variety of expertise. Knowledge of promisingness can only come from deep and long immersion in progressive problem solving within a domain. If creative experts are just experts who have learned from being more venturesome, wise experts are just experts who have learned from exercising more concern with human values and far-reaching consequences.

But what of the popular image of wisdom, embodied in the elderly sage who is not much of an expert at anything other than sound judgment? These may be wise experts in the sense we have been proposing, whose expert knowledge is of human relations or domestic life. But there are also people who acquire a reputation for wise judgment on matters related to technological progress and social change but who are not involved in the disciplines that are producing the change and are not experts in them. Some, indeed, base their wisdom on a knowledge of ancient texts. To press the matter further, there are probably millions of people, including most of those who will be reading these lines, who feel that they have wisdom to offer on such matters as television, politics, law enforcement, transportation, medical care, environmental protection, and so on, and who feel that their wisdom derives partly from the fact that they are not immersed in the work of these domains and can view them from a less compromised perspective.

Certainly, nonspecialist wisdom exists. Culture critics of today, like prophets in earlier times, exercise it in telling us where we have gone astray and in redirecting our attention to higher values. But such wisdom is not the same as the active wisdom we hope to find in the people who generate progress. It helps in making judgments but not in creating solutions. It helps us understand where we are heading, but not what we can do to change our course. As Neil Postman said near the end of *Technopoly: The Surrender of Culture to Technology,*

> Anyone who practices the art of cultural criticism must endure being asked, What is the solution to the problems you describe? Critics almost never appreciate this question, since, in most cases, they are entirely satisfied with themselves for having posed the problems and, in any event, are rarely skilled in formulating practical suggestions about anything. This is why they became culture critics.[7]

There are exceptions. Paul Goodman was full of practical suggestions, and said his audiences resented it, preferring to be told that problems are unsolvable. Most pundits, if they do not entirely avoid the issue of what to do, end with some lame call for a change in values or for better education (which is more or less how Postman met the challenge he posed).

If we are correct about how wisdom gets brought into progress, pundits should not be blamed for their lack of positive proposals. Proposals, to be worth much, have to be based on knowledge of promisingness, which can only be gained through progressive problem solving in a field. And a division of labor does not seem realistic. On occasion the experts could present what they consider to be promising ideas for a panel of wise people to judge. In principle, this is what happens when a legislature is asked to appropriate money for a large particle accelerator, for instance. But it is not just lack of sagacity and high principles that keep the legislators from dealing wisely with such proposals. They can call in experts to advise on the feasibility and cost and scientific merit of the proposal, but finally who is to judge what the accelerator will do for society, what the prospective long-term consequences are of supporting that proposal instead of some other one—to invest equivalent money in supplying universities with electron microscopes, for instance, or in creating a high-speed national network for computer data transfer, or not investing it in technical infrastructure at all but in some social program aimed at bringing more women and minorities into science?

A. N. Whitehead saw the problem already in the 1920s, and attributed it to uncoordinated specialization:

> The leading intellects lack balance. They see this set of circumstances, or that set; but not both sets together. The task of coordination is left to those who lack either the force or the character to succeed in some definite career. In short, the specialized functions of the community are performed better and more progressively, but the generalized direction lacks vision. The progressiveness in detail only adds to the danger produced by the feebleness of coordination.[8]

Whitehead implied, however, that if politicians or bureaucrats of sufficient vision and strength could be installed, the necessary coordination could be achieved. Had he witnessed the fiasco of social management in Eastern Europe, he might have been less inclined to look to government at all as a potential way of coordinating progress for the greater public good. The fault, in this context at least, is not an inherent weakness of government management. The fault is that the necessary wisdom does not exist, either in government or outside it.

We always think of wisdom as existing 'out there' someplace, in private or collective minds, and needing to be brought into practical affairs. But on many complex issues, such as investment in scientific infrastructure, the necessary wisdom is nowhere to be found. The physicists and the biologists and the computer scientists, each with their stake in certain lines of progress, do not have the wisdom, and neither do the philosophers or the culture critics or members of the general public. And it cannot be said that it exists in some suprapersonal form within the aggregate of such people. It doesn't exist at all!

The challenge for an expert society is not to find but to generate wisdom. If we are correct that wisdom is generated through problem solving, then this should be possible. The necessary endogenous processes already exist to some extent but without an organizing idea that gives people something to work toward. The expert society can be that organizing idea. The endogenous processes are ones that generate active wisdom—an enlightened and effective concern with human values and far-reaching consequences—by broadening the scope of progressive problem solving that goes on within the disciplines, institutions, and agencies that produce progress.

Some Positive Tendencies

One common scenario for the future depicts a society divided between a small proportion of highly trained experts and a multitude of people performing humdrum, routine services.[9] This scenario does not depict an expert society. It depicts a nonexpert society run by experts.

A nonexpert society run by experts is more or less what we already have. The futuristic scenario is not an imaginative one, merely an extrapolation of current trends, which show more and more societal functions being taken over by experts of increasing technical sophistication. Our challenge is to direct the course of history away from this kind of society and toward an expert society in which everyone's capacity for expertise is given a chance to contribute to the public good. Yet at first blush there seems no way to bring about such a redirection. Regulatory laws can at best impede a process that seems unalterable. Hence the culture critics' despair.

There are, however, some positive glimmerings. They are no more than that, but they indicate possibilities that can be worked toward. None of the tendencies, by itself, could take society very far. But they have the potential to reinforce one another and thus consolidate into what could be a major cultural shift. It is a shift in the direction of a society in which the process of expertise becomes increasingly prominent at the level of individual careers, in the functioning of professions and industries, and in such major societal activities as education and health care.

Among the positive glimmerings are the following: Within most professional societies there are at least pockets of concern about the profession's coercive tendencies and interest in 'giving expertise away', as we put it in the first chapter. Correspondingly, there is an increasing tendency, aided by 'support' groups of various kinds, for the clients of professional services to become more knowledgeable and assertive, insisting on a more collaborative relationship with the professionals. This is even starting to happen among clients of the welfare system. The result we would look for in these developments is not just a redistribution of power in the relationship between professionals and clients. The result should be partnerships that function at a higher level of expertise than would be possible for the professionals and their clients functioning independently.

In the industrial world, the idea of expert groups composed of people who did not previously collaborate is rapidly becoming a standard management concept. Its manifestations include quality circles, job enrichment, and horizontal management structures replacing hierarchical ones. To enlightened managers, these are not simply strategies for getting better work out of lower-level employees, they are strategies for getting better work out of the organization as a whole, through processes that go on above the individual level. Thus they represent definite movement toward an expert society.

It is easy to be cynical about these developments, especially if one is inclined to see all social relationships in terms of power. It can usually be shown that in the very act of giving away power at one level, professionals or managers are reasserting it at a higher level. But to fixate on that aspect of social change is to overlook the possibility of an overall increase in people's power to achieve goals in their life and work. The process of expertise, whether carried out at the individual or the societal level, is the very antithesis of a zero-sum game. If you gain expertise in some craft, you gain power without taking it away from someone else. If doctor and patient or engineer and machinist work effectively together, they both gain in power irrespective of whether there is a proportional shift in how power is distributed between them. If a whole company reorganizes to function as an expert unit, one of the things it will need is a shared vision that goes beyond beating the competition. In order to make the investments of effort required for the process of expertise, people generally need to see their work, both individually and collectively, as having social value. On the whole, therefore, movements toward an expert society are also movements toward democracy and social betterment. Indeed, it could well be that, beyond the basic human rights and entitlements already established in liberal democracies, the further advancement of democratic ideals is better achieved by working toward more expertlike social institutions than by concentrating directly on rights and entitlements.

The Expert Society as Something to Work Toward

Point to any aspect of society and you will find widespread agreement about what needs improving, and often quite a bit of public will ready to support meliorative efforts. But there is seldom anything for this will to harness itself to. We know the kinds of results we want, and focus on those, while giving little thought to the kind of process that might be expected to produce those results. We want higher levels of knowledge and skill, better thinking, increased productivity, less crime, better quality goods, a cleaner environment, medical care that is both cheaper and better. Intelligent people are hard at work trying to achieve these and many other kinds of betterment, but all working in isolation without a unifying purpose. Improvement is not a unifying purpose; it has too many divergent possibilities. Excellence, to the extent that it merely means improvement, is not a unifying purpose, either. International competitiveness is probably the closest thing we have to a unifying purpose. We need something better than that.

Something better is not likely to come in the form of a plan or a manifesto. Enthusiasm for grand social schemes is probably at a record low for the modern era. What we need is something that can be worked toward by degrees, with discernible benefits along the way. That is what we have been trying to suggest in this chapter—not a plan, but a variety of tendencies which, if strengthened, would seem to constitute progress toward a more effective society than we have now.

In taking what some people may regard as a vague and even aimless approach to achieving an expert society, we have been trying to apply the very concept of progress that we propose. There is an oft-repeated joke about an airline pilot who announces over the loud speaker, 'I have some bad news and some good news. The bad news is that we're lost. The good news is that we're ahead of schedule.' The pilot is claiming progress with respect to emergent goals. It is not movement toward a prefigured destination. It is movement in a direction that educated intuition identifies as promising. Such a conception of progress may not be appropriate to airline travel, but it is appropriate to all those conditions in which the destination does not pre-exist but is a product of creative efforts put into getting there. That is how it is in art and science and we have argued that it must also be that way with social progress. Those who demand a destination and a plan for getting there are asking for something that is more likely to impede than to promote progress in the long run.

And there seems to be a widespread feeling that something deeper, something at the level of the ethos, does need changing. It is implicit in the catchword, 'excellence'. We are getting beaten out by quality—not by superior numbers or cheaper labor but by people who seem to be doing things better than we do. This suggests, to the reactionary mind, that we have gotten slack and need sterner treatment. To the reflective mind, however, it suggests a more pervasive insufficiency that shows up at all levels, including the boardrooms, and in all our institutions. There isn't any 'we' who can set 'them' straight. Massive cultural bootstrapping is required.

Expertise and the Quest for Quality
Cultural bootstrapping means generating progress for a whole society from the bottom, without any group who are already at the summit and helping pull the rest of us up. As with

scientific or technical progress, goals emerge out of the process itself rather than being available at the beginning as targets. In the absence of definite goals, cultural bootstrapping requires an ideal, something that people will find worthy of sustained commitment.

Expertise, as we have conceived of it here, could serve as such an ideal, except that the term itself lacks inspirational value. Furthermore, it brings a lot of unpleasant baggage with it, which we have been trying hard to cast off in these chapters; but in ordinary usage, connotations such as elitism and specialization are bound to remain. Some more attractive and less contaminated word will have to stand in its place to represent the ideal.

'Excellence' is a term that gained currency during the 1980s in talk about cultural betterment. It has inspirational value and is relatively clean, except for a hint of competitiveness (which may not be altogether out of place). The trouble is that the word is so clean that it is practically devoid of meaning. You can point to examples of excellence, but what are we supposed to learn from them, except to try harder? Even for inspirational purposes we need a concept with more meat on it than that.

A term that has more recently begun to attract attention is 'quality'. There is a quality movement developing in U.S. industry, partly in response to competition from Japan, where the idea of systematic pursuit of quality improvement took hold much earlier. Quality has even achieved something of an official status through the U.S. Congress's passing of the Malcolm Baldrige National Quality Improvement Act of 1987 (public law 100–107), which establishes awards to organizations that meet a comprehensive set of criteria of quality in all aspects of their functioning.

Although 'quality' is no easier to define than 'excellence', and in everyday language means approximately the same thing, the quality movement has given the idea substance. As conceived by W. Edwards Deming and other gurus of the movement, quality bears a very close resemblance to the concept of expertise that we have been trying to develop here. It is a continuing process, not a state or outcome. It involves all the members of an organization cooperating in pursuit of an ideal goal that can never be attained, but that can be approached endlessly. Although not identified as such, progressive problem solving seems to be implicit in the idea. The ideal, for instance, may be to eliminate defects in a manufactured product. A short-term goal might be to bring a rate of defects that currently stands at 15 per million to below 10 per million. When that goal is achieved, a goal of 6 per million might be set, and so on. Although the goal may be simple, the changes in practice required to meet it may be very complex. The change from 15 to 10 defects might require reorganization of work on the shop floor, but the next level of defect reduction might require changes throughout the organization, and the level after that might require a major technological breakthrough. Thus, although the ideal goal remains the same, the actual problems to be solved keep being reformulated as progress is made, which is the essence of progressive problem solving.[10]

So close is the resemblance of quality improvement to the process of expertise, that we might even characterize it as the process of expertise translated into a practical program for organizations. The quality movement comes, not just with a philosophy, but with management procedures and statistical techniques for organizing and assessing programs of quality improvement. This is surely a benefit for companies in search of a method, but it also poses a danger. Total Quality Management or TQM, as it is being called, sounds reassuring when applied to an airline or an electronic parts manufacturer, but somewhat chilling when applied to a school system or an opera company or to a household. One large school system has, in fact, embarked on TQM, complete with elaborate statistical accounting and the idea that every aspect of the schooling enterprise from the janitorial services to the superintendent's office will be organized to work together toward total quality. Good enough. But then when we read that the parents are to be considered the suppliers, that the entering skills and attributes of the students are the raw materials, and that the graduates are the products, whose defect rate is to be minimized, it begins to sound Orwellian. In fairness, it should be noted that W. Edwards Deming, a leading thinker in the quality movement, would probably also condemn such a distortion of the quality idea. His own thinking was solidly humane and broad in scope, but of course one has no control over where one's ideas will be taken.

Expertise, we believe, is a deeper and ultimately more enspiriting concept than quality. Quality connects to the human desire for perfection, whereas expertise connects to the human capacity to rise above present competence. 'Quality', or something like that, may serve as the watchword, the word to build slogans around, and the word to incorporate into policies, legislation, and new programs of many progressive kinds. But for those who want to engage in deeper planning and thinking, there is one important idea that is not captured in the concept of quality. That is the idea, reiterated in this chapter, of *making better use of the human capacity for expertise.*

Concepts of expertise can provide a common way of thinking about many otherwise unrelated strivings for quality and excellence. The following are central ideas that can apply to many different circumstances and thus give coherence to a society-wide effort at cultural bootstrapping:

1. **Second-order environments.** This is a concept that can apply to schools, workplaces, associations, and government services. As elaborated in this chapter, it is the idea of a social environment in which progress or growth is a continuing requirement of adaptation to the environment.

2. **Reinvestment of mental resources.** This, we might say, is the psychological basis of progress. It is not necessary to keep finding new mental resources, new energy. These keep coming available as a natural result of practice, so that fewer resources are needed to do what we have been doing and more are available for new challenges.

3. **Progressive problem solving.** This is the dynamic element in the process of expertise. As time and mental resources become available, they are reinvested in

addressing problems at higher levels. This keeps experts from becoming habit-bound and makes genuine progress possible.

4. Working at the edge of competence. A natural consequence of progressive problem solving, it means that expertise keeps growing.

5. Creative expertise. This is the kind of creativity that develops through adventurous problem solving, where one is required to make decisions on the basis of judgments of promisingness. It can be developed in any expert domain, may be helped by but does not depend on creative traits of personality.

6. Active wisdom. This is a special kind of expertise marked by the ability to make decisions that turn out to have been wise ones. Like creative expertise, it is based on knowledge of promisingness—in this case, promisingness with respect to human values and far-reaching consequences.

None of these concepts is simple or a part of common knowledge. As we observed at the beginning of this book, expertise has been with us since the dawn of civilization, but until recently people have not thought about it in any general sort of way. They have not thought about it in ways that would make expertise something that could be pursued and cultivated on purpose rather than being left as an occasional fortunate outcome of training and experience focused on more limited goals. As a result, we lack concepts that enable us to discuss and plan ways of advancing toward an expert society. The preceding six concepts are offered as a start.

Conclusion

In Chapter 1 we offered the prospect of discovering a "method" of expertise, comparing it to the "method of invention", which Alfred North Whitehead called the nineteenth century's greatest invention. It is time now to evaluate that idea. From what has been said in the intervening chapters, it might seem that nothing could be more remote from practical possibility than a method of expertise. We have continually represented expertise as a matter of going beyond one's well-learned procedures, of resisting downsliding into routines, and of reformulating problems at new and more complex levels. But that is the point. That is the method.

That is the method, so far as it can be specified at the individual level. But what we have been working toward in the last two chapters is a conception of expertise at a communal or societal level. Interestingly, this is the level at which Whitehead conceived of the method of invention. It was not a method that could be learned and exercised by an individual. Rather, it was, like the Industrial Revolution of which it was a part, an invention at the societal level.

Indeed, much of what Whitehead said about invention resembles what we have been saying about expertise. It is based on knowledge: "The whole change has arisen from the new scientific information." Its essence is progressive problem solving: "It is a process of disciplined attack upon one difficulty after another." But it did not so much come about through individual achievement as through the social reorganization of the pursuit of knowledge—"the full self-conscious realization of the power of professionalism in knowledge in all its departments, and of the way to produce the professionals, and of the methods by which abstract knowledge can be connected with technology, and of the boundless possibilities of technological advance." The result has been an entire cultural context oriented toward "disciplined progress."[11]

Accordingly, we may think of the method of expertise as an extension or broadening of the method of invention Whitehead wrote about. For invention is but one of the manifestations of a process that can go on in every sphere of human activity. This process, which consists of reinvesting mental resources in efforts to go beyond what can be achieved with present competence, is what we have tried to show is the underlying process of expertise.

Looking at expertise as a process seems strange, is hard for people to sustain. They keep slipping back into the easier and more natural way of thinking of it—as a state achieved by talented people after lengthy training and experience. Our effort is not to rewrite the dictionary, but only to introduce ways of thinking about expertise that have hope of leading somewhere, to something other than the most banal of conclusions. As we have conceded, 'expertise' is probably not the word to use on posters or in pronouncements by heads of state. Some other word, such as 'quality', will have to take the limelight. But for people who want to think creatively about transforming society, such words are mere ornaments. We believe that, for serious thinkers in all areas of human affairs, it is worth trying to learn to think about expertise as something that people can *do,* can be encouraged to engage in, can adopt as a way of life.

Notes

Chapter One: The Need to Understand Expertise

1. Whitehead 1925/1948.
2. Gladwin 1970.
3. Dreyfus and Dreyfus 1986.
4. Welker 1991.
5. Welker 1991.
6. Berliner 1986.
7. The teaching profession, as it happens, provides a nice case for dismantling the stereotypes of expertise. Public education has managed to acquire most of the ills associated with expertise, without ever managing to convince the public that its practioners are experts. It has made its services obligatory. Credentialling and over-specialization are rife. Schools have typically been authoritarian and paternalistic, with a penchant for quick-fix solutions to complex human problems. And they are frequently accused of perpetuating social inequalities and playing into the hands of the powerful. There are widely differing proposals of what to do about public education, but we have yet to hear of one from any quarter that suggests education would be improved by having less expert teachers.
8. Vallas 1990.
9. Attewell 1990, 429–430.
10. Harper 1987. Willie's analysis is that, in trying to keep the file level, people press down with equal force on both ends. But as the file moves across the blade, the leverage changes, so that the effect of equal force is that the front end goes down, creating a rounded edge. To keep the file level, one must hold the file lightly and change the balance of pressure between the two hands as the file moves, so as to compensate for the change in leverage.
11. Chi, Glaser, and Farr 1988; Ericsson and Smith 1991.
12. Harper 1987.
13. Harper 1987.
14. Hirschhorn 1984.
15. Lesgold and Lajoie 1991.
16. Jacobs 1961; 1984.
17. Hayes (1985) argues that this is true even for a Mozart. See also Bhaskar, Herstein, and Hayes 1983.
18. Simon 1957, 198.

Chapter Two: Experts are Different from Us: They Have More Knowledge

1. de Groot 1965.
2. Marjoram 1987.
3. Chase and Simon 1973.
4. Egan and Schwartz 1979.
5. Allard and Burnett 1985.
6. Halpern and Bowe 1982.
7. Charness 1991.
8. Ericsson and Harris 1989 (cited in Ericsson and Smith 1991).
9. Allard and Starkes 1991.
10. Patel and Groen 1991.
11. Dreyfus and Dreyfus 1986.
12. Charness 1991.
13. Newell and Simon 1972.
14. Larkin, McDermott, Simon, and Simon 1980; Patel and Groen 1986; Sweller, Mawer, and Ward 1983.
15. Joseph and Patel 1986.
16. In medical diagnosis studies, experts do produce wrong diagnoses with disturbing frequency. There are various ways to account for this, however, without concluding that the problems strain the limits of their competence. Participants in the studies are required to make a diagnosis on the available facts, whereas in real life they might call for more tests. Also (this is the disturbing possibility) medical diagnosis may be inherently chancy, so that even optimum use of information may result in a fairly high rate of misdiagnosis.
17. Bereiter, Burtis, and Scardamalia 1988; Scardamalia and Bereiter 1987.
18. Snow and Yalow 1982, 520.
19. Buchanan and Shortliffe 1984. Good nontechnical discussions of expert systems are provided in Winston and Prendergast 1984.
20. This is a disputable point, since there are intelligent systems that learn (Klahr, Langley, and Neches 1987). But it is probably fair to say that what they demonstrate is the gradual augmenting and editing of crystallized expert knowledge, rather than modeling the learning that comes from wrestling with a tough problem.

Chapter Three: Expert Knowledge and How It Comes About

1. Anderson 1983.
2. Ryle 1949.
3. Roedinger III and Craik 1989.
4. Polanyi 1964; 1967.

5. Dreyfus and Dreyfus 1988.
6. Rumelhart 1989; Rumelhart, McClelland, and the PDP Group 1986; McClelland, Rumelhart, and the PDP Group 1986; Smolensky 1988.
7. A nontechnical explanation of how connectionist programs do this can be found in Bereiter 1991b. The program described here and a number of other simple but thought provoking programs are available on diskettes (MS-DOS or Macintosh) accompanying McClelland and Rumelhart's *Explorations in Parallel Distributed Processing* (1988).
8. Dennett 1986; Hofstadter 1985.
9. Fodor and Pylyshyn 1988.
10. de Kleer and Brown 1985, 13.
11. Lave and Wenger 1991; Suchman 1987.
12. Scribner 1984.
13. Osgood, Suci, and Tannenbaum 1957.
14. Eliot 1871/1977.
15. A classic study showing the astonishing rate of forgetting school-learned factual information is Tyler 1930. For a modern theoretical treatment of memory as re-experiencing, see Minsky 1980.
16. Hirschhorn (1988) has used a problem similar to this in training workshops, and reports these as common strategies administrators use.
17. Broudy 1977, 1988.
18. Plimpton 1992.
19. Brown, Bransford, Ferrara, and Campione 1983; Garner 1987.
20. See Popper's *Objective Knowledge* (1972). For a modern psychological treatment of this issue, see Margolis 1987 Also see Harré 1984.
21. Whitehead 1929. We may have been the first to reintroduce it into discourse about cognition and learning, at a conference in 1980 (Bereiter and Scardamalia 1985).
22. Boshuizen and Schmidt 1992.
23. This is the main point of E. D. Hirsch's frequently misunderstood book, *Cultural Literacy* (1987). We discuss it further in Bereiter and Scardamalia 1992.
24. Anderson 1982, 1987.
25. Vosniadou and Brewer 1987.
26. Voss 1988.
27. Brown, Collins, and Duguid 1989; Carraher, Carraher, and Schlieman 1985; Lave 1988; Lave and Wenger 1991.
28. More 1934.

Chapter Four: Expertise As Process
1. Simon 1957, 198.
2. Salthouse 1991.

3. There is a claim that has been passed around for years in self-improvement circles, that we normally use only 10 percent of our mental capacity. Having heard it so many times, people are inclined to believe there must be some basis for it, but as far as we have been able to make out, there is none, and it isn't even clear what the claim means. The point that this pseudo-fact is usually enlisted to support, however, is not far off from the one we are making here: that it is possible through learning to make much more effective use of the capacity given us by nature.

4. Camerer and Johnson 1991.

5. Anderson 1985.

6. The most promising work has used computer models that at some level simulate the nervous system rather than simulating rational behavior. These have proved more adept and humanlike in their ability to recognize patterns in the environment and to adapt behavior to them (McClelland et al 1986; Beer 1991).

7. James 1914.

8. Murnighan and Conlon 1991.

9. Bhaskar et al. 1983.

10. Csikszentmihalyi and Csikszentmihalyi 1988, 29.

11. Csikszentmihalyi and Csikszentmihalyi 1988, 30.

12. Mitchell 1988, 36.

13. Hirschhorn 1988.

14. Suomi 1991.

15. Marmot 1986.

16. Bereiter and Scardamalia 1987b; Scardamalia and Bereiter 1991b.

17. Piaget 1960, 10.

18. Case 1985. Various neo-Piagetian theories are presented in Siegler 1978.

19. Vygotsky 1978; Wertsch 1985.

20. For a general treatment of reading ability from a cognitive point of view, see Perfetti 1985 or Stanovich and Richardson 1991. The poverty of the diagnostic-remedial approach is documented by Arter and Jenkins (1979). Dependency in adult nonreaders is reported by Johnston (1985). Our analysis of reading difficulties is presented in Bereiter 1988 and Brett and Bereiter 1989, the latter also containing a detailed report of the case summarized here. Valerie Anderson's work is reported in Anderson and Burtis (in press).

21. Gladstein 1984.

Chapter Five: Creative Expertise

1. Barron 1969; MacKinnon 1965.

2. This does not mean that the creative expert produces many noncreative theories, symphonies, or whatever. Unsuccessful attempts may seldom

get beyond the idea stage. The high output of publications or finished works is a reflection of the much larger amount of productive activity that never reaches the finished state (Simonton, 1984, 1988).

3. McClelland and Rumelhart 1988.
4. Margolis 1987.
5. Margolis 1987, 63.
6. Beer 1991.
7. Newell, Shaw, and Simon 1962, 145–46.
8. Dillon 1982; Getzels 1979.
9. Greeno (1978), in his analysis of problem types, calls all these "composition" problems, noting that a main task in all of them is elaborating the goals.
10. Explicit creative goals may re-enter at difficult points in solving the main problem, however. The problem solver says, in effect, 'I'm stuck. I'm not getting anywhere with the way I'm approaching this problem. I've got to look for a more creative approach.'
11. Wallas 1926.
12. Khatchadourian 1977.
13. Perkins 1981.
14. D. T. Campbell (1960) has propounded a theory of creativity as luck. It is a theory not even a mother could love, but it survives because of the extraordinary difficulty of coming up with a better one. As noted above (Note 2), Simonton has developed this theory further by incorporating the hypothesis that an extraordinarily high rate of idea production, by increasing the incidence of fortunate connections, explains creative careers.
15. Dostoyevsky 1874–75/1969.
16. The resulting novel, *A Raw Youth,* is not one of Dostoyevsky's major works. Wasiolek, editor of the notebooks from which we have quoted, suggests, in effect, that the failure of the book resulted from a top-down decision that nullified the promising ideas that surfaced early in the planning of the novel.
17. Simonton 1988.
18. Brown and Day 1983; van Dijk and Kintsch 1983.
19. Another recourse is to shift to a slower-moving field like education or social planning and try to make a contribution there. Nobel laureates often do this, with results that are usually disappointing and sometimes pathetic. Physical scientists who try this usually grossly underestimate the amount of knowledge required, naively imagining that their scientific experience has equipped them with a process unknown to practitioners of the more retarded sciences. See the *Omni Interviews* (Weintraub 1984) for examples.
20. E. H. Gombrich (1959) has argued, however, that the great painters were not the great innovators, not the people who introduced new forms. The great painters, rather, were ones who most fully developed

the potentialities of forms originated by other, lesser artists. A similar argument could perhaps be made in science. Butterfield, in his *Origins of Modern Science* (1949), commented that the more one learns about Newton's predecessors and contemporaries, the harder it becomes to indentify anything original that Newton did. Newton ends up being credited with having 'seen what it was all about', having 'put it all together'. Still, there is no question that what was done by Newton— and by Raphael and Mozart—was bold and risky. The difference is not between risky creativity and safe and conservative elaboration, it is between being the first with a seminal idea and being someone who achieves a major creative synthesis. Both are bold; both venture beyond the limits of existing competence.

21. Gruber 1974.
22. Art dealers have told us about factories that produce oil paintings in an impressionistic style using production line techniques. One person paints skies, another adds buildings, another rapidly sketches people and vehicles in the street, and—*voilà!*—Paris street scenes blossom on each canvas. But at the end, the master painter, using only a fine brush and black paint, adds a creative touch here, another there, and, of course, a signature. It could be maintained that such a process has nothing to do with creativity at all. Thousands of customers appear to have thought otherwise, however, at least at the time of purchase. We suggest that this factory process be thought of as one that exploits automated parts of creative expertise. The painters employed in such factories are typically experienced artists hard up for money. In the course of their serious artistic efforts they have mastered various creative techniques, and it is the most fully automated of those techniques, the ones that can be run off rapidly and repeatedly, that they use in their factory work. The master artist is probably using equally automated procedures, although ones that operate at a some-what higher level. The resulting paintings may not be judged creative by   people   of   discernment,   but   they   contain   many   of the features. As someone remarked, when viewed out of the corner of the eye they create the general impression of a work of art.
23. Schön 1987.
24. Graves 1983.

Chapter Six: Expertlike Learners
1. Ghent 1989.
2. Tal 1992.
3. Patel and Groen 1991.

4. This is what Harman (1986) calls "argument to the best explanation", and which Thagard (1989) takes to be the essential process in scientific theorizing. Thus, although the outcome of expert diagnosis of problematic cases is not a general theory, its process seems to be essentially the same as what goes on in the construction of scientific theories. We like to call it 'building a theory of the case'.

5. Biggs 1984; Marton and Säljö 1976; Ng and Bereiter 1991; van Rossum and Sehenk 1984.

6. Bloom 1985; Resnick and Omanson 1987.

7. Ng and Bereiter 1991.

8. Scardamalia and Bereiter 1985.

9. A common measure of consistency is Cronbach's Coefficient Alpha, which can range from 0 to 1. Coefficient Alpha for deep planning in the three areas combined was .92, which is on a par with the best of mental tests.

10. Fodor 1980.

11. There have been various efforts to explain how this bootstrapping occurs (Bereiter 1985; Boom 1991; Juckes 1991). The 'learning paradox', according to which learning is impossible, results, we now believe, from the way language forces us to describe knowledge—in the form of propositions, rules, and so forth. The paradox disappears if we abandon the assumption that knowledge in the mind actually consists of such objects (Bereiter 1991a).

12. Carey 1978. So as to prevent the children from linking the new color to the possibly familiar fruit, Carey actually referred to the color as 'chromium', but we omit that complication from the narrative account.

13. van Daalen-Kapteijns and Elshout-Mohr 1981.

14. Chan, Burtis, Scardamalia, and Bereiter 1992.

15. Chan et al. 1992.

16. But not necessarily all domains. The difficulties adults have in learning foreign languages may, for instance, be partly due to their applying general knowledge building schemas that are appropriate for learning conceptually organized material, as in science, but that lead to the wrong kind of learning when language proficiency is the goal (Krashen 1981).

17. The cognitive implications of the way business is conducted in schools are only beginning to be studied in depth. An important early work is John Holt's *How Children Fail* (1964). Like workers in any other occupation, students may be expected to evolve strategies to minimize effort, including mental effort. There is evidence that students tend to resist assignments that call for higher-level thinking and to bargain down intellectual work demands (Doyle 1983, 1986).

18. Brown and Day 1983; Fillion and Mendelsohn 1979; Hidi and Klaiman 1983; Scardamalia and Bereiter 1984.

19. Bloom 1985.
20. Bereiter and Scardamalia 1989.
21. Bloom 1985.
22. Bloom and his co-investigators note, in fact, that in some cases the child who received this heroic dedication from parents was not the one judged to be most talented but the one most willing to work hard. According to our analysis, this makes sense. It is the performance of the parent-child combination, not of the child alone, that determines early progress, and so a high premium would be placed on the child's willingness and ability to work in that combination.
23. Bull and Davis 1980; Howieson 1981; Segal, Busse, and Mansfield 1980.
24. Galway 1974; Ostrander 1979.
25. Scardamalia and Bereiter, in press-b.

Chapter Seven: Schools as Nonexpert Societies

1. Evans and Patel 1989.
2. Soloway and Iyengar 1986.
3. Nock 1936.
4. It is simply not true, for instance, that the upper occupational classes have been highly successful in passing status on to their children. Both U.S. and Canadian census data over several decades show that about 40 percent of the sons of men in professional or managerial occupations end up in lower-level occupations. This was true even in times of economic expansion, when the number of professional and managerial jobs increased greatly (Bereiter 1977; Blau and Duncan 1967).
5. Remillard 1991.
6. Remillard 1991.
7. Bereiter and Scardamalia 1987a.
8. Taylor 1970; Zahorik 1975.
9. Fredericksen 1984.
10. The debate is likely to center on how seriously one is to take standardized test performance. Studies generally show an advantage for didactic schools, especially with disadvantaged students. The standard criticism is that this advantage reflects the similarity of the teaching to the test. However, child-centered educators have not been able to show valid indicators that favor their approach to schooling (Evans 1979; Steller 1988; Squires, Huitt, and Segars 1983).
11. A further obstacle to progressivity is the tendency of some child-centered pundits simply to deny unfavorable results. See Bereiter and Kurland (1981) and the subsequent responses.
12. Graves 1983; Calkins 1983.
13. Bradford and Cohen 1984; Clemmer and McNeil 1988; Peters 1987.

14. On learning by discovery, Shulman and Keislar 1966. On cognitive apprenticeship, Collins, Brown, and Newman 1989.

15. Lewis 1991.

16. Gladstein 1984.

17. A whole issue of the journal, *The Behavioral and Brain Sciences*, was devoted to airing problems of the journal system. The discussion is focused on an experiment by Peters and Ceci (1982), in which slightly disguised versions of published articles were submitted to the same journals in which the originals had appeared. In most cases the manuscripts were rejected, even though their duplication was not recognized.

18. Betts 1910; Hoetker and Ahlbrandt 1969.

19. Heap 1985.

20. "Communities of learners and thinkers" comes from an article of that name by Ann Brown and Joseph Campione (1990). "Reflective community" is from Matthew Lipman (1988), who has pioneered the introduction of philosophy into school curricula.

21. Resnick, Bill, Lesgold, and Leer 1991; Brown, Campione, Reeve, Ferrara, and Palincsar 1991.

22. Scardamalia and Bereiter 1991a; Scardamalia and Bereiter, in press-a; Scardamalia and Bereiter, in press-b; Scardamalia, Bereiter, Brett, Burtis, Calhoun, and Smith Lea 1992; Scardamalia, Bereiter, McLean, Swallow, and Woodruff 1989.

23. Brown, Ash, Rutherford, Nakagawa, Gordon, and Campione, in press; Scardamalia et al. 1992; Scardamalia, Bereiter, and Lamon, in press.

24. It is worth noting that adult scientists and scholars do not spend all their time advancing the frontiers of knowledge. For most of them that is a rare event. They spend a great deal of their time trying to make sense of what others have found or proposed, and that is not fundamentally different from what we have reported school children to be doing.

Chapter Eight: Toward an Expert Society

1. This norm creates a well-known problem when scientists work in competitive industries. When at work they may uphold their company's interest in protecting trade secrets and then go off to a conference where—their competitors now turned into 'colleagues'—they give everything away in a public presentation.

2. Kitto 1954.

3. Lasch 1991.

4. The belief that progress is autonomous and automatically addressed to needs has an interesting counterpart in people's naive beliefs about evolution. On the basis of interviews with university students, Stellan

Ohlsson (1991) concluded that most of them view evolution as something that just happens, without any mechanism, Darwinian or Lamarkian. It seems quite possible that for many people evolution and progress are one and the same concept. Evolution/progress is not caused by anything but is just how the world works, inevitably answering to creatures' needs by providing long necks for giraffes and cellular telephones for commuters.

5. Lieberman's *The Tyranny of the Experts* (1970) exemplifies the more outraged response, Hoffman's *The Politics of Knowledge: Activist Movements in Medicine and Planning* (1989) the more measured and analytic response. Both, however, convey severe pessimism about the possibilities of salvation.

6. Beer 1991.

7. Postman 1992, 181.

8. Whitehead 1925/1948, 176.

9. Collins and Tanner 1984.

10. Dobyns and Crawford-Mason 1991; Deming 1986.

11. Quotations are from Whitehead 1925/1948, 92.

Bibliography

Allard, F., and Burnett, N. 1985. Skill in Sport. *Canadian Journal of Psychology, 39,* 294–312.

Allard, F., and Starkes, J. L. 1991. Expertise in Human Motor Performance. In K. A. Ericsson and J. Smith (eds.), *Toward a General Theory of Expertise* (New York: Cambridge University Press).

Anderson, J. R. 1982. Acquisition of Cognitive Skill. *Psychology Review, 89,* 369–406.

———. 1983. *The Architecture of Cognition.* Cambridge, MA: Harvard University Press.

———. 1985. *Cognitive Psychology and its Implications* (2nd ed.). San Francisco: Freeman.

———. 1987. Skill Acquisition: Compilation of Weak-Method Problem Solutions. *Psychological Review, 94,* 192–210.

Arter, J. A., and Jenkins, J. R. 1979. Differential Diagnosis— Prescriptive Teaching. A Critical Appraisal. *Review of Educational Research, 49,* 517–555.

Attewell, P. 1990. What is Skill? *Work and Occupations, 17,* 422–448.

Barron, F. 1969. *Creative Person and Creative Process.* New York: Holt, Rinehart, and Winston.

Beer, R. D. 1991. *Intelligence as Adaptive Behavior.* Cambridge, MA: M.I.T. Press.

Bereiter, C. 1977. IQ and Elitism. *Interchange, 7,* 36–44.

———. 1985. Toward a Solution of the Learning Paradox. *Review of Educational Research, 55,* 201-226.

———. 1988. A Cognitive Adaptational Interpretation of Reading Disability. In C. Hedley (eds.), *Reading and the special learner* (21–34). Norwood, NJ: Ablex.

———. 1991a. Commentary. *Human Development, 34,* 294–98.

———. 1991b. Implications of Connectionism for Thinking about Rules. *Educational Researcher, 20,* 10–16.

Bereiter, C., Burtis, P. J., and Scardamalia, M. 1988. Cognitive Operations in Constructing Main Points in Written Composition. *Journal of Memory and Language, 27,* 261–278.

Bereiter, C., and Kurland, M. 1981. A Constructive Look at Follow Through Results. *Interchange, 12,* 1–22.

Bereiter, C., and Scardamalia, M. 1985. Cognitive Coping Strategies and the Problem of 'Inert Knowledge'. In S. F. Chipman, J. W.

Segal, and R. Glaser (eds.), *Thinking and Learning Skills: Vol. 2. Research and Open Questions* (65–80). Hillsdale, NJ: Erlbaum.

Bereiter, C., and Scardamalia, M. 1987a. An Attainable Version of High Literacy: Approaches to Teaching Higher-Order Skills in Reading and Writing. *Curriculum Inquiry, 17* (1), 9–30.

Bereiter, C., and Scardamalia, M. 1987b. *The Psychology of Written Composition.* Hillsdale, NJ: Erlbaum.

Bereiter, C., and Scardamalia, M. 1989. Intentional Learning as a Goal of Instruction. In L. B. Resnick (ed.), *Knowing, learning, and instruction: Essays in honor of Robert Glaser* (361–392). Hillsdale, NJ: Erlbaum.

Bereiter, C., and Scardamalia, M. 1992. Cognition and Curriculum. In P. W. Jackson (eds.), *Handbook of research on curriculum* (517–542). New York: Macmillan.

Berliner, D. C. 1986. In Pursuit of the Expert Pedagogue. *Educational Researcher, 15,* 5–13.

Betts, G. H. 1910. *The Recitation.* Boston: Houghton Mifflin.

Bhaskar, R., Herstein, J. A., and Hayes, J. R. 1983. How to Decide How to Decide. *Instructional Science, 12,* 267–277.

Biggs, J. B. 1984. Learning Strategies, Student Motivation Patterns and Subjectively Perceived Success. In J. R. Kirby (ed.), *Cognitive Strategies and Educational Performance* (111–134). Orlando: Academic Press.

Blau, P., and Duncan, O. D. 1967. *The American Occupational Structure.* New York: Academic Press.

Bloom, B. S. (ed.). 1985. *Developing Talent in Young People.* New York: Ballantine Books.

Boom, J. 1991. Collective Development and the Learning Paradox. *Human Development, 34,* 273–287.

Boshuizen, H. P. A., and Schmidt, H. G. 1992. On the Role of Biomedical Knowledge in Clinical Reasoning by Experts, Intermediates and Novices. *Cognitive Science, 16,* 153–184.

Bradford, D., and Cohen, A. 1984. *Managing for Excellence: The Guide to Developing High Performance in Contemporary Organizations.* New York: Wiley.

Brett, C., and Bereiter, C. 1989. A cognitive-adaptationist approach to remediating reading problems. *Reading, Writing, and Learning Disabilities, 5,* 281–291.

Broudy, H. S. 1977. Types of Knowledge and Purposes of Education. In R. C. Anderson, R. J. Spiro, and W. E. Montague (eds.), *Schooling and the Acquisition of Knowledge* (1–17). Hillsdale, NJ: Erlbaum.

Broudy, H. S. 1988. *The Uses of Schooling.* New York: Routledge.

Brown, A. L., Ash, D., Rutherford, M., Nakagawa, K., Gordon, A., and Campione, J. C. (in press). Distributed Expertise in the Classroom. In G. Salomon (ed.), *Distributed Cognitions.* New York: Cambridge University Press.

Brown, A. L., Bransford, J. D., Ferrara, R. A., and Campione, J. C. 1983. Learning, Remembering, and Understanding. In J. H. Flavell and E. M. Markman (eds.), *Handbook of Child Psychology: Vol. 3, Cognitive Development* (77–166). New York: Wiley.

Brown, A. L., and Campione, J. C. 1990. Communities of Learning and Thinking, or A Context by Any Other Name. *Contributions to Human Development, 21,* 108–126.

Brown, A. L., Campione, J. C., Reeve, R. A., Ferrara, R. A., and Palinscar, A. S. 1991. Interactive Learning, Individual Understanding: The Case of Reading and Mathematics. In L. T. Landsmann (ed.), *Culture, Schooling and Psychological Development.* Hillsdale, NJ: Erlbaum.

Brown, A. L., and Day, J. D. 1983. Macrorules for Summarizing Texts. The Development of Expertise. *Journal of Verbal Learning and Verbal Behavior, 22,* 1–14.

Brown, J. S., Collins, A. and Duguid, P. 1989. Situated Cognition and the Culture of Learning. *Educational Researchers, 18,* 32–42.

Buchanan, B. G., and Shortliffe, E. H. 1984. *Rule-Based Expert Programs: The MYCIN Experiments of the Stanford Heuristic Programming Project.* Reading, MA: Addison-Wesley.

Bull, K. S., and Davis, G. A. 1980. Evaluating Creative Potential Using the Statement of Past Creative Activities. *Journal of Creative Behavior, 14,* 249–257.

Butterfield, H. 1949. *The Origins of Modern Science, 1300–1800.* London: G. Bell.

Calkins, L. M. 1983. *Lessons from a Child: On the Teaching and Learning of Writing.* Exeter, NH: Hienemann.

Camerer, C. F., and Johnson, E. J. 1991. The Process-Performance Paradox in Expert Judgment: How Can Experts Know So Much and Predict So Badly? In K. A. Ericsson and J. Smith (eds.), *Toward a General Theory of Expertise: Prospects and Limits* (195–217). Cambridge: Cambridge University Press.

Campbell, D. T. 1960. Blind Variation and Selective Retention in Creative Thought as in Other Knowledge Processes. *Psychological Review, 67,* 380–400.

Carey, S. 1978. The Child as Word Learner. In M. Halle, J. Bresnan, and G. A. Miller (eds.), *Linguistic Theory and Psychological Reality* (264–293). Cambridge, MA: M.I.T. Press.

Carraher, T. N., Carraher, D. W., and Schlieman, A. D. 1985. Mathematics in the Streets and in Schools. *British Journal of Developmental Psychology, 3,* 21–29.

Case, R. 1985. *Intellectual Development: Birth to Adulthood.* Orlando, FL: Academic Press.

Chan, C. K. K., Burtis, P. J., Scardamalia, M., and Bereiter, C. 1992. Constructive Activity in Learning from Text. *American Educational Research Journal, 29* (1), 97–118.

Charness, N. 1991. Expertise in Chess: The Balance Between Knowledge and Search. In K. A. Ericsson and J. Smith (eds.), *Toward a General Theory of Expertise: Prospects and Limits* (39–63). Cambridge: Cambridge University Press.

Chase, W. G., and Simon, H. A., 1973. Perception in Chess. *Cognitive Psychology, 4,* 55–81.

Chi, M. T. H., Glaser, R., and Farr, M. (eds.) 1988. *The Nature of Expertise.* Hillsdale, NJ: Erlbaum.

Clemmer, J., and McNeil, A. 1988. *The VIP Strategy: Leadership Skills for Exceptional Performance.* Toronto: Key Porter Books.

Collins, A., Brown, J. S., and Newman, S. E. 1989. Cognitive Apprenticeship: Teaching the Crafts of Reading, Writing, and Mathematics. In L. B. Resnick (ed.), *Knowing, Learning, and Instruction: Essays in Honor of Robert Glaser* (453–494). Hillsdale, NJ: Erlbaum.

Collins, E. L., and Tanner, L. D. 1984. *American Jobs and the Changing Industrial Base.* Cambridge, MA: Ballinger.

Csikszentmihalyi, M., and Csikszentmihalyi, I. S. (eds.) 1988. *Optimal Experience: Psychological Studies of Flow in Consciousness.* New York: Cambridge University Press.

de Groot, A. D. 1965. *Thought and Choice in Chess.* The Hague: Mouton.

deKleer, J., and Brown, J. S. 1985. A Qualitative Physics Based on Confluences. In D. G. Bobrow (eds.), *Qualitative Reasoning about Physical Systems* (7–84). Cambridge, MA: M.I.T. Press.

Deming, C. W. 1986. *Out of the Crisis.* Cambridge, MA: M.I.T. Center for Advanced Engineering Study.

Dennett, D. C. 1986. The Logical Geography of Computational Approaches: A View from the East Pole. In R. Harnish and M. Brand (eds.), *The Representation of Knowledge and Belief.* Tucson, AZ: University of Arizona Press.

Dillon, J. T. 1982. Problem Finding and Solving. *Journal of Creative Behavior, 16,* 97–111. Dodyns, L., and Crawford-Mason, C. 1991. *Quality or Else: The Revolution in World Business.* Boston: Houghton Mifflin.

Dostoyevsky, F. (1874–75/1969). *Notebooks for A Raw Youth* (V. Terras, trans.). Chicago: University of Chicago Press.

Doyle, W. 1983. Academic Work. *Review of Educational Research, 53,* 159–199.

Doyle, W. 1986. Classroom Organization and Management. In M. C. Wittrock (ed.), *Handbook of Research on Teaching* (392–431). New York: Macmillan.

Dreyfus, H. L., and Dreyfus, S. E. 1988. The Socratic and Platonic Basis of Cognitivism. *AI and Society, 2,* 99–112.

Dreyfus, H. L., and Dreyfus, S. E. 1986. *Mind Over Machine.* New York: Free Press.

Egan, D. E., and Schwartz, B. J. 1979. Chunking in Recall of Symbolic Drawings. *Memory and Cognition, 7,* 149–158.

Eliot, G. (1871/1977). *Middlemarch.* New York: Norton.

Ericsson, K. A., and Smith, J. 1991. Prospects and Limits of the Empirical Study of Expertise: An Introduction. In K. A. Ericsson and J. Smith (eds.), *Toward a General Theory of Expertise: Prospects and Limits* (1–38). Cambridge: Cambridge University Press.

Evans, D., and Patel, V. (eds.) 1989. *Cognitive Science in Medicine.* Cambridge, MA: M.I.T. Press.

Evans, M. A. 1979. A Comparative Study of Young Children's Classroom Activities and Learning Outcomes. *British Journal of Educational Psychology, 49,* 15–26.

Fillion, B., and Mendelsohn, D. 1979. *A Pilot Investigation into the Effects of Writing on Learning* (Unpublished report No. Ontario Institute for Studies in Education.)

Fodor, J. A. 1980. Fixation of Belief and Concept Acquisition. In M. Piattelli-Palmerini (ed.), *Language and Learning: The Debate between Jean Piaget and Noam Chomsky* (142–149). Cambridge, MA: Harvard University Press.

Fodor, J. A., and Pylyshyn, Z. 1988. Connectionism and Cognitive Architecture: A Critical Analysis. In S. Pinker and J. Mehler (eds.), *Connections and symbols* (3–71). Cambridge, MA: M.I.T. Press/Bradford Books.

Fredericksen, N. 1984. The Real Test Bias: Influences of Testing on Teaching and Learning. *American Psychologist, 39,* 193–202.

Galway, W. T. 1974. *The Inner Game of Tennis.* New York: Random House.

Garner, R. 1987. *Metacognition and Reading Comprehension.* Norwood, NJ: Ablex.

Getzels, J. W. 1979. Problem-Finding: A Theoretical Note. *Cognitive Science, 3,* 167–171.

Ghent, P. 1989. *Expert Learning in Music.* Master's thesis. University of Toronto.

Gladstein, D. L. 1984. Groups in Context: A Model of Task Group Effectiveness. *Administrative Science Quarterly, 29,* 499–517.

Gladwin, T. 1970. *East is a Big Bird: Navigation and Logic on Puluwat Atoll.* Cambridge, MA: Harvard University Press.

Gombrich, E. H. 1959. *Art and Illusion: A Study in the Psychology of Pictorial Representation.* London: Phaedon Press.

Graves, D. R. 1983. *Writing: Teachers and Children at Work.* Exeter, NH: Heinemann.

Greeno, J. G. 1978. Natures of Problem-Solving Abilities. In W. K. Estes (eds.), *Handbook of Learning and Cognitive Processes: Vol. 5. Human Information Processing* (239–270). Hillsdale, NJ: Erlbaum.

Gruber, H. E. 1974. *Darwin on Man: A Psychological Study of Scientific Creativity.* New York: Dutton.

Halpern, A. R., and Bower, G. H. 1982. Musical Expertise and Melodic Structure in Memory for Musical Notation. *American Journal of Psychology, 95,* 31–50.

Harman, G. 1986. *Change in View: Principles of Reasoning.* Cambridge, MA: M.I.T. Press.

Harper, D. 1987. *Working Knowledge: Skill and Community in a Small Shop.* Chicago: University of Chicago Press.

Harré, R. 1984. *Personal Being: A Theory for Individual Psychology.* Cambridge, MA: Harvard University Press.

Hayes, J. R. 1985. Three Problems in Teaching General Skills. In S. F. Chipman, J. W. Segal, and R. Glaser (eds.), *Thinking and Learning Skills: Vol. 2. Research and Open Questions* (pp. 391–405). Hillsdale, NY: Erlbaum.

Heap, J. L. 1985. Discourse in the Production of Classroom Knowledge: Reading Lessons. *Curriculum Inquiry, 15* (3), 245–280.

Hidi, S., and Klaiman, R. 1983. Notetaking by Experts and Novices: An Attempt to Identify Teachable Strategies. *Curriculum Inquiry, 13* (4), 377–395.

Hirsch, E. D., Jr. 1987. *Cultural Literacy: What Every American*

Needs to Know. Boston, MA: Houghton Mifflin.

Hirschhorn, L. 1984. *Beyond Mechanization.* Cambridge, MA: M.I.T. Press.

—. 1988. *The Workplace Within: Psychodynamics of Organizational Life.* Cambridge, MA: M.I.T. Press.

Hoetker, J., and Ahlbrandt, W. P. 1969. The Persistence of Recitation. *American Educational Research Journal, 6,* 145–167.

Hoffman, L. M. 1989. *The Politics of Knowledge: Activist Movements in Medicine and Planning.* Albany, NY: SUNY Press.

Hofstadter, D. R. 1985. *Metamagical Themas: Questing for the Essence of Mind and Pattern.* New York: Basic Books.

Holt, J. 1964. *How Children Fail.* New York: Pitman.

Howieson, N. 1981. A Longitudinal Study of Creativity—1965–1975. *Journal of Creative Behavior, 15,* 117–134.

Jacobs, J. 1961. *The Death and Life of Great American Cities.* New York: Random House.

—. 1984. *Cities and the Wealth of Nations.* New York: Random House.

James, W. 1914. *Habit.* New York: Holt.

Johnston, P. H. (1985). Understanding Reading Disability: A Case Study Approach. *Harvard Educational Review, 55,* 153–177.

Joseph, G. M., and Patel, V. L. 1986. Specificity of Expertise in Clinical Reasoning. In *Program of the Eighth Annual Conference of the Cognitive Science Society* (331–345). Hillsdale, NJ: Erlbaum.

Juckes, T. J. 1991. Equilibration and the learning paradox. *Human Development, 34,* 261–272.

Khatchadourian, H. 1977. The Creative Process in Art. *British Journal of Aesthetics, 17,* 230–241.

Kitto, H. D. F. 1954. *The Greeks.* Baltimore, MD: Penguin Books.

Klahr, D., Langley, P., and Neches, R. (eds.) 1987. *Production System Models of Learning and Development.* Cambridge, MA: M.I.T. Press.

Krashen, S. D. 1981. *Second Language Acquisition and Second Language Learning.* Oxford: Pergamon.

Larkin, J. H., McDermott, J., Simon, D. P., and Simon, H. A. 1980. Models of Competence in Solving Physics Problems. *Cognitive Science, 4,* 317–345.

Lasch, C. 1991. *The True and Only Heaven: Progress and Its Critics.* New York: Norton.

Lave, J. 1988. *Cognition in Practice.* Boston: Cambridge University Press.

Lave, J., and Wenger, E. 1991. *Situated Learning: Legitimate Peripheral Participation.* Cambridge, England: Cambridge University Press.

Lesgold, A. M., and Lajoie, S. 1991. Complex Problem Solving in Electronics. In R. J. Sternberg and P. A. Frensch (eds.), *Complex Problem Solving: Principles and Mechanisms* (287–316). Hillsdale, NJ: Erlbaum.

Lewis, R. W. B. 1991. *The Jameses: A Family Narrative.* New York: Farrar, Straus, and Giroux.

Lieberman, J. K. 1970. *The Tyranny of the Experts: How Professionals are Closing the Open Society.* New York: Walker.

Lipman, M. 1988. *Philosophy Goes to School.* Philadelphia, PA: Temple University Press.

MacKinnon, D. W. 1965. Personality and the Realization of Creative Potential. *American Psychologist, 20,* 273–281.

Margolis, H. 1987. *Patterns, Thinking, and Cognition.* Chicago: University of Chicago Press.

Marjoram, D. T. E. 1987. Chess and Gifted Children. *Gifted Education International, 5,* 48–51.

Marmot, M. G. 1986. Social Inequalities in Mortality: The Social Environment. In R. G. Wilkenson (eds.), *Class and Health: Research and Longitudinal Data* (21–33). London: Tavistock.

Marton, F., and Säljö, R. 1976. On Qualitative Differences in Learning: I—Outcome and Process. *British Journal of Educational Psychology, 46* (1), 4–11.

McClelland, J. L., and Rumelhart, D. E. 1988. *Explorations in Parallel Distributed Processing: A Handbook of Models, Programs, and Exercises.* Cambridge, MA: M.I.T. Press.

McClelland, J. L., Rumelhart, D. E., and the PDP Research Group, (ed.) 1986. *Parallel Distributed Processing: Explorations in the Microstructure of Cognition: Vol. 2. Psychological and Biological Models.* Cambridge, MA: M.I.T./Bradford.

Minsky, M. L. 1980. K-lines: A Theory of Memory. *Cognitive Science, 4,* 117–133.

Mitchell, R. C., Jr. 1988. Sociological Implications of the Flow Experience. In M. Csikszentmihalyi and I. S. Csikszentmihalyi (eds.), *Optimal Experiences: Psychological Studies of Flow in Consciousness.* (36–59). New York: Cambridge University Press.

More, L. T. 1934. *Isaac Newton.* New York: Scribner.

Murnighan, J. K., and Conlon, D. E. 1991. The Dynamics of Intense Work Groups: A Study of British String Quartets. *Administrative Science Quarterly, 36,* 165–186.

Newell, A., Shaw, J. C., and Simon, H. A., 1962. The Processes of Creative Thinking. In H. E. Gruber, G. Terrell, and M. Wertheimer (eds.), *Contemporary Approaches to Creative Thinking* (63–119). New York: Atherton Press.

Newell, A., and Simon, H. A. 1972. Human Problem Solving. Englewood Cliffs, NJ: Prentice-Hall.

Ng, E., and Bereiter, C. 1991. Three Levels of Goal Orientation in Learning. *The Journal of the Learning Sciences, 1* (3 & 4), 243–271.

Nock, A. J. (1936). *Jefferson.* New York: Blue Ribbon Books.

Ohlsson, S. 1991. *Young Adults' Understanding of Evolutionary Explanations: Preliminary Observations.* Tech. Rep. to OERI No. University of Pittsburgh, Learning Research and Development Laboratory.

Osgood, C. E., Suci, G. J., and Tannenbaum, P. 1957. *The Meaning of Meaning.* Urbana, IL: University of Illinois.

Ostrander, S. 1979. *Superlearning.* New York: Delacorte Press.

Patel, V., and Groen, G. 1986. Knowledge Based Solution Strategies in Medical Reasoning. *Cognitive Science, 10,* 91–116.

Patel, V. L., and Groen, G. J. 1991. The General and Specific Nature of Medical Expertise: A Critical Look. In K. A. Ericsson and J. Smith (eds.), *Toward a General Theory of Expertise: Prospects and Limits* (93–125). Cambridge: Cambridge University Press.

Perfetti, C. 1985. *Reading Ability.* New York: Oxford University Press.

Perkins, D. N. 1981. *The Mind's Best Work.* Cambridge, MA: Harvard University Press.

Peters, D. P., and Ceci, S. J. 1982. Peer-Review Practices of Psychological Journals: The Fate of Published Articles, Submitted Again. *Behavioral and Brain Sciences, 5* (2), 187–255.

Peters, T. 1987. *Thriving on Chaos: Handbook for a Management Revolution.* New York: Knopf.

Piaget, J. 1960. *The Psychology of Intelligence.* Paterson, NJ: Littlefield, Adams.

Plimpton, G. (ed.) 1992. *The Paris Review Interviews, Ninth Series.* New York: Penguin.

Polanyi, M. 1967. *The Tacit Dimension.* Garden City, NJ: Doubleday.

Polanyi, M. 1964. *Personal Knowledge: Towards a Post-Critical Philosophy.* New York: Harper and Row.

Popper, K. R. 1972. *Objective Knowledge: An Evolutionary*

Approach. Oxford: Clarendon Press.

Postman, N. 1992. *Technopoly: The Surrender of Culture to Technology.* New York: Knopf.

Remillard, J. 1991. *Conceptions of Problem Solving in Commonly Used and Distinctive Elementary Mathematics Curricula* No. East Lansing, MI: Michigan State University, Center for Learning and Teaching of Elementary Subjects.

Resnick, L. B., Bill, V., Lesgold, S., and Leer, M. 1991. Thinking in Arithmetic Class. In B. Means, C. Chelemer, and M. S. Knapp (eds.), *Teaching Advanced Skills to At-Risk Students: View from Research and Practice.* San Francisco: Jossey-Bass.

Resnick, L. B., and Omanson, S. F. 1987. Learning to Understand Arithmetic. In R. Glaser (eds.), *Advances in Instructional Psychology* (41–95). Hillsdale, NJ: Erlbaum.

Roedinger III, H. L., and Craik, F. I. M. (eds.) 1989. *Varieties of Memory and Consciousness: Essays in Honor of Endel Tulving.* Hillsdale, NJ: Erlbaum.

Rumelhart, D. E. 1989. The Architecture of Mind: A Connectionist Approach. In M. I. Posner (eds.), *Foundations of Cognitive Science* (133–159). Cambridge, MA: M.I.T. Press.

Rumelhart, D. E., McClelland, J. L., and the PDP Research Group, (eds.) 1986. *Parallel Distributed Processing: Explorations in the Microstructure of Cognition: Vol. 1. Foundations.* Cambridge, MA: M.I.T. Press.

Ryle, G. 1949. *The Concept of Mind.* London: Hutchinson.

Salthouse, T. A. 1991. Expertise as the Circumvention of Human Processing Limitations. In K. A. Ericsson and J. Smith (eds.), *Toward a General Theory of Expertise: Prospects and Limits* (286–300). Cambridge: Cambridge University Press.

Scardamalia, M., and Bereiter, C. 1984. Development of Strategies in Text Processing. In H. Mandl, N. L. Stein, and T. Trabasso (eds.), *Learning and Comprehension of Text* (379–406). Hillsdale, NJ: Erlbaum.

Scardamalia, M., and Bereiter, C. 1985. Fostering the Development of Self-Regulation in Children's Knowledge Processing. In S. F. Chipman, J. W. Segal, and R. Glaser (eds.), *Thinking and Learning Skills: Vol. 2. Research and Open Questions* (563–577). Hillsdale, NJ: Erlbaum.

Scardamalia, M., and Bereiter, C. 1987. Knowledge Telling and Knowledge Transforming in Written Composition. In S. Rosenberg (ed.), *Advances in Applied Psycholinguistics: Vol. 2. Reading,*

Writing, and Language Learning (142–175). Cambridge: Cambridge University Press.

Scardamalia, M., and Bereiter, C. 1991a. Higher Levels of Agency for Children in Knowledge Building: A Challenge for the Design of New Knowledge Media. *The Journal of the Learning Sciences, 1* (1), 37–68.

Scardamalia, M., and Bereiter, C. 1991b. Literate Expertise. In K. A. Ericsson and J. Smith (eds.), *Toward a General Theory of Expertise: Prospects and Limits* (172–194). Cambridge: Cambridge University Press.

Scardamalia, M., and Bereiter, C. (in press-a). An Architecture for Collaborative Knowledge Building. In E. D. Corte, M. Linn, H. Mandl, and L. Verschaffel (eds.), *Computer-Based Learning Environments and Problem Solving (NATO-ASI Series F: Computer and Systems Sciences)* Berlin: Springer-Verlag.

Scardamalia, M., and Bereiter, C. (in press-b). Schools as Knowledge-Building Communities. In S. Strauss (eds.), *Human Development: The Tel Aviv Annual Workshop: Vol. 7. Development and Learning Environments* Norwood, NJ: Ablex.

Scardamalia, M., Bereiter, C., Brett, C., Burtis, P. J., Calhoun, C., and Smith Lea, N. 1992. Educational Applications of a Networked Communal Database. *Interactive Learning Environments, 2* (1), 45–71.

Scardamalia, M., Bereiter, C., and Lamon, M. (in press). CSILE: Trying to Bring Students into World 3. In K. McGilley (ed.), *TBA* Cambridge, MA: M.I.T. Press.

Scardamalia, M., Bereiter, C., McLean, R. S., Swallow, J., and Woodruff, E. 1989. Computer-Supported Intentional Learning Environments. *Journal of Educational Computing Research, 5,* 51–68.

Schön, D. 1987. *Educating the Reflective Practitioner.* San Francisco: Jossey-Bass.

Scribner, S. 1984. Studying Working Intelligence. In B. Rogoff and J. Lave (eds.), *Everyday Cognition: Its Development in Social Context* (9–40). Cambridge, MA: Harvard University Press.

Segal, S. M., Busse, T. V., and Mansfield, R. S. 1980. The Relationship of Scientific Creativity in the Biological Sciences to Predoctoral Accomplishments and Experiences. *American Educational Research Journal, 17,* 491–502.

Shulman, L. S., and Keislar, E. R. (eds.) 1966. *Learning by Discovery: A Critical Appraisal.*

Siegler, R. S. (ed.). 1978. *Children's Thinking: What Develops?* Hillsdale, NJ: Erlbaum.

Simon, H. A. 1957. *Models of Man: Social and Rational: Mathematical Essays.* New York: Wiley.

Simonton, D. K. 1984. *Genius, Creativity, and Leadership.* Cambridge, MA: Harvard University Press.

Simonton, D. K. 1988. Creativity, Leadership, and Chance. In R. J. Sternberg (ed.), *The Nature of Creativity: Contemporary Psychological Perspectives* (386–426). Cambridge: Cambridge University Press.

Smolensky, P. 1988. On the Proper Treatment of Connectionism. *Behavioral and Brain Sciences, 11,* 1–74.

Snow, R. E., and Yalow, E. 1982. Education and Intelligence. In R. J. Sternberg (eds.), *Handbook of Human Intelligence* (493–585). Cambridge: Cambridge University Press.

Soloway, E., and Iyengar, S. (ed.) 1986. *Empirical Studies of Programmers.* Norwood, NJ: Ablex.

Squires, D. A., Huitt, W. G., and Segars, J. K. 1983. *Effective Schools and Classrooms: A Research-Based Perspective.* Alexandria, VA: Association for Supervision and Curriculum Development.

Stanovich, K. E., and Cunningham, A. E. 1991. Reading as Constrained Reasoning. In R. J. Sternberg and P. A. Frensch (eds.), *Complex Problem Solving: Principles and Mechanisms* (3–60). Hillsdale, NJ: Erlbaum.

Steller, A. W. 1988. *Effective Schools Research: Practice and Promise.* Bloomington, IN: Phi Delta Kappa Educational Foundation.

Suchman, L. A. 1987. *Plans and Situated Actions: The Problem of Human-Machine Communication.* Cambridge: Cambridge University Press.

Suomi, S. J. 1991. Primate Separation Models of Affective Disorders. In J. Madden (ed.), *Neurobiology of Learning, Emotion, and Affect.* New York: Raven Press.

Sweller, J., Mawer, R. F., and Ward, M. R. 1983. Development of Expertise in Mathematical Problem Solving. *Journal of Experimental Psychology: General, 112,* 639–661.

Tal, N. F. 1992. *Diagnostic Reasoning of Difficult Internal Medicine Cases: Expert, Proto-expert, and Non-expert Approaches.* Doctoral thesis, University of Toronto.

Taylor, P. H. 1970. *How Teachers Plan Their Courses.* Slough, England: National Foundation for Educational Research.

Thagard, P. 1989. Explanatory Coherence. *Behavioral and Brain Sciences, 12,* 435–502.

Tyler, R. W. 1930. What High School Pupils Forget. *Educational Research Bulletin, 9,* 490–97.

Vallas, S. P. 1990. The Concept of Skill: A Critical Review. *Work and Occupations, 17,* 379–398.

van Daalen–Kapteijns, M. M., and Elshout-Mohr, M. 1981. The Acquisition of Word Meanings as a Cognitive Learning Process. *Journal of Verbal Learning and Verbal Behavior, 20,* 386–399.

van Dijk, T. A., and Kintsch, W. 1983. *Strategies of Discourse Comprehension.* New York: Academic Press.

van Rossum, E. J., and Schenk, S. M. 1984. The Relationship Between Learning Conception, Study Strategy and Learning Outcome. *British Journal of Educational Psychology, 54,* 73–83.

Vosniadou, S., and Brewer, W. F. 1987. Theories of Knowledge Restructuring in Development. *Review of Educational Research, 57,* 51–67.

Voss, J. F. 1988. Problem Solving and the Educational Process. In A. M. Lesgold and R. Glaser (eds.), *Foundations for a Psychology of Education* (251 294). Hillsdale, NJ: Erlbaum.

Vygotsky, L. S. 1978. *Mind in Society: The Development of Higher Psychological Processes* (M. Cole, V. John-Steiner, S. Scribner, and E. Souberman, trans.). Cambridge, MA: Harvard University Press.

Wallas, G. 1926. *The Art of Thought.* New York: Harcourt Brace.

Weintraub, P. 1984. *The Omni Interviews.* New York: Ticknor and Fields.

Welker, R. 1991. Expertise and the Teacher as Expert: Rethinking a Questionable Metaphor. *American Educational Research Journal, 28,* 19–35.

Wertsch, J. V. (ed.). 1985. *Culture, Communication, and Cognition: Vygotskian Perspectives.* Cambridge: Cambridge University Press.

Whitehead, A. N. (1925/1948). *Science and the Modern World* (Mentor edn.). New York: New American Library.

————. 1929. *The Aims of Education.* New York: Macmillan.

Winston, P. H., and Prendergast, K. A. (eds.). 1984. *The AI Business: Commercial Uses of Artificial Intelligence.* Cambridge, MA: M.I.T. Press.

Zahorik, J. A. 1975. Teachers' Planning Models. *Educational Leadership, 33,* 134–139.

Index

unpromisingness, 139
unskilled labor, complex skills and, 9
van Daalen-Kapteijns, M. M., 171
virtual reality, 210, 234
Voss, James, 67–68
Vygotsky, Lev, 114

Welker, Robert, 8
Whitehead, Alfred North, 1, 63, 64,
  67, 200, 231, 237, 245–46

whole language, 197, 198
Willie, 11–12, 13, 15, 18–19
wisdom, 15
  active, 232: as concept of
    expertise, 245; and
    promisingness, 235–36, 245;
    as variety of expertise,
    235–36, 238
  passive, 232